Spare Time in Texas

Number Twenty-one

JACK AND DORIS SMOTHERS SERIES IN TEXAS HISTORY, LIFE, AND CULTURE

Spare Time in Texas

RECREATION AND HISTORY IN THE LONE STAR STATE

By David G. McComb

University of Texas Press Austin

PUBLICATION OF THIS WORK WAS MADE POSSIBLE IN PART BY SUPPORT FROM THE J. E. SMOTHERS, SR., MEMORIAL FOUNDATION AND THE NATIONAL ENDOWMENT FOR THE HUMANITIES.

Printed in the United States of America
First edition, 2008

Requests for permission to reproduce material from this work should be sent to:

Permissions
University of Texas Press
P.O. Box 7819
Austin, TX 78713-7819
www.utexas.edu/utpress/about/bpermission.html

♾ The paper used in this book meets the minimum requirements of ANSI/NISO Z39.48-1992 (R1997) (Permanence of Paper).

LIBRARY OF CONGRESS CATALOGING-IN-PUBLICATION DATA

McComb, David G.
Spare Time in Texas : Recreation and history in the Lone Star State / by David G. McComb.
p. cm. — (Jack and Doris Smothers series in Texas history, life, and culture ; 21)
Includes bibliographical references and index.
ISBN 978-0-292-71889-0

1. Recreation—Texas—History. 2. Leisure—Texas—History. I. Title. II. Series
GV54.T59M33 2008
790.09764—dc22

2008017080

To Mary Alice

Contents

Spare Time in Texas

Introduction

For many people recreation, or leisure, is a trivial subject. Work is what is important—an opinion shared by psychoanalyst Sigmund Freud, sociologist Max Weber, and four centuries of Puritans. John Adams of Massachusetts, second president of the United States, proclaimed, "I was not sent to this world to spend my days in sports, diversions, and pleasures. I was born for business; for both activity and study."[1] A century later, another president, Theodore Roosevelt of New York said, "Far and away the best prize that life offers is the chance to work hard at work worth doing."[2] To be sure, making a living, or work, is vitally important, but Adams also developed a taste for Parisian theater, and Roosevelt rode his horse every afternoon in Washington's Rock Creek Park.

Upon meeting someone for the first time our initial question is usually, "What kind of job do you have?" It is a means of economic identification and a measurement of worth. The Southern variant is, "Where do you come from?" This is meant to establish family lineage and social status. We might gain greater insight, however, by asking an additional question, "What do you do in your spare time?" This is the activity that a person freely chooses. How people spend their leisure time is an indication of their true interests, since they are not under the direction of a job or boss. A person's choice of recreation, therefore, may well be a better measurement of individual character than vocation or family, the usual standards. In larger terms, the recreational preferences of a people reveal the character of the people.

After time spent for work and everyday life maintenance, such as grocery shopping and house cleaning, there are about as many leisure hours left over per week as those used for a job. This can be roughly calculated by assuming forty hours per week for work, fifty-six hours for sleeping, and thirty-two hours for meals and errands. What is left over—forty hours—is leisure. Of course, there are variations. Some people labor many more hours, or sleep less, or have their spare time taken up with the demands of children, or they eat fast foods, or may be unemployed, or may be retired. But as sociologist John R. Kelly put it, "Leisure is what we don't have to do."[3] In general, people have a large quantity of discretionary time.

"Recreation," although often used interchangeably with the word "leisure," implies a certain amount of organization, self-direction, benefit, and purpose. Leisure is left-over time—the quantity; recreation is what is done with the time—the quality. Recreation history, thus, is the study of how people have used their leisure.[4] It includes entertainments, diversions, festivities, vacations, sports, and games. It should be noted, moreover, that there have long been a recognition and concern about the use of leisure. A royal Egyptian official, Ptahhotpe, wrote in the twenty-fourth century BCE, "Do no more than you are ordered to, nor shorten the time accorded to leisure. It is hateful to the spirit to be robbed of the time for merriment."[5] In Genesis the Old Testament God created heaven and earth in six days and then rested on the seventh. Ancient Greeks thought leisure necessary for self-development and for political participation.[6]

In modern American society there is the thought that recreation is necessary in order to recover from work and to prepare to go back to work. It is "re-creation." The seventeenth-century proverb from English writer James Howell, "All work and no play makes Jack a dull boy," has become a part of the vernacular. Thus, recreation is rationalized to be beneficial, if not necessary. It is certainly demanded by the public. About one-half trillion dollars were spent in the United States on recreation at the turn of the twenty-first century, and the number of visitors to national parks equaled the population of the nation.[7]

Still, there is little documented evidence that recreation is vital for human beings, and indeed, there has been some cynical comment. At the end of the nineteenth century, economist Thorstein Veblen (1857–1929) wrote scathingly about the non-productive leisure class. About conspicuous leisure and consumption by the upper class, he commented, "In the one case it is a waste of time and effort, in the other it is a waste of goods."[8] University of Chicago educator Robert Hutchins (1899–1977) later grumped about the lower class, "More free time means more time to waste. The worker who used to have only a little time in which to get drunk and beat his wife now has time to get drunk, beat his wife—and watch TV."[9]

THE EVOLUTION AND COMMERCIALIZATION OF LEISURE

Amounts of leisure, of course, have varied over time—generally, declining during the Industrial Revolution (1775–1900) and increasing during the twentieth century. The "three eights" became the modern standard: eight hours for work, eight hours for rest, and eight hours for leisure along with a two-day free weekend and two weeks or more of vacation. During this transformation into the modern world, railroads spun a spider web of connections across the United States and hard surface roads spread within and between cities for the benefit of trucks, buses, and cars. At first, the recreational ambitions of bicycle riders and automobile enthusiasts inspired the construction of good roads. Air travel became an important mass transport system after 1945.

People who had increasing amounts of time and money thus could travel to distant recreation areas. Not surprisingly, the American playground movement began in 1885 and cities with public parks expanded from one hundred in 1892 to sixteen hundred in 1926. Central Park, the model for all urban parks, opened in New York City in 1853, and the National Park system began with Yellowstone in 1872. Motels started as experiments in the 1920s and Holiday Inn, the first motel chain, began in 1952.

Commercial recreation blossomed with the innovations of P. T. Barnum, who put circuses on trains in 1872, and Thomas Cook, who put people on trains for grand tours of England and Europe in the mid-nineteenth century. The 1893 Columbian Exposition in Chicago with its midway, displays, Ferris wheel, and exotic dancer "Little Egypt" demonstrated the potential of amusement parks. Seaside resorts for the wealthy have a long history reaching back into the eighteenth century, but Coney Island in New York City was the first to entertain the American masses beginning in 1890.

Professional baseball began its storied history with the formation of the Cincinnati Red Stockings in 1869, a team that toured all the way to California aboard the newly completed transcontinental railroad. Professional baseball and later professional football required the building of large stadiums in order to provide playing fields and control admission. Within the cities by the end of the nineteenth century, in addition, music halls, horse-racing tracks, bawdy houses, theaters, saloons, and nickelodeons offered a variety of entertainment.[10] More forms of mass entertainment developed in the twentieth century with movies in the 1900s, radio in the 1920s, and television in the 1950s. Zoos, theaters, sports, libraries, parks, bars, and nightclubs continued to offer their varied attractions throughout the century. Americans, including Texans, consequently had plenty of choices for the expenditure of free time.

THE ACADEMIC STUDY OF LEISURE

Psychologists, sociologists, geographers, economists, physical educators, and philosophers have all studied the phenomenon of leisure. Business people who at first were only mildly interested became vitally interested when the tourist trade became the second largest employer in the United States and in Texas after World War II. Notably for academics the *Journal of Leisure Research* began in 1969. Yet, historians have ignored the leisure phenomenon. As Gary Cross, a comparative historian at Pennsylvania State University, explained: "To be sure, leisure has had a place in the study of everyday life and popular culture. But scholars have usually undertaken these topics for ulterior purposes—like the study of class, gender, or political change. As a result, historians have neglected the story of the modern emergence of free time and the changing meaning of leisure as an activity of intrinsic value."[11]

Cross has written one of the few general accounts of recreation, *A Social History of Leisure Since 1600* (1990), and it compares favorably with the pioneering study by

Foster Rhea Dulles, *A History of Recreation: America Learns to Play* (1940). Only an incomplete, unorganized, and unrecognized collection of writings about recreation history, however, exists for Texas. The major bibliographies of Texas, *A Guide to the History of Texas* (1988), edited by Light T. Cummins and Alvin R. Bailey Jr., and *Basic Texas Books* (1983) by John H. Jenkins, list nothing about recreation. Moreover, there are no entries for "recreation" or "leisure" in the *New Handbook of Texas* (1996). The *Handbook*, however, does include an article about tourism by Keith Elliott and entries about specific recreation places, such as the Armadillo World Headquarters and the Astrodome. A few references to recreation events can be found in the lengthy indexes of the *Southwestern Historical Quarterly*. Coverage of the topic of recreational history in Texas, therefore, is spotty.

ORGANIZATION BY PLACE

One of the great difficulties in dealing with such an amorphous subject as recreation is the enormous variety that can be found not only at a single moment, but also over time. There is, consequently, a great problem of organization. How can the topic of recreation be described, arranged, and analyzed? There are always ethnic, age, and gender differences to consider and economic and social trends to think about. Also, what might be a delight to one segment of society may be a sin to another. Geography, or location, could be a factor. What about architecture? How can a historian gain a grip on such a slippery topic?

Specific events, such as the 1936 Texas State Fair, can be examined, or perhaps topics such as poker, Texas line dance, or jazz might be described and traced. Anthropologists and folklorists like to do that. Another way, seemingly, is to study the places of recreation in a historical sense—how they started, how they were used, why they endured, who was involved, how and why they have changed, and what they have meant to the people who used them. Places are tangible reminders of events, and people are tied by their emotions to locations. They are historical artifacts, in a sense.

Certain places in Texas, when threatened by economic adversity, bulldozers, or greed, have the power to bring citizens into the streets, flood the newspapers with angry letters, and threaten the well-being of local politicians. These are places where memories have been created, sometimes in quiet, sometimes in tumult, but always with remembered emotion. Indeed, battlegrounds such as the Alamo or San Jacinto with their dramatic stories of violent death have become sacred. There are places of infamy, such as the Sixth Floor Museum in Dallas and the observation tower of the Main Building at the University of Texas, where an insane sniper peered through a narrow gun sight at unsuspecting people far below. Historic sites are important lest we forget our past.

Less shocking, less time locked, and less obvious are places such as the zoos, libraries, stadiums, parks, saloons, and theaters that have provided memories and moments of relaxation for thousands of people. Such unassuming places reflect an important part of Texas culture, an aspect that has been mainly neglected in the portrayal of the state history, a history devoted mostly to straightforward provincial narratives of politics, war, and economics. Recreation represents the activities of entertainment, rest, and rejuvenation. These activities illuminate aspects of class, income, race, ethnicity, education, age, gender, technology, and geography just as do the more common topics of study. Recreational sites thus can be historically significant.

In this series of essays, consequently, I take a look at Texas places—zoos, libraries, stadiums, parks, saloons, brothels, and theaters—in order to extract some knowledge about the significance of recreation in Texas life. In addition, I comment about the ephemeral entertainment provided by movies, radio, and television. Although decentralized, this electronic extension of theater cannot be ignored. There are other places and activities of recreation, of course, but these subjects seem to be an obvious point to start.

THE HISTORICAL ESSAY

The format for discussion is a historical essay. Essays in the literary sense usually deal with one topic or theme; they are generally short, opinionated, and flow easily to a conclusion. These essays, however, contain a lot of information, reach back to historical antecedents, and slice through the entire history of the state from the beginning to the present. They are dense with descriptive information and spiky with footnotes, something not usual for traditional literary essays. As one English professor put it to me, "These essays are like fruitcake, rather than cake." I did not particularly like the analogy, but it is one way to explain the difference. I focus upon Texas, of course, but I usually attempt to place Lone Star developments into a broad national and sometimes international historical context. Recreation in Texas did not evolve in isolation, although often there was a local wrinkle in the story.

CHAPTER 1

The Licit and the Illicit

If prostitution is the world's oldest profession, as folklore claims, then drinking and gambling are handmaidens in attendance. When a dusty, stinking nineteenth-century cowboy, with money jingling in his pocket, came to town after spending three weeks chasing range cattle, he took a bath, shaved, ate a good meal, took a drink of whiskey, gambled, and thought about women. In Big Spring, Texas, in the 1880s the first establishments that catered to that frontier cowboy were combination saloons, gambling places, dance halls, and restaurants. It was an explosive situation as experience proved, and the town shortly separated the activities. "In other words," recalled Shine Philips, a druggist who grew up in the town, "folks decided that when a man ate he got to drinking and when he drank he got to looking around for a woman and it was best not to have all three in the same building—too handy and convenient. So these three prime entertainments were segregated."[1] Gambling and drinking, thus, remained within the province of the saloon while prostitution and restaurants moved into separate housing. This division was the general pattern for these recreational businesses in Texas until the mid-twentieth century, but the vice triad of gambling, drinking, and prostitution have danced together in a loose historical rhythm, at times legal and at other times illegal, even unto the present time.

PROSTITUTION

Sexual activity and prostitution, the exchange of sex for money, have always been a part of the human story. In the *Epic of Gilgamesh* (2000 BCE), one of the oldest pieces of literature in Western civilization, the hero, Gilgamesh, sends a temple prostitute to weaken a savage rival with six days and seven nights of lovemaking. The words come down to us from the ancient Middle East: "She used not restraint but accepted his ardour, / She put aside her robe and he lay upon her."[2] Moreover, as most Christians know, Mary Magdalene of Jesus' time was once thought to be a repentant harlot. "And behold," states the Gospel of Luke, "a woman of the city who was a sinner when she learned that he [Jesus] was sitting at table in the Pharisee's house, brought an alabaster flask of ointment and standing behind him at his feet, weeping, she began to wet his feet with her tears, and wiped them with the hair of her head, and kissed his feet, and anointed them with the ointment."[3] Jesus forgave her sins and nineteenth-century American Christian rescue groups for prostitutes called themselves Magdalen Societies.[4]

Prostitution can be tracked in European history and it shows up in accounts of colonial cities—Benjamin Franklin, for example, cavorted with the bawds of Philadelphia. In Texas, Susanna Dickinson (1814–1883) who, with her infant child, survived the fall of the Alamo and carried the news of the defeat to Sam Houston, later lived in a bagnio and was labeled a whore by her husband during a divorce in 1857. Her daughter Angelina, the "Babe of the Alamo," died as a Galveston prostitute in 1869.[5]

Modern researchers have provided some explanations for the raging sexual behavior of human beings, an activity that both ensures the propagation of the species and, incidentally, provides the opportunity for prostitution. Men with their production of testosterone and sperm require periodic ejaculation—around three times per week for younger men, according to zoologist Alfred C. Kinsey, the pioneer of sex research.[6] From puberty into old age, the human male experiences a short-cycled sexual urgency that nags for repeated relief again and again. This is the origin of lust. The periodic urge encourages marriage and emboldens visits to prostitutes. Men are easily aroused by the glimpse of a woman and have straightforward sex goals: easy access, control over the act, rapid withdrawal after satisfaction, and unencumbered departure.[7]

Kinsey commented, "Men go to prostitutes because they can pay for the sexual relations and forget other responsibilities, whereas coitus with other girls may involve them socially and legally beyond anything which they care to undertake."[8] More bluntly, Leonard Shlain, a physician and historian, cited a young whore who marveled that a man would pay for such a brief experience. Her madam explained that she was being paid not only for the sex, but also for her to go away when it was over.[9] Of course, it is more complicated than that. Men visit prostitutes for many reasons: curiosity, novelty, variety, companionship, and cost (it is cheaper than courtship or marriage), as well as to lose virginity, to fulfill a fantasy, and to express comradeship for male friends.[10] Considering the absence of women on the frontier, on shipboard, and in newly established cities; and considering a society and culture dominated by men, the prostitution of women for male needs is comprehensible.

But what about the women's side of the equation? Women do not sexually arouse as easily as men, can go for days without sexual interest, are not nearly as concerned about orgasm, and reach a peak of sexual interest some ten years later than men.[11] They also can be lustful, but there is usually no short-term cyclical urgency. Without the estrus cycle of other mammals, the human female, however, possesses a year-round receptivity with a physical capacity for many sexual partners. Because ovulation is cryptic, frequent coitus is necessary for pregnancy, and the female ability to respond to restimulation is much quicker than that of the male.[12] Females, therefore, are more capable of frequent intercourse. According to Desmond Morris, the zoologist who wrote *The Naked Ape* (1967), for all of these biological reasons sex among humans was raised to a status of recreation.[13]

Prostitution, however, has been largely a one-way street—men have paid for sex, not women. "As in past eras," commented feminist historians Bonnie S. Anderson and Judith P. Zinsser, "the most lucrative item a woman could sell on the streets was the sexual use of her body. Well into the twentieth century, prostitution remained a woman's most profitable means of earning income, and a prostitute could earn in a day what other working-class women made in a week."[14] Mrs. Ardie Smith, the madam of the "Brick House" bagnio in Galveston in the 1930s, said, "I have something that men want and are willing to pay for. It's my property, so why shouldn't I sell it?"[15]

This commercial argument resonates today. Alexa Albert, a medical student who studied legal prostitution at the Mustang Ranch in Nevada during the 1990s, found the same attitude. The "girls" told her that from their point of view all women sold sex—for a household, for status, for jewelry, for children—but that prostitutes were just more honest about it. As one of them pronounced, "If you're going to put out, why not get paid for it? There're too many women giving their bodies away for free and getting nothing but heartache and pain."[16] This argument, of course, has split modern feminist thinkers. Isn't prostitution exploitation of women by men? But shouldn't free women be allowed to do as they wish with their bodies? The answers are "yes" and "yes."[17]

The commercial argument, however, underscores the fundamental reason that women become prostitutes—the need to make money. It is the timeless answer to the trite question, "What's a nice girl like you doing in a place like this?" Only rarely has the answer been recorded. Women drifted in and out of the business, moved, changed their names, died, and remained silent. There was a tacit understanding between madams and magistrates: don't carry harassment too far or the names of patrons and activities will be revealed to the public. Thus, authorities did not push too much, and information remained hidden. It was considered a shameful business and so people did not talk about it. Moreover, the prostitutes were often young and inarticulate. They did not write books, give interviews, pen diaries, pose for pictures, record oral histories, or mail descriptive letters home. It is almost impossible to track the life of an individual whore; they just appeared and disappeared. So, researchers have culled bits of information from court records, census data, jail notations, newspapers, military records, cemeteries, and anecdotes.[18] The story of prostitution is thus incomplete and lacks an intimate voice.

Prostitution in Texas and the West

Still, a broad picture can be painted. Historian Anne Butler studied the institution in the Old West and published the results in *Daughters of Joy, Sisters of Misery: Prostitutes in the American West, 1865–90* (1985). Her assessment was generally gloomy. The women came from poor circumstances and from all racial groups, although most were white. They were as young as fifteen, and after age thirty, when they were hard used and less attractive, they became saloon operators and madams. While remaining in the business, they married and raised sons who drifted and daughters who repeated the life of the mother. With low wages and high costs, lasting poverty was their fate. All prostitutes—from those in the fancy houses to those of the lowly "cribs," the one-room shacks that lined the alleys of vice districts—had to pay the costs of fines, rents, medical inspections, clothes, extortion, and pimps.

Violence and disease hovered around the corner, drug addiction and alcoholism were expected, and suicide with laudanum, a tincture of opium, became the means of escape. Society referred to them as "frail sisters," "fallen angels," "nymphes du pave," "queens of the night," "courtesans," "soiled doves," "Jezebels," "ladies of the lamplight," "hookers," "fair Cyprians," "scarlet women," and "abandoned women." Although often they were considered a necessary evil, they were shunned and isolated by polite society. In the oil boomtown of Wink, Texas, for instance, the prostitutes could patronize the same shops as others, but the beauty salons placed a folded newspaper on the seats of chairs for the respectable women to sit upon.[19] And people told jokes about the profession such as the one about a Dallas madam in the 1880s who borrowed $5,000 from a banker and promised to repay it after the state fair in October. She returned, however, a month before the fair and repaid the amount. The curious banker asked how she and her girls had been able to do that. "Ah well," the madam replied, "I forgot all about the preachers' convention in August."[20]

People laughed, but with shallow sympathy. There were few relief agencies and almost no work for widowed or abandoned females—perhaps some employment in schools, boardinghouses, and stores, but not enough. The labor of mining, running cattle, cutting trees, constructing railroads, and building towns required male strength. The thought that good men married such women was a myth: even though "decent men" patronized bawdy houses, they married "decent women" when they could. There is little evidence of upward mobility. According to Butler, prostitutes married the worst of men, often a pimp, and led lives filled with arrests, bribes, and brutality. The rape of a prostitute was a crime not possible, so it was thought at the time, because her virtue was already gone, leaving nothing to protect. The plight of the nineteenth-century female was reflected in the sympathetic comment of W. L. Lincoln, an Indian agent in Montana in 1885: "The Indian maiden's favor had a money value, and what wonder is it that, half clad and half starved, they bartered their honor . . . for something to cover their limbs and for food for themselves and their kin."[21]

Butler bristled at "heart of gold" prostitute stories such as that of Ella Hill of Amarillo, as related by Judge James Hamlin. Hill ran an honest bagnio and dance hall in the 1890s, according to Hamlin, where visiting cowmen left their money with the madam at the front door. After the men cavorted, Hill deducted expenses and returned the remainder. She contributed money to a local church and required her "girls" to dress up and go to special Sunday afternoon services. Hill eventually retired to run a laundry service in Wichita, Kansas, but the surprising part of the story was that she successfully reared two daughters, boarded with a worthy family in Fort Worth, who never knew of her profession. Butler dismissed Judge Hamlin's sentimental, folksy, distant portrayal of Hill as a partial folktale. Still, the Judge claimed to be her lawyer and confidant.[22] Where was the truth? Perhaps, in the miserable detritus of prostitution there could be some human gold.

Prostitution, anyway, was present in Texas for the entirety of its history. It was common along cattle trails, in railroad towns, oil boomtowns, large cities, and near military encampments. Wherever there were large numbers of single men, "soiled doves" swarmed and competed with one another for the money. They were the bane and curse of military commanders who wished to keep their men fit for duty, a frustration for ministers, and a puzzle for city officials. Reliable numbers are not available, but in 1886 in El Paso an estimated 150 prostitutes marched to a city council meeting to protest $10 monthly fines, and a grand jury in 1913 counted 367 in the city's red-light district. Austin reported at least 100 prostitutes in 1880 and Houston listed 239 in the census of 1910. San Antonio claimed 630 in 1915, and 1,600 registered with that city's health department in 1939.[23] "The legions of prostitutes in the West did not march to a gentle drummer; rather, they caroused across the frontier," concluded historian Anne Butler.[24]

FRENCHY AND MY MACK

A sordid gathering of prostitutes—including "Frog Lip Sadie," "Rowdy Kate," and "Slippery Sue"—along with assorted gamblers, criminals, and con artists at Tascosa, a Panhandle cattle town, nevertheless produced one of the great love stories of Texas. It was like a flower emerging from a human garbage dump. Elizabeth McGraw, of Irish descent, was born in 1852 near Baton Rouge, learned to speak French, grew up pretty with blue eyes and black hair, and ran away from home in her mid-teens. She worked the dance halls of Dodge City, called herself "Frenchy," and arrived to sample the hot cowboy action in Mobeetie, Texas, in 1880. There she met Mickey McCormick from Tascosa who was a gambler, hunter, and livery owner. The small, mild-mannered Mickey found his lady luck when Frenchy stood beside him at the poker tables, and he took her with him back to Tascosa, a town known as the "Prodigal Queen of the Panhandle." When Oldham County formed in 1881, they married and the certificate became Frenchy's most treasured possession. Mickey built her a two-room adobe house among the cottonwood trees of nearby Atascosa Creek and they pledged to stay together forever.

The town began to decline in the late 1880s due to the end of the cattle drives and the railroads that ran southward to Amarillo. In October 1912, Mickey, not feeling well, fell across their bed; murmured to his wife, "I wonder what you'll do"; and died. He was buried on a nearby ridge to the east under a white marble grave marker. Frenchy pretended "My Mack" just went off on a trip and would soon return. Tascosa lost the county seat in 1915 and people left, but Frenchy remained steadfast as the last resident in a crumbling town. Enduring spring floods, black dust storms, and blue northers, Frenchy lived on alone in the small adobe house in the cottonwoods for almost three decades. She refused to leave Mickey.

Friends and the county supplied her with food, coal, and kerosene. Her well caved in, rattlesnakes denned under the house, and Frenchy became deaf, toothless, thin, and enfeebled. She finally allowed a friend in nearby Channing, Texas, to take her in after the friend promised to bury her in Tascosa. Frenchy revealed little about her past, kept her trunks locked, slept with her purse under her pillow, and said that she was too embarrassed to go to church. Cal Farley's Boys Ranch took over the site of Tascosa in 1939, and the old woman died in her sleep in 1941. Promises were kept, however, and friends buried her next to "My Mack" while the boys of the new school sang "Home on the Range." The students later raised the money for a gravestone and the devoted couple, their promise fulfilled, now slumber side by side, overlooking an institution dedicated to bringing hope to the lost children of the country.[25]

Red-light Districts

Elsewhere, in the larger, more successful towns, as the state matured vice districts congealed—"Guy Town" in Austin, "Two Street" in Waco, "Frogtown" in Dallas, "Happy Hollow" in Houston, "Postoffice Street" in Galveston, "Utah Street" in El Paso, "The District" in San Antonio, the "Flats" in Corpus Christi, the "Reservation" in Beaumont, the "Bowery" in Amarillo, and "Hell's Half Acre" in Fort Worth. Often located near the railroad depot and downtown businesses, these areas featured bawdy houses, saloons, dance halls, and gambling places. Supposedly, red-light districts were a necessary evil and the theory was to confine vice to a certain area of town. Said Christopher E. Bryne, the Roman Catholic bishop of Galveston, "We segregate mental and physical diseases. Let us do the same for moral sickness, for soul sickness. . . . As long as man has free will some of us will fall into impurity."[26] People entering a vice district knew where they were going and there could be little excuse. In 1882, for example, when a visiting Canadian accused Duckie Belcher, a prostitute at Sallie Daggett's brothel in Austin, of stealing his $65, the woman calmly testified that the man was drunk and spent the money. The court agreed and dismissed the charge.[27] The districts, nonetheless, presented a mixed blessing for cities.

The bordellos were licensed and the prostitutes regularly fined, which provided needed income for municipalities.[28] Routinely, towns passed vague laws to control "disorderly houses" and set up vagrancy ordinances in order to periodically tax the "fallen angels." In Canadian, Texas, in the late 1880s, for instance, the court allowed impoverished prostitutes to pay part of a fine and then return to their practice in order to earn the remainder.[29] The complicity was licit and illicit at the same time. Cities thus became a part of the corruption and had to tolerate the dissipation and frequent violence that came with it. In 1890 at Hattie Tyree's bawdy house in Waco, for example, Eva Clinton stole Lily Murphy's best customer. Promising to "do up" the "damn bitch," Lily attacked Eva with spittoons and Eva fought back with a penknife.

Lily died from a stab wound and Eva was fined $1,000 by the court. Lily's young daughter was placed in a convent.[30] Waco had to preside and intervene in order to maintain civic order.

El Paso in 1886 provided another example of the unruly bawdy houses and, incidentally, a classic Texas newspaper typographical error. Six-foot "Fat Alice" Abbott and five-foot Etta Clark were rival, across-the-street madams. After arguing with Abbott over fees and cheating, her best whore, Bessie, crossed the street to work for Clark. Bellowing, the 200-pound Fat Alice charged through Clark's front door, demanding the return of Bessie. A fight broke out between the madams. Petite Etta hit Fat Alice with a small tube used to light gas fixtures and Alice struck Etta in the face. When Alice turned on Bessie, Etta fetched a .44 caliber pistol from her room and ordered her rival to leave. Alice charged Etta, and Etta fired. She hit Fat Alice in the pubic area, which caused her to reel out the door and collapse in the street. Three of Alice's prostitutes retrieved her from the road and called a doctor who found that the bullet had passed on through and struck no vital organs. Alice readily recovered, and the news account in the *El Paso Herald* reported that she had been hit in the "public arch." Etta was acquitted of attempted murder on the grounds of self-defense.[31]

The red-light districts, as they came to be known, became tourist attractions. In San Antonio, as in East Coast cities, an annual guide was published for the "Sporting District," dedicated to "those whose creature desires impel them to saunter forth to the enjoyment of the clinking glass, sports, and good fellowship. . . ." The guide listed saloons, restaurants, athletic events, and bawdy houses ranked into three classes (one dollar, fifty cents, and twenty-five cents).[32] "The District," moreover, was more egalitarian than others in Texas. As Sam Johnson, a black man recalled, "You'd see bankers and politicians alongside us working men. The colored could go to any house they wanted. Nobody paid no never mind to nothing like that. If you had the money, they had the time." The San Antonio vice area, however, was just as corrupting as the rest. A city official remembered as a school boy walking past the line of cheap cribs west of San Pedro Creek: "The whores would get a kick out of shocking us gawk-eyed kids by jerking back the curtains to expose their all and shouting, 'You ever seen any of this?' We'd just drop our jaws and take off running . . . but the older we got the longer we looked."[33]

As might be expected as cities and their societies matured, with mothers wanting to protect their sons, there was a demand to turn off the red lights. It took a national reform movement and two world wars to accomplish the task. Long smoldering reform groups came together to fire a purity crusade during the Progressive Era at the last of the nineteenth century and into the first part of the next. The Women's Christian Temperance Union, organized in 1874, clasped hands with the Federation of Women's Clubs (1889) and later with the American Social Hygiene Association (1913) to attack alcoholism and prostitution. Church officials, ministers, and civic reformers joined the crusade and railed against the red-light districts.

In Dallas, for example, James T. Upchurch of the Berachah Rescue Society wrote: "The brothel is a breeding place for crimes of all description, and the feeding place for the 'unchained Demon.' It is a grossly immoral place and NO MORAL MAN CAN SUPPORT AN IMMORAL INSTITUTION AND REMAIN MORAL HIMSELF."[34] As a result of the push for change, the age of consent in Texas jumped from ten in 1886 to twelve in 1893 to fifteen in 1895. The districts in Dallas, Austin, and Amarillo closed by 1914. In Dallas, at least, the reformers provided a home for the "wayward sisters." Sheltering Arms, a mission in South Dallas, provided a refuge for 2,640 women and 1,460 children from 1911–1934.[35]

Other vice districts persisted, however, and in El Paso's Utah Street the soldiers awaiting their turn lined the stairs and hallways of brothels.[36] World War I closed Utah Street and the remaining red-light districts in 1917 under orders from Newton Baker, Secretary of War. Young men in training camps had to be protected from venereal disease so that they would be "fit to fight" in the war effort.[37] Venereal disease could take a soldier out of action for thirty days.

POSTOFFICE STREET

Following the war, the battered brothels made a partial recovery, but prostitutes increasingly worked out of hotels, motels, and call girl services that found advantage with the technology of telephones and automobiles. In the "Free State of Galveston," as residents called their city, all styles of procurement flourished and the old-time district endured. There in 1929–1930 Granville Price, a former police reporter for the *Galveston Daily News*, put together the most noteworthy report on prostitution in Texas. In researching "A Sociological Study of a Segregated District" for a master's thesis at the University of Texas, he visited bawdy houses, described them, and interviewed the inhabitants. He asked the kind of questions that historians would want—as did Alexa Albert later at the Mustang Ranch.

Price counted fifty-four houses in the Postoffice Street district with an average of six prostitutes per house. The 150–200 black whores in the nearby streets and alleys, plus a number of occasional trollops resulted in an estimated total of 800–900 prostitutes in the town of 50,000. That was a world-class ratio that rivaled the greatest sin cities of the world. The "ladies" attracted the sailors of the 15–30 ships in port, the 600-man garrison of soldiers at Fort Crockett, students from the University of Texas Medical Branch, residents, conventioneers, and tourists.[38]

Lacking paint, the old wooden, two-story bawdy houses on Postoffice Street appeared dingy, rundown, and quiet during the daytime. "By night, however, the lighted doorways, the faces in the windows where the lower shutters are missing, the muffled sound of music and sliding feet, the parked automobiles, the pedestrians—swaggering, grinning seamen; furtive, hurrying young men; and slouchy nonchalant denizens—are evidence of normal activity." The experience for a visitor, according to Price, was as follows: upon ringing a doorbell, the customer was escorted by a black maid into a parlor of worn furnishings, a jukebox, obscene pictures, perfume, and subdued light. In spite of Prohibition, the maid offered wine or whiskey at fifty cents per glass, or beer at twenty-five cents. Depending upon the madam's choice of uniform, the "girls" then displayed themselves dressed in an evening gown, or frock, or underwear so that the man could make a choice. He was invited to buy drinks and to go upstairs. Afterward he was asked to leave. The cost was $3 to $5, and the madam kept track of the money.[39] Compared to the modern-day Mustang Ranch, the routine for the customer and for the prostitutes was almost the same then as it is now.

The whores explained to Price that they came to the houses because of poverty, desertion by husband or family, the need to support a child, and bad company. They dreamed of becoming authors, aviators, or brokers, but never about being shopgirls, stenographers, or housewives. They read little and their obscenity-laced conversations centered on the weather and solicitation. Jealousy was common, and Price thought that mental tests would reveal capabilities below the general population. Most were U.S. citizens, had worked in other places—as far away as New York City—and plied their trade without coercion. They were free to go as they pleased during the day, but were on duty from 6:00 p.m. until 2:00 a.m. They were constrained by city ordinance from having sex across racial lines and by an unwritten rule that they were neither to solicit outside the district nor to seduce minors. They were subject to police inspection for venereal disease and at times used bribery to avoid quarantine. Their expenses included room and board at $40 to $75 per month, clothing, and beauty expenses. Price met only a few who had savings accounts. Their ages ranged from seventeen to forty-seven, but by age twenty-five, liquor and narcotics had so eroded their looks that, if possible, they became madams who no longer entertained customers.[40]

The madams worked as independent entrepreneurs and their property was owned by a variety of investors—widows, a policeman, a grocery owner, a fireman, a customs guard, the wife of a real estate man, the owner of a Negro mortuary, the manager of a piano company, the wife of a railway express agent. There was no evidence of organized crime in the Galveston district and few pimps worked the area. Theft and fighting were the major offenses. Although there was some homosexual activity in Galveston, there was none in the district. Prostitution was essentially a female business operating with the consent of the city. J. E. Pearce, Galveston's mayor at the time, said that prostitution was impossible to stop and it was better to segregate it. But, he added, "People who care for their future will not frequent the place."[41]

Venereal disease, particularly gonorrhea and syphilis, was a problem. Medical inspections were of little use since an infection could take place within hours after an inspection. The latent and hidden stage of syphilis, moreover, could last two years and was highly infectious. The frequently used douches of vinegar, carbolic acid, or bichloride of mercury did not halt these diseases. During the world wars and the time between them, Galveston operated a VD clinic and tried to keep track of the "girls" with only limited success. In 1941 military officials threatened to order Galveston "off limits" for the troops, but when the anxious city fathers hurriedly closed the district the 800 harlots simply scattered across town. Inspection of a roundup of 206 whores in May 1942 revealed that one-fourth of them were infected with gonorrhea or syphilis or both. Disease continued.

At this point, the army learned to issue condoms, along with venereal disease literature, to men going on leave and to inspect and treat the men it controlled rather than to depend upon city officials to catch evasive women. This policy and the availability of penicillin in 1944 brought disease rates to acceptable levels. Following the end of the war, the Galveston red-light district roared back into short-lived glory. In 1957, however, the Postoffice district died in a crossfire from the state that killed illegal drinking and gambling in the "Free State of Galveston."[42] Without her handmaidens, the institution of prostitution in the red-light district withered, declined, and disappeared into shadowy memory.

THE CHICKEN RANCH

The single most notorious bawdy house in Texas, however, was the Chicken Ranch, a place made famous by the 1979 Broadway musical *The Best Little Whorehouse in Texas*, written by Larry King, Peter Masterson, and Carol Hall. It began in 1844, persevered as the oldest operating bordello in the United States, moved a half-dozen times around LaGrange, Texas, and finally settled on the outskirts of the town. The tolerant people of Fayette County stuck to their motto, "Work hard, play hard, and mind your own business." Jesse Williams from Waco took over the house in 1905 in order to escape poverty. She did well in World War I and struggled during the Great Depression like everyone else. The price for a sex act was $1.50 in 1932, but in this rural area a chicken could be traded for the service. Hence the name, the Chicken Ranch. There were plenty of eggs and chickens, and no one went hungry.[43]

Williams died in 1961, eighty years old, at an age that belies the idea that prostitutes die young, and Edna Milton, thirty-one years old, took over the single-story, clapboard house. Like Williams, she added a room at a time as business increased. The Chicken Ranch attracted blue-collar workers from Houston, college boys from College Station, and politicians from Austin. Working with twelve to fourteen "girls," at a rate of $15 for fifteen minutes, Milton made a profit of $500,000 per year and became a local philanthropist. The prostitutes, who would display themselves in sports clothes during the day and cocktail dresses at night, lived at the ranch and kept half of their income. An off-duty policeman provided protection and maintained order. Jim Flournoy, who was county sheriff from 1946 until 1980, stated, "That Chicken Ranch has been here all my life and all my daddy's life and never caused anybody any trouble."[44]

In 1973, however, Martin Zindler, a flamboyant consumer affairs reporter for Houston's KTRK-TV, telecast a week-long exposé that led to the end of the Chicken Ranch. Under political pressure, Governor Dolph Briscoe ordered Wilson Spier of the Department of Public Safety to close the place. Spier called Flournoy, Flournoy called Milton, and she shut down her Chicken Ranch. The women scattered to the winds.[45] A dustup occurred eighteen months later when Zindler brought a television crew to LaGrange to assess the change. Flournoy angrily tried to pull the reporter out of his car, failed, but yanked off Zindler's white wig and went whooping around the street like an Indian with a scalp. As Zindler later said, "We both looked like jackasses to the public."[46] Two Houston lawyers bought the property with its twelve bedrooms in 1977. The house was dismantled, sent to Dallas, and reassembled as a restaurant and disco. It failed in four months, and the remains of the Chicken Ranch disappeared when the owners auctioned off bits and pieces as souvenirs.[47]

The Decline of Prostitution

This was the fate of most bawdy houses and cribs. They were demolished, disassembled, and paved over. Only a few structures remain as curiosities of a bygone day. Hattie's in old town San Angelo that the Texas Rangers closed in 1945, for example, reopened in 1977 as a museum.[48] Following the police assaults in Galveston and elsewhere, wide-open, flagrant violations ceased to exist in Texas. Overall, the amount of prostitution in the United States seems to have declined. At least, men did not visit prostitutes as often. A survey in 1992 revealed that among men who came of age in the 1990s only 1.5 percent had paid for sex. This compared to 7 percent in the 1950s.[49] Kinsey had detected a shift in societal attitudes toward premarital sex starting in the World War I era that was reinforced by the looser morality of the 1920s.[50]

Evolving technology with latex condoms, diaphragms, and contraceptive pills and legal abortions took care of unwanted pregnancies; and penicillin and advancing medical knowledge knocked out major venereal diseases. Both sexes thus became less constricted and more equal in their sexual behavior.[51] Female chastity became less valued in American society; Kinsey and others provided accurate information about sex; pornography boomed as big business ($8 billion in 1996, $10 billion in 2001); divorce was more readily accepted; women gained greater economic opportunity; living together without marriage was tolerated; casual "hooking up" began to occur; and the population aged. In 1900 the median age in the United States was twenty-three years and in 2000 it was thirty-six years. Age, of course, is the great enemy of the physical passions. As Kinsey documented, after age thirty, men experience less and less interest in sex. All of this contributed to the shifting attitudes and to a decline in prostitution.

The Enduring Delusion

The oldest profession, however, lived on in Texas through escort services, massage parlors, streetwalking, and call girl services. Automobiles became the modern crib. Bars, taverns, hotels, and motels became places of assignation with the heat of activity regulated by fluctuations in local police suppression.[52] San Antonio officials clamped down on tanning salons, escort services, and streetwalkers in the parks. The city began using decoy prostitutes for the first time in 1979 to snare "johns" soliciting sex. The men could be embarrassed by publicity and charged with a misdemeanor. It was the first time in Texas that men shared the blame and the shame.

In 1980 the San Antonio police closed down the small, quiet suburban brothel of Theresa Brown that had operated for twenty years. She had a list of 3,000 customers that she kept under her bed. She was friendly with the police and one veteran cop commented that when he began work two decades earlier he was advised that he could not do three things (in a paraphrase of a song of the time): "Spit into the wind, pull Superman's cape, and mess with Theresa Brown."[53] With a plea bargain and twelve good-character witnesses, Brown was sentenced to five years probation.[54]

In Dallas, adult bookstores, nude modeling studios, lingerie shops, and "hot sheet" motels mixed in with other businesses along Harry Hines Boulevard. Streetwalkers, most of them black, solicited men in passing cars and sought customers from a mattress discount store with such comments as, "Hey baby, you want to try that out?" With a vigorous effort the police made 649 arrests in the first five months of 1991.[55] Arresting both men and women, the Dallas vice police periodically swept the streets, raided the shops, and ran sting operations to temporarily suppress prostitution. At times, the stings went awry. An undercover policewoman was insulted by an offer of only $1 when the going rate was $20, and a lawyer was outraged when he was handcuffed and arrested at a bar after complimenting an undercover officer, "You look like a million dollars worth." She claimed it was an offer for sex.[56]

In Fort Worth in 1991, the police broke a call girl service that charged $100 per half-hour, made $10,000 per week, and had 1,500 clients while claiming to be a stress management service.[57] The Plano police in 2001 arrested two women who were using teenage girls, a fourteen-year-old and a thirteen-year-old, to service eight to nine men per night in a residential home.[58] Houston police in 1995 raided a spa where padlocked immigrant Asian women were held in "white slavery." The women received nothing of the $120 a "pop" that men were charged.[59] In Austin police arrested James A. Bunch for running Aimes Escorts from his job at the state Department of Human Services, of all places. Men paid $50 to the escort agency and $150 to the supplied woman. A receptionist told the men that it was illegal in Texas to pay for sex and that what they paid was for the ladies' time. One customer had an account of $11,000 over eighteen months. Bunch was released on bond, but several days later he shot himself to death outside the department headquarters where he had worked for twenty-three years.[60]

Even Odessa made headlines. In 2003, two lesbians opened the Healing Touch massage parlor between a carpentry shop and a revivalist ministry in a small strip mall. The experienced madams hired three discreet women and charged the prostitutes $30 for a half-hour rent on a massage room. The whores then charged the men $100 for straight sex plus tips for extras.

Outstanding at her work was "Lexus," a dark-haired, twenty-two-year-old former cheerleader and homecoming queen from Big Spring who needed the money to free her family from debt. She had a bubbly personality, remembered flattering details about her clients, and attracted dozens of prominent men from the community. Lexus replaced a woman who quit when her pastor began showing up as a client. In time, Lexus developed a cocaine habit and separated from her husband. Following a raid in May 2004, Lexus and her coworkers provided the names that indicted sixty-eight men, including a city planner, assistant district attorney, several teachers, and a well-known rancher. Their names, ages, and addresses appeared on the front page of the *Odessa American*. For punishment the men generally faced a fine of $500, community service, and a test for venereal disease; the prostitutes, a fine of $1,000 and fifteen days in jail; the madams, two years and a day in prison for drug and prostitution charges.[61]

The Odessa scandal once more underscored the time-old foundation for the world's oldest profession—a woman's need for money and a man's need for sexual release. There was also the shared hypocrisy by all involved that resulted in embarrassment, fines, imprisonment, and divorce. But, deeper than that, the Odessa episode revealed the sad delusion of prostitution, part of the existential loneliness of human beings. Men came from Germany, New York, Colorado, and San Antonio to meet with Lexus. She was flattered and liked the attention. "I was like, 'You want *me*?' And they were like 'Yeah!'"[62] The men also liked the attention, but had to purchase the illusion of affection. They thought that they were special to the prostitute and they were flattered that Lexus remembered them. She did, but only because she had a photographic memory and was a good businesswoman.

A Nevada prostitute recently posted her feelings in an Internet chat room that unveiled the charade. When asked how she felt about being a prostitute, she wrote, "The first words that come to mind are: degraded, dehumanized, used, victim, ashamed, humiliated, embarrassed, insulted, slave, rape, violated." And about the men who came to her she wrote, "99% of them fit these words: pig, dog, animal, uncaring, user, slave owner, asshole, mean, thoughtless, rude, crude, blind."[63] She did not use these words, of course, with a customer. Prostitution provided an illusion. Essentially, the world's oldest profession is a recreation without a heart, where the men and women involved restlessly search for the recognition, appreciation, love, and devotion of Frenchy and her Mack.

DRINKING

Intimately associated with prostitution, as the people of Big Spring figured out in the nineteenth century, was the drinking of intoxicating beverages. Every society that grew grain or fruit discovered fermentation and how the consumption of ethyl alcohol can blunt the sharp edges of reality. Drinking became a recreation of escape that emanated from three sources: beer (3–8 percent alcohol), wine (8–12 percent alcohol), and distilled spirits such as whiskey (40–50 percent alcohol). Alcohol acts as a depressant and impairs the functioning of the brain. Inhibitions drop, happy people become gregarious, and unhappy individuals turn belligerent.

Absorbed into the bloodstream, alcohol begins to interrupt brain function when it reaches .05 percent of the blood-alcohol concentration—current state traffic laws define .08 percent as intoxicated. At .20 percent, which can be attained by drinking a little more than a cup of spirits, a person will have trouble walking, and at .30 percent, which can be achieved by rapidly drinking a pint of whiskey, the guzzler will become unconscious. (Even Noah, after the great flood, got drunk on wine and passed out.) Higher concentrations than this disrupt the autonomic brain centers that control heart action and breathing and may cause death. Weight, gender, time, and food can influence absorption rate, but year in and year out in American and Texan society drunkenness and its consequences have resulted by far in the greatest number of police offenses. Historically, alcohol has been the drug of choice.[64]

Moderate amounts slowly sipped pose no problem because the body can metabolize about one ounce per hour. The traditional western measurement of three fingers of whiskey—the depth of liquid that equals the distance of three fingers grasping a glass—amounts to about four ounces, however, and most people drink at a faster rate than their body can handle. That, of course, is the purpose—to become intoxicated. Habitual, heavy drinking leads to addiction, cirrhosis of the liver, fetal alcohol syndrome, hallucinations, tremors, and delirium tremens. There was a joke, probably universal, in the cattle town of Big Spring about two drunk cowboys who accosted the town doctor. One of the cowboys insisted that his friend had gone blind, but an examination revealed no such thing. "The hell they ain't anything the matter with him," insisted the soused partner. "The room is full of alligators and elephants and he must be blind because he can't see them!"[65]

Alcoholic drinks came to America with the first immigrants—there were no local intoxicants. The Pilgrims brought with them a vat of sour English beer; the elite of the seaboard colonies learned to imbibe expensive, imported Madeira wine; and Franciscan priests planted vineyards in El Paso. "Spirits," a term that refers to any distilled liquor—gin, brandy, rum, and whiskey—were considered medicinal, nutritious, and necessary. Polluted water and raw milk could make a person sick, and tea and coffee, both imported and taxed, were rare and expensive. Although the rum from the triangular trade and the hard cider made in apple-growing regions were especially popular during the colonial and Revolutionary era, lager beer, whiskey, and wine to a lesser extent were the important alcoholic beverages of later periods. Drinking, but not drunkenness, was a pervasive and an accepted part of life. Stagecoaches stopped every five miles in 1830, according to a foreign observer, "to water the horses and *brandy the gentlemen*!"[66] Shopkeepers in the early trading town of Dallas in the 1840s, moreover, kept a barrel of whiskey at the rear of their stores with a tin cup for free drinks.[67]

Scots and Whiskey

It is a rough truism that immigrant Scots brought a taste for whiskey to America; the Germans produced the first worthy beer; and the Italians, French, and Spanish popularized wine in the young country. The Scots of western Pennsylvania, remembering their skills of distillation, discovered that they could convert a bushel of unwanted grain into three gallons of welcome whiskey. This precipitated the short-lived "Whiskey Rebellion" of 1794, which was basically a protest about taxes. The Scots, erecting small stills wherever they went, migrated to Tennessee and Kentucky and made whiskey from rye and corn. They learned to recycle old fish barrels by charring the inside and discovered to their surprise that the taste of the whiskey improved. The charcoal removed impurities from the whiskey and, over time, water escaped through the oak staves, leaving behind a smooth-drinking product. Sloshing in the casks, the liquor traveled well, and by 1812 mellow Kentucky whiskey was an item of commerce in the eastern United States and down the Mississippi River.[68]

On an early business venture, John J. Audubon (1785–1851), the famous painter of American wildlife, for instance, floated three hundred barrels on a flatboat from Henderson, Kentucky, to St. Genevieve, Missouri, to sell for two dollars per gallon. He had paid twenty-five cents per gallon.[69] Sam Houston, the great icon of Texas history, provides another historical example. After his disastrous marriage to Eliza Allen, he resigned from the governorship of Tennessee and migrated westward to live among the Cherokees. He set up a trading post and imported, among other items, four barrels of Monogahela whiskey and one barrel each of cognac, gin, rum, wine, and corn whiskey. Selling liquor to the Indians was illegal, and it is debatable that Houston ever did, but officials temporarily seized forty barrels from his business associates. Houston claimed his supply was for personal use. "Refreshments," he called them. Perhaps so, because the local Indians shortly began to call him "The Big Drunk."[70]

Whiskey came down the Mississippi River to river towns and to New Orleans, where it was transhipped on small packets to the seacoast ports of Texas. From these points, the casks moved by oxcart to the interior. Later, the consolidated distilleries that formed in Kentucky and Tennessee following the Civil War transported their products over railroads and made them readily available to barroom entrepreneurs. A saloon was among the easiest businesses to start. All that was needed was a cask, cups, a few planks, and a customer. And in the boomtowns of Texas, the saloon was nearly always the first local business on the ground. For example, after the legislature announced the new town of Houston to be the capital in 1836, Francis R. Lubbock went to look for it early in 1837. He found a street leading from Buffalo Bayou, some stakes and footprints, several small houses under construction, and a few tents, one of which was a saloon.[71] Years later, in 1875, the buffalo hunter Dick Bussel observed soldiers in the Texas Panhandle unloading one hundred wagons to set up Fort Elliott, and nearby he noted employees of the supply company Lee and Reynolds raising a tent. These sutlers had a bar in operation by midafternoon of the first day.[72]

Saloon owners filled and refilled bar bottles from the casks, and in the process added various diluents such as water, tobacco, molasses, red pepper, fusel oil, ethyl alcohol, turpentine, and prune juice. These diluted drinks along with inferior whiskey acquired local names such as "Tangle Leg," "Stump Puller," "Phlegm Cutter," "Red Eye," "Stagger Soup," "Coffin Varnish," "Taos Lightning," "Pop Skull," "Bug Juice," "Dynamite," "Bust Head," "Brain Scorch," "Rot Gut," and "Tiger Spit." The federal government in 1893 stopped this dangerous custom by requiring a bottled-in-bond from the seller that declared what was in a bottle. This was a part of the drive for pure food and drugs and was a law that also protected the integrity of trade names such as Old Crow and Sunny Brook.[73]

With the coming of railroads, an entrepreneur could order a ready-made bar including an operating manual from Chicago or St. Louis. A classic style thus emerged that featured a bat-wing swinging door at the entry and a long, varnished hardwood stand-up bar with a low brass rail in front. Cowboys notoriously suffered from sore backs and a rail on which to prop one leg and a bar top on which to place an elbow was a great relief. There would also be tobacco for sale and so saloons featured well-placed cuspidors with sawdust scattered around them to absorb errant expectoration. Behind the bar was a narrow passage for the bartender and lining the back bar would be the glittering bottles of whiskey, brandy, rum, and gin. Beer might be available from an iced keg.

Above the display, likely, would be placed a mirror so customers could watch other people, or paintings of nude women, or Custer's Last Stand, or sports scenes. The bartender—traditionally dressed in a long-sleeved white shirt, black vest, black bow tie, and white apron—presided as server, peace officer, neighborhood psychologist, and news source. A few tables with chairs, a stove in the corner, a room for storage, perhaps a billiard table, and a back door to the outhouse completed the scene.

The saloon of the nineteenth century was essentially a male refuge where drinks sold almost uniformly for twenty-five cents per shot of whiskey or ten cents for a large glass of beer. There were other drinks, of course, such as whiskey punches and juleps along the coast where ice was available. The saying about juleps was that one was a revelation, two was pure heaven, and three was a serious mistake.[74] William Bollaert, an early Texas diarist, recorded this wisdom and listed a variety of such drinks available in Galveston bars in 1842.[75]

Mixing cocktails, however, was an art not easily mastered. There is a story from Old Tascosa about a young apprentice left in charge of the Griffin Saloon. A huge man in a buffalo robe coat entered, shook the snow off like a dog, hugged the warm stove, and demanded a cocktail. Knowing nothing, the young man stirred together the contents of several bottles and handed it to the man. The stranger drank it in one swallow, gasped, and demanded another. Delighted with his success, the youngster mixed another and took it to the man standing by the stove. In a rapid movement the stranger pressed a gun barrel into the barkeep's ribs. "Now drink it yourself," he growled, "and we will die together."[76]

The saloon was a place of jokes, comradeship, songs, and escape from daily life. In Texas and the West, barrooms generally excluded minorities, children, and women, but any white man could enter, buy a drink, treat the house, and take an empty chair at a poker game. Women drank at home, often alcohol-based tonics that were supposedly good for their health. Respectable women were thus protected from rough men, as historian Madelon Powers noted, and rough men were protected from decent women.[77] Prostitutes, according to historian Richard Selcer, existed in a gray area of saloon culture, "both there and not there."[78] They were not allowed in high-class places. It was at the saloon that cattlemen, oilmen, and merchants met to carry on business, confirm a friendship, and eat lunch. The breweries in large cities sponsored free cold lunches for their beer drinkers, a custom that lasted from the 1880s until World War I.[79]

Germans and Beer

Although the whiskey punch served during the Christmas season in coastal hotels was considered the national drink of Texas, for most saloons straight whiskey and beer were the staples of trade. It had been known from the time of ancient Egypt that yeast added to fermented grain can produce a carbonated alcoholic drink. It was chancy, however, because the yeast floating on top also attracted bacterial growth that soured the beer. Chemists Louis Pasteur and Emil Hansen helped solve this problem with pasteurization, but meanwhile the Germans discovered a yeast that would sink to the bottom of the malt. After aging in cool conditions, usually over the winter, the mixture produced a sweet-tasting lager beer. Unlike whiskey, however, beer did not travel well because it was bulky and began to lose carbonation almost immediately upon leaving the brewery. Germans, consequently, established local brew houses for neighborhood consumption wherever they went.[80]

William A. Menger (1827–1871), who arrived in San Antonio with the initial thrust of German migration in the 1840s, established the first Texas commercial brewery and the best-known hotel in Texas next door to the Alamo. Menger's Western Brewery (1855–1878) used the cool water of the Alamo Madre ditch to chill and age the lager beer in a stone cellar with three-foot walls. The cellar is still there at the hotel. By 1860 there were eleven small breweries in Texas and twenty-seven in 1870, all in places of heavy German settlement. These immigrants were by far the largest group from Europe and in 1880 San Antonio was about one-third German in population. Three years later, Adolphus Busch of St. Louis, another German immigrant, built the Lone Star Brewery (1884–1918) in the Alamo City. Busch's brewery distributed bottled beer not only in Texas, but also in Mexico and California. This was a major operation that marked the influence of outside investors, technical advances in bottling, and commercial expansion, but Prohibition killed it and the Lone Star name passed to another company in 1940. The second Lone Star, marketed as "the national beer of Texas," developed a filter system to make nonrefrigerated draft beer. The company sold out to Olympia Brewing Company of Washington state in 1976.

As in the case of the first Lone Star, the dragons of Prohibition and the skeletons of the Great Depression ended the life of most Texas breweries. The San Antonio Brewing Association that established Pearl Beer in 1886, however, survived the dragons by marketing near-beer, ice, and soft drinks. Pearl rolled out one hundred trucks and twenty-five boxcars of beer within fifteen minutes of the end of Prohibition, went on to become a national brand in the 1970s, and was purchased by Californians in the 1990s. Kosmos Spoetzl, a German immigrant brewmaster, who took over a small, failed brewery in Shiner, Texas, in 1915 also managed to survive. His company outlasted Prohibition not only by selling ice and near-beer, but also by using family money from construction work in Florida. Ownership of the Spoetzl Brewery has passed through several hands, but it is still Texan controlled and has found a regional niche market with its heavy, dark bock beer. Interestingly, the history of beer-making in Texas and the United States returned in full circle during the 1990s with the construction of microbreweries in the larger cities to serve neighborhoods once again with unique tastes and brands.[81]

The nineteenth-century Germans, about five percent of the total state population, introduced Texans not only to good beer, but also to a family joy of drinking and amusement. In their communities that spread across south-central Texas, they established clubs for shooting, athletics, singing, and dancing. They organized masquerade balls, plays, concerts, song festivals, and parades. *Maifest* and *Oktoberfest* as well as the Fourth of July were times for exuberant celebration, and between those times, the Germans valued the drinking, conversation, and storytelling of friendly visits. According to Texas historian Glen E. Lich, "The German immigrant showed his busy Anglo-American neighbor how to relax after toil, since what marked the German perhaps most of all was his passion for 'organized fun.'"[82] Time, declining immigration at the end of the nineteenth century, and the prejudice of two world wars have eroded appreciation of the German contribution to Texas history. Ghosts, however, linger in Texas place names such as New Braunfels, Schulenburg, Fredericksburg, Pflugerville, and Luckenbach and in the scattered old dance halls of Anhalt, Cat Spring, Gruenau, Kendalia, Lindenau, and Cypress.

THE *GARTEN VEREIN*

In Galveston 180 German citizens established a private park in 1874 for "social entertainment" and "innocent sports." They charged a $10 membership fee, required stockholders to speak German, bought two city blocks, hired architect Nicholas J. Clayton, and erected an open-air pavilion in 1879. It could be reached by trolley car and became a center for middle- and upper-class entertainment. The *Garten Verein* functioned during the summertime and provided weekly music, food, bowling, tennis, and romance. Red-faced German waiters with flowing mustaches served platters of cold meat, salads, ice cream, lemonade, and steins of foaming beer. A reporter in 1897 commented, "The Wednesday night concerts and picnics have been responsible for more changes of heart in the last twenty years than all the other agencies combined which Cupid has established in Galveston."[83]

The *Garten Verein* had to be rebuilt and the grounds replanted following the devastation of the hurricane of 1900. After that it continued on its merry way, and an archival dance card from 1918 for the Conway Shaw orchestra indicated a program of three waltzes and nine one-step dances. The first one-step tune was "Liberty Bell" and the last waltz song was "Somewhere a Voice is Calling." Use of the park declined in the early 1920s, in part because of World War I prejudice against Germans, and in 1923 Stanley E. Kempner, a member of an elite Galveston family, bought the property for use as a free city park. Following a fire in 1979, the city rebuilt the pavilion with the use of donated funds from the Moody and Kempner foundations and today the ornate facility is used for receptions, weddings, dances, and parties.[84] It is a tribute to the city's heritage.

GRUENE HALL

A rougher history awaited another famous Texas German gathering place, Gruene Hall. Heinrich D. Gruene (?–1920) built a cotton gin, store, bar, and social hall for his neighbors and tenants on the stagecoach road between Austin and San Antonio in the 1870s. By 1900 Gruene (pronounced "Green"), Texas, was the ginning and social center for the area's cotton farmers, but a boll weevil infestation struck in the 1920s. It was devastating, and at the end of the decade the Gruene family was not able to produce a single bale on their eight thousand acres. The Great Depression and highways that bypassed the village turned it into a ghost town. In 1976, however, entrepreneurs Pat Molak and Mary Jane Nalley bought the old dance hall and gristmill as a place for arts, crafts, and tourism. Gruene Hall reopened in 1979 and rode a wave of popular country-western music to success.[85] The beer thus began to flow and dancers returned to stomp, scoot, and shuffle on the hardwood floor of this reminder of German hospitality.

SCHOLZ GARTEN

Probably the oldest, continuously operating German drinking establishment in Texas is Scholz Garten of Austin. August Scholz (1825–1891) opened it in 1866, and after 1908 the Austin *Saengerrunde*, a German singing club, ran it as a place where families could sit under the trees to eat, drink, and listen to music. An 1871 newspaper advertisement described it as a "rallying point for light-hearted youth and a place of recreation for weary business people," and its location near the University of Texas—with its perennial supply of "light-hearted" students and "weary" faculty—has ensured its popularity to the present.[86] The elm trees still provide shade in the back where Scholz Garten still offers beer and music, albeit of a different sort. It is the best example today of what the nineteenth-century German immigrants had in mind.

GAMBLING

Most nineteenth-century Texas saloons, however, lacked the family conviviality of the German social halls. Instead, they were places of male amusement and gambling. Behind the swinging doors were not only a long bar, foot rail, and spittoons, but also tables and chairs for games of chance. Poker, roulette, blackjack, craps, chuck-a-luck (tumbled dice), monte (played with a special deck of forty cards), three-card monte (trying to select the highest of three face-down cards), and keno (like bingo) games were likely, but the most popular was faro. It was a French gambling game named for the early cards that displayed an Egyptian pharaoh on the back. The dealer used an oilcloth printed with the thirteen cards of one suit, usually spades. Participants would place bets on the layout and then the dealer would pull two cards from a slot in a spring-loaded box. If matched, the first card won bets for the dealer; the second won for the players. When played honestly, faro gave the participant an almost even chance to win against the house.

Gambling was as widespread as drinking and whoring and just as deeply embedded in history. After all, at the crucifixion of Christ, Roman soldiers cast lots for the possession of his clothing. Through all times, people have seemed willing to take a risk for a quick, easy profit. Beyond the greed, the allure of gambling was excitement. A football game or horse race became personal once money was wagered on the outcome. During the settlement of western Texas at Fort Chadbourne north of San Angelo, for example, some officers challenged a band of Comanches to a 400-yard horse race. The seemingly reluctant Indians produced a shaggy "sheep of a pony" and placed bets. When a large, 170-pound native mounted the pony with a club, the sympathetic soldiers, thinking they had an advantage, matched it with their third-best horse. The Comanches, of course, won and gathered up the flour, sugar, and coffee that had been wagered against their buffalo robes.

The insulted officers demanded a second race that matched their second fastest horse against the mustang pony. Once more the Indian horse with its heavy rider won and the outraged soldiers demanded a third match. Betting became serious and heavy, and the officers brought out a Kentucky thoroughbred mare. In the race the Indian jockey whooped, threw away his club, bolted into the lead, and, fifty yards from the finish, turned backward on the mustang to jeer at the army loser.[87]

The story demonstrates the endurance of the mustang, the sagacity of the Comanches, the hubris of the U.S. soldiers, and the eagerness of people to gamble. But, there is something more to be said. To some extent, all human life is a speculation, and on the frontier, the gamble was heightened. People hoping for gold, land, and opportunity moved westward on wagons, horses, and foot. The trip was a risk, a gamble, but men and women grasped at the chance in spite of dangers, disease, and death. They dreamed of success, of being winners. The recreation found in unrestrained western gambling was symbolic of the greater wager people had made with their lives.[88]

A small, itinerate group of professional gamblers, honest and dishonest, emerged to make a living by playing cards. It was easier than being a cowboy or farmer, but as eastern places became respectable, the citizens pushed the sharpies out. They too went West. At Vicksburg in 1835, town vigilantes hanged five blacklegs and the rest escaped to live on Mississippi riverboats. The professionals migrated to the places of action—cow towns, forts, red-light districts, the larger western cities—and readily moved when pushed out or when opportunity appeared somewhere else. Their names repeatedly show up in western and Texas history—Bat Masterson, Luke Short, Lottie Deno, the Earp brothers, Ben Thompson, John Wesley Hardin, and Timothy Courtright. They often walked both sides of the law—sometimes licit and sometimes illicit—seldom accumulated a large fortune, lived nocturnally in smoke-filled rooms, and frequently ended their lives abruptly in a flash of gunfire and splatter of blood.

The Violence of the Saloons

There are some famous stories about these gamblers and gunmen of nineteenth-century Texas, but it should be remembered that, with the influence of whiskey and the excitement of gambling, the saloon could be a very dangerous place for anyone. Consider an anecdote from the early history of Houston when it was the capital of the new Republic. An uncle of Charles Hedenberg arrived from New Jersey to set up a carriage shop. After landing, he had his trunks transferred from the wharf to his nephew's merchant house, Hedenberg and Vedder. Busy at the moment, Charles suggested that the uncle look about town. After hearing gunshots at the new capitol, the uncle witnessed the carting off of Algernon Thompson, who had been severely wounded by a fellow senate clerk. Shaken, the uncle quickly walked down the west side of Main Street where a soldier, shot by another, almost landed upon him as he passed by the Round Tent Saloon. The uncle then ran across the street and arrived in front of John Carlos' Saloon just as a man rushed out the door with his bowels protruding from a huge Bowie knife wound. Reaching his nephew's store, the uncle gasped, "Charley, have you sent my trunks to the house?"

"No, Uncle, not yet."

"Well, do not send them. Get me a dray so I can at once take them to the boat that leaves for Galveston this afternoon."

"Why Uncle, what do you mean? Why, you have seen nothing; have not had time to look at the town."

"Charley, I have seen enough. I wish to return home immediately. I do not wish to see any more of Texas." And with that, the man left and never returned.[89]

The effusive and sometimes unreliable Sam Chamberlain of *My Confession*, a diary about the War with Mexico, recorded an incident at the Bexar Exchange, a San Antonio saloon, that again demonstrates the inherent danger of such places. In a dispute over euchre, a betting game played with the highest cards of a deck, a short, thick man in Mexican clothes threw a glass of liquor into the face of his opponent, a tall Ranger dressed in a red shirt and buckskin leggings. The Ranger sprang to his feet and poked the muzzle of a revolver against the chest of his antagonist and demanded an apology or he would blow a hole that a rabbit could jump through. "Shoot and be d—d, but if you miss, John Glanton won't miss you," was the reply. The Ranger pulled the trigger. Misfire. Glanton leaped up and, with the quick slash of a Bowie knife, cut halfway through the Ranger's neck.

Placing his foot on the bleeding corpse and glaring about the room, Glanton announced, "Strangers! Do you wish to take up this fight? If so, step out. If not we'll drink." All went to the bar to touch glasses with Glanton as he wiped the dripping knife clean on his leather sleeve. Bar attendants hauled away the body and sprinkled sawdust on the bloody floor. Glanton, a professional gambler and Indian fighter, then calmly returned to his game of euchre.[90]

Richard Selcer, the leading historian of nineteenth-century Texas saloons, estimates that somewhere in the bars of Fort Worth, Austin, El Paso, or San Antonio gunfire aligned with insult at least once every week.[91] Ty Cashion, the historian of Fort Griffin, notes on the other hand that gratuitous killing was rare and that neither legal authorities nor the public took violence lightly.[92] A few events nevertheless are emblazoned on the pages of Texas history.

FATAL CORNER

Such is the case of Jack Harris and Ben Thompson. His background is sketchy, but Harris (1834?–1882) was born in Connecticut, became a scout for the U.S. Army, joined the San Antonio police force in 1860, and fought for the Confederacy. He returned to the Alamo City and established a saloon in 1872 at West Commerce and Soledad. Jack Harris' Vaudeville Saloon and Theatre developed into a profitable combination bar, gambling hall, and variety theater.

The variety theater, or concert saloon, started in New Orleans in 1849 and used short acts of comedy, juggling, singing, music, and dance to entertain and attract customers for drinking and gambling. In the West and Texas, it replaced the old cowboy dance halls as cattle drives decreased. Harris and others used women in the theaters as actresses as well as waitresses in the bar to hustle drinks. Although such women were often prostitutes, their presence meant that the saloon was no longer an exclusive male club. A line had been crossed and the crossing pointed to the future. The variety theater was a forerunner of burlesque, vaudeville, and the strip clubs of today. Texas passed a law in 1910 that banned theatrical productions in places that served liquor and allowed women in the audience.

Ben Thompson (1842–1884), a professional gambler and gunman with a mean temper, was born in England, but grew up in Texas. His checkered career was punctuated by killings—fifteen homicide warrants in his lifetime—and he spent two years in the Texas state penitentiary for slaying his brother-in-law. He participated in a railroad war in Colorado, received $5,000, invested in Austin property, and purchased the second-floor gambling concession of the Iron Front Saloon at Sixth (Pecan) Street and Congress Avenue. This concession gave him the exclusive right to direct the games, mainly keno and faro, and he split the profits with the owners. The dapper, urbane, somewhat portly Thompson gained a reputation for running an honest house that featured high stakes. In 1880, he was elected marshal, which gave him the protection of the law while he continued to wager. He was a success, but trouble dogged Thompson like a shadow.

On a pleasure trip with his family to San Antonio, he visited Jack Harris' Vaudeville Saloon and Theatre. Gambling, after all, was Thompson's profession. Drunk, he lost his money and jewelry playing monte. In a rage, he pulled a pistol on Joe Foster, the dealer, and at gunpoint took it all back. Harris, who was not there at the time, pronounced that Thompson was never to return to his saloon. Thompson, of course, took that as a challenge.

Back in San Antonio on July 11, 1882, Thompson, again drinking heavily, prowled the streets and the Vaudeville, looking for Harris. A deputy sheriff prevented bloodshed on the street during a chance meeting of the two men when words, not bullets, were exchanged. Tension mounted. Still drinking, Thompson raged at a bartender at the Vaudeville, "I'm going to close this damned whore house. You tell Joe Foster and Jack Harris that they are a damned lot of thieving SOBs and living off the produce of their whores."[93] Thompson then left the saloon and a friend warned the absent Harris, who slipped into his bar, picked up a shotgun, and waited.

Thompson arrived at the entrance and saw Harris in the shadowy evening interior. "What are you doing with that shotgun?" he yelled, and Harris replied, "Kiss my ass, you son of a bitch!"[94] Thompson jerked up his pistol and fired twice through the latticework of the swinging door. Harris fell, mortally wounded in the chest, and Thompson hastened back across the plaza to his room in the Menger Hotel. There, Thompson turned his gun over to a friend and surrendered to the police. He was shortly indicted and, four months later, acquitted. The attitude of the courts was that gunmen and gamblers could settle their disagreements as they wished so long as it was a fair fight. In this case, it was agreed that both men were armed and that it was a private matter. When Thompson returned to Austin, a crowd at the train station greeted him as a hero. They unhitched the horses of his hack and in adulation hand-pulled the carriage up Congress Avenue to the steps of the capitol. The killing, however, was not yet done.

Ben Thompson returned to the Harris saloon on March 11, 1884, with King Fisher, a friend of like ilk. Thompson had traveled to San Antonio on a lark and, at the end of a night of carousing, he and Fisher ended up at Harris' old establishment. Forewarned, the current owners of the saloon, Billy Simms and Joe Foster, awaited them. Simms and Jacob Coy, the bouncer, greeted Thompson and Fisher at the bar and, after casual conversation and a drink, the four went upstairs to watch a variety act from the theater balcony. Foster joined them there as Thompson gave a drunken triumphal recounting of how he shot Jack Harris. Foster seethed. He was a friend of Harris and the dealer Thompson had robbed. The group stood up to move down to the bar, and Thompson offered Foster his hand in reconciliation. When Foster refused the handshake, Thompson slapped him across the face. Then he drew his pistol and struck Foster across the mouth. Coy grabbed the six-shooter as the room exploded with gunfire.

There is a debate about the number of shots fired, somewhere between ten and twenty-two. The stage show and music abruptly halted as people ducked and scrambled to get out of the way of stray bullets. There were curses and screams, but the place was empty and quiet in a few moments.

Bullet holes and gore spattered the saloon walls. The curious theater actresses lifted their skirts above the blood dripping down the stairwell to obtain a glimpse of the dead. Thompson, his lifeless gray eyes open, his waxed mustache still curled, had been hit two times in the forehead, once in the chin, another in the abdomen. He had fired five times, but his buddy Fisher, also dead, had never taken his gun from the holster. Foster was hit below the knee and bled to death eleven days later after a doctor cut an artery while probing the injury. Coy had a flesh wound and Simms was unharmed.

An immediate coroner's inquest cleared the surviving combatants with a ruling of justified self-defense, but an official autopsy later in Austin raised doubts. It reported that Thompson had been hit by eight bullets, some fired from above, and one of them from a Winchester rifle. Possibly Thompson's death was an assassination, a murder planned in advance. No one knows for certain because there was no evidence, and the original coroner's verdict was allowed to stand. Afterward, however, the intersection of West Commerce and Soledad near Main Plaza became known as the "Fatal Corner."[95]

SHOWDOWN AT THE WHITE ELEPHANT

A similar explosive event ended the infamous feud between Luke Short and Timothy Courtright in Fort Worth. It was one of the few actual face-to-face showdowns in the history of the West. Timothy "Longhair Jim" Courtright (1845–1887) was born in Iowa, served bravely with the Seventh Iowa Infantry in the Civil War, worked as an army scout where he let his hair grow long, made money as a hired gun in New Mexico, and served as marshal in Fort Worth for three terms (1876–1879). Courtright was moody, overbearing, and mean. He always wore two six-guns, butts forward, drew with the right hand from the right hip, and was considered faster than Wild Bill Hickok, Wyatt Earp, or Bat Masterson. In the last millisecond of his life, however, he must have been surprised with the lightning speed of Luke Short.

Short (1854–1893) grew up in the Red River Valley of Texas. He became a cowboy, barkeeper, professional gambler, and a successful saloonkeeper in Dodge City, Kansas. He drifted to Fort Worth in 1883 and began to run the upstairs gambling concession of the White Elephant Bar in 1887. It was located in the uptown business section of the city, well away from the downtown red-light district that featured the Black Elephant Saloon for African-Americans. With a superb bar, upscale restaurant, thick carpets, drapes, and expensive chandeliers, the White Elephant was considered an exclusive gambling house for high-class society. Bat Masterson characterized it as one of the best in the Southwest. The small, well-dressed Short—who carried a concealed, short-barreled Colt revolver in a special leather-lined hip pocket—provided a variety of games and popularized keno in Fort Worth. He made a lot of money for himself and his partners.

Courtright, meanwhile, skidded downward. He tried unsuccessfully to run a detective agency and then, through intimidation, began to force protection upon unwilling businessmen. Short, who would give money to almost anyone, would not accept extortion and refused Courtright's demands. A brooding Courtright drank heavily and bragged that he would kill the gambler. Short remained calm and had his shoes shined. At 8:00 p.m. on February 8, 1887, Courtright, big pistols strapped on, called Short to the street in front of the saloon. They moved up the street about three to four feet apart. There was a brief exchange of words and Longhair Jim pulled a gun for the last time. Short was faster and his first bullet hit Courtright in the thumb of his gun hand. Then Short made a surprising move. He closed the gap between them and fired four more shots at point-blank range—bam! bam! bam! bam!—that struck the drunk Courtright in the shoulder and heart. Courtright, without returning a bullet, sprawled dead and bleeding halfway into the doorway of a neighboring shooting gallery.[96]

There was no indictment of Short. His action was considered self-defense, as indeed it was. The shootout between Short and Courtright, however, symbolized the zenith of the Wild West. Although violence at the bars continued, the old wide-open saloon, gambling, and prostitution were forced to change. The respectable people of Fort Worth shunned Luke Short, and it was a shock, even to the rowdy element, when a few days later Sally, a little-known dance hall girl from Hell's Half Acre, was found dead and nailed to an outhouse door.[97]

New Attitudes and New Laws

The Progressive Era with its dynamic forces of temperance and increased respect for women won power at the juncture of the new century. Reform politicians gained traction in Texas, red-light districts dimmed their lights, gambling was suppressed, and saloons began to limit their hours. In response to a local ordinance in 1889, even the famous White Elephant had to close on Sundays. A 1913 Texas law went further and closed all bars, including associated businesses such as restaurants, from 9:30 p.m. to 6:00 a.m. on weekdays and from 9:30 p.m. on Saturday until 6:00 pm on Monday. Owners could not even enter their saloons to clean up on Sundays.[98]

In 1905 the Texas legislature passed a law that allowed injunctions to stop the use of any building for gaming purposes. It bolstered the ignored 1881 anti-gambling law. That ended open casino gambling, and, wherever possible, such as in El Paso, the gamblers, prostitutes, saloon owners, brewers, and distillers moved across the Rio Grande into Mexico. The final hammer came down with the 1917 passage by the U.S. Congress of the Eighteenth Amendment to the Constitution, which prohibited the manufacture, sale, or transportation of intoxicating beverages. America's moral crusaders had won, at least for a while.

PROHIBITION AND BEYOND

The Texas legislature ratified the amendment in 1918 and Texas voters approved a state prohibition amendment in 1919. Carrie Nation, the beetle-browed, hatchet-wielding harridan from Kansas was no longer a joke as the breweries shut down and the saloons sold out lock, stock, and barrel. At the horseshoe-shaped bar in Thurber, Texas, where thirsty miners washed the coal dust from their mouths and throats with seven railroad cars of beer per week, the furnishings were liquidated for ten cents on the dollar.[99] As saloon men and dealers in Texas sold their supplies to anxious purchasers, it was reported that one man, Zach White, bought the entire stock of the Paso del Norte Hotel for his personal use. Elsewhere in El Paso, as the final minutes ticked off, the bartenders at the Gem, the city's most famous saloon, simply placed the bottles, mixers, and beer on the bar and let the customers serve themselves.[100] In San Antonio, barroom owner Dan Breen told his patrons, "Drink up the stuff, boys, this is the last day." He joined them and dropped dead in the late afternoon.[101] Thus began Texas' longest drought.

It lasted fourteen years, but of course, illegal gambling, drinking, and whoring continued albeit at a suppressed, furtive level. Taos Lightning (corn liquor) made a comeback as clandestine stills popped up to supply the thirsty element of society. Enforcement of the law was difficult, and worse, it became amusing for normal, law-abiding people to tweak the law, at least some of the time. They joked about the regulations. A standard jest was about the arrested moonshiner who insisted that it was simple spring water he carried in his jug. An agent, however, tasted it and found alcohol. The moonshiner also tasted, confirmed the corn liquor, and said, "Well what do you know, the good Lord has gone and done it again!"[102]

Rural counties such as Harrison, Trinity, Somervell, and Freestone with hilly hiding places, a fresh water supply, cooperative officials, and access to big cities became centers of illegal production. About Trinity County Ranger Carl Busch commented: "Those were the bootleg days, and it was a terribly bad bootleg-whiskey-making county. Everybody was related from river to river—first, second, or third cousins. They had thirteen speakeasies in the city of Trinity that were all paying off the deputy sheriff, and he was first cousin to the sheriff!"[103]

Citizens, moreover, could make wine at home. Bricks of dried grapes came from California with a warning: Don't immerse in so many gallons of water with so much sugar, and don't keep it at a certain temperature for so many days, because it will produce fermentation, and that is illegal.[104] Specialty stores in Corpus Christi sold corks and bottles, and local welders made stills for South Texas.[105] Sister Mary Keaveney concluded after studying Fort Worth, "There were a few people who neither bought, traded, or made liquor, beer, nor wine during the epoch. But they were only a few."[106] And it was not hard to find small-scale gambling. In 1929 "The Stroller," a reporter for the *San Antonio Light*, easily uncovered poker, blackjack, dice, and lottery games accessible to the public in San Antonio hotels and residences.[107]

The same could be found in the Deep Ellum settlement of Dallas that formed around the old Houston and Texas Central Railroad depot. Blacks, Jews, and others who didn't fit easily into society began to move there following the Civil War, and it became a place of shops where you could buy anything from "a concrete mixer to second-hand false teeth." Between the world wars, rowdy Deep Ellum (an early mispronunciation of "Elm") became the "Broadway of the Dallas Black Belt" with cafes, nightclubs, domino parlors, dice games, pawnshops, flophouses, and whorehouses lining Indiana Alley. Most important, Deep Ellum nurtured the blues and jazz music of Huddie "Leadbelly" Ledbetter, Sam "Lightnin'" Hopkins, and Blind Lemon Jefferson in its nightclubs and bars. The area declined in the 1950s after the railroad removed the depot and a segment of Central Expressway slashed through the neighborhood. Interestingly enough, in the 1990s gentrification restored Deep Ellum as a place of artists, bars, music, and avant-garde shops for young Dallas urbanites.[108]

Enthusiasm for Prohibition waned in Texas by the mid-1920s and faded for the nation with the coming of the Great Depression. The Twenty-first Amendment repealed Prohibition in 1933, and Texas voters ratified a repeal of the statewide dry law in 1935. Thereafter, the question of alcohol was left to local authorities, but liquor could only be sold in full bottles. For years respectable Texans looked somewhat foolish carrying around bottles in plain paper bags. In 1970 counties could also choose "liquor by the drink" to offset the 1935 law. Texas thus became wet, dry, and damp (beer and wine sales allowed). As Austin columnist Billy Porterfield explained, a thin, dry line could be drawn from El Paso to Orange with the wet to the south and the dry to the north and west. "The jigger, the rule of thumb," he said, "is that you're usually on wet ground in the heart of the cities. But if you are out in the sticks in the top half of the state . . . the hope that a saloon awaits just over the ridge is a mirage."[109]

The Balinese Room

Out of the unsteady conditions of Prohibition emerged Texas' most famous nightclub. Galveston Island became a smuggler's haven again, a precise century after the demise of the pirate broker Jean Laffite. Racketeers shipped high quality liquor from Canada to British Honduras, placed it on large freighters and sent it to "rum row," forty miles at sea from Galveston. Bootleggers with small, fast speedboats met the freighters outside the jurisdictional waters of the United States, carried the liquor to the city in small quantities, and then transported it, disguised as scrap, on railroad cars as far north as Detroit and Cleveland. Gangsters competed for control of the operation, but after shootouts, murders, and jail terms, Rosario "Rose" and Sam Maceo surfaced as the underworld leaders in Galveston.

Although smuggling gave them their start, the Maceo brothers were really interested in gambling, which remained illegal in Texas. They organized, distributed, and took over wagering on lotteries, slot machines, casino games, and horse racing on the island and nearby mainland. They built the Hollywood Dinner Club in 1926 that featured dining, cocktails, dancing, big name bands, and gaming. The idea of such nightclubs evolved in the big cities before World War I and flourished between the wars. In 1942 the brothers transferred much of this activity to their Balinese Room, a remodeled nightspot at the end of a long pier that extended into the Gulf surf.

Since places with open gaming and drinking could be closed by injunction, the Maceos operated the Balinese Room on a loose membership basis as a private club. This was not much protection, so a guard at the front of the long pier screened patrons and warned of unwanted visitors. The Maceo organization usually received tips about gambling raids and stored away the illegal paraphernalia before getting caught. When the red lights flashed and bells rang a warning, it took only thirty-two seconds to clear a dice table. It took three minutes to walk the length of the pier. Supposedly, on one such raid, after the state officers clumped down the pier and burst into the dining area, the orchestra struck up "The Eyes of Texas" as the band leader announced, "And now, ladies and gentlemen, we give you in person, the Texas Rangers!"[110] The Rangers, however, had the last laugh.

The state received no help from either Galveston politicians or the local sheriff, Frank L. Biaggne, who claimed that, try as he might, he just could not find any gaming equipment on the island and that he could not inspect the Balinese Room because he was not a member. Meanwhile, reformer Will Wilson won the position of state attorney general in 1956. Wilson looked upon gambling in Galveston as the symbol of vice in Texas, but was frustrated because his plans for raids always leaked to the Maceos. He therefore switched to a successful tactic that he had used earlier when he was county attorney in Dallas.

Two undercover couples from Texas City quietly visited the gambling and drinking places, talked to prostitutes over several months time, and kept notes. With this evidence, Wilson, brandishing injunctions, swooped onto the island in June 1957 and closed forty-seven clubs, bingo parlors, and brothels as public nuisances. State police officers on the Galveston causeway intercepted gaming equipment being sent off the island while Texas Rangers systematically searched premises for hidden paraphernalia. They found some two thousand slot machines, illegal since 1951, that they smashed and dumped into Galveston Bay. Wilson maintained the pressure for a year—Rangers visited the Balinese Room every night—and the criminal element scattered. The madams abandoned the brothels on Postoffice Street and, while the gentle waves at the beach licked at the forlorn wooden pilings of a locked and darkened Balinese Room, Galveston subsided into the role of a quiet family resort.[111]

Thunder Road

A similar story can be found on a three-and-a-half mile strip of the Jacksboro Highway of north Fort Worth in the 1940s and 1950s. The population of Fort Worth jumped by one-third during World War II with the building of training camps and aircraft factories. On the strip, known as "Thunder Road," were six liquor stores, eighteen restaurants, seven nightclubs, and ten "no tell" motels. It was the place for soldiers, laborers, and refugees from dry West Texas to recreate with booze, sex, and gambling. There was a Chicago gang element too, and, as reporter Mack Williams commented, "Crime became organized, mean, and played for high stakes."[112] Car bombings, fights, police payoffs, muggings, and murders mark the history of the strip.

The story of Edell Evans, a pudgy, disliked pimp and gambler, illustrates the violence of the strip. In 1955 two hit men shot Evans in the back of the head in his own car. Evans had hired them to kill someone else, but the intended victim had simply paid the somewhat dim-witted assassins more money to turn their guns on Evans. As they dragged the heavy body to a shallow grave near Lake Worth, Evans regained consciousness and bit one of the men on the ankle. They shot him again, dumped him in the grave, covered the body with dirt, and left. It all unraveled, of course, and the two hit men were both killed, whacked, by others before they came to trial.[113]

Fort Worth recorded sixteen gangland murders before Thunder Road fizzled out in 1960. In the glare of newspaper exposures, the state watched a 1951 grand jury investigation led by John B. Honts, an honest special attorney. The jury indicted more than sixty gamblers and prepared to move on the corrupt police department. District Attorney Stewart Hellman, however, worked out deals to spare the police and to reduce charges against the gamblers from felonies to misdemeanors. The people's attack had been blunted by a public official, but the sheriff resigned to fight an income tax evasion charge, a new police chief began to suppress gambling, and the district attorney lost the next election.[114] Eventually, over the decade, the gamblers found it easier to go to Las Vegas where wagering was legal, the mobsters killed each other, the shabby dance halls closed, the strip became a six-lane highway, and the era of Thunder Road came to a close.

Armadillo World Headquarters

A gentler tale can be told about a more recent place of recreation, the Armadillo World Headquarters in Austin. The saga began when rock band manager Eddie Wilson ducked out the back door of a honky-tonk one night to relieve his bladder on the side of an abandoned National Guard armory next door at South First Street and Barton Springs Road. He noted not only the broken windows, but also the size of the building he was anointing. It looked like a huge dark armadillo that was big enough to hold a lot of people. Inside were high cinder block walls, a concrete floor, small vent windows, exposed steel beam superstructure, and a corrugated steel roof. The parking lot had daunting chug-holes. Nonetheless, Wilson, lawyer Mike Tolleson, Bobby Hederman, and artist Jim Franklin opened the Armadillo World Headquarters as a live music venue on August 7, 1970. It became important, not for the funky, seedy structure, but because of what happened inside.

For ten years the Armadillo offered an eclectic menu of musicians, ranging from Count Basie, Ray Charles, Bette Midler, Waylon Jennings, Jimmy Buffet, to Frank Zappa. Also it included performances by the Austin Ballet Theatre and the San Francisco Mime Troupe. It became the center of the Texas music scene and a magnet for aspiring artists to perform for an enthusiastic audience of fifteen hundred fans sitting on a floor covered with sewn bits of carpet. It was a place where Birkenstocks happily mixed with Bostonians and Tony Lamas.

Waylon Jennings, for example, played on the same bill with Commander Cody and the Lost Planet Airmen to a full house. Afterward in astonishment he said to his friend Willie Nelson, who was looking for a home for his country music, "You have to come see this place. We've got all these long-haired hippies listening to our music."[115] Bruce Springsteen from New Jersey, who became a star between two engagements at the Armadillo in 1974, commented: "I knew for sure that we didn't look like cowboys and I didn't know how they [the audience] would act. All I'd heard was that they listened to country. I didn't know what to think. But you know, they were up and dancing by the second song. . . . I didn't think there were people like that anywhere, able to shift from one extreme to the other so quickly."[116]

There was something special about the outgoing, friendly atmosphere—maybe because it was charged with marijuana, nachos, and Lone Star beer. As one fan recalled about the Armadillo, you didn't have to smoke in order to smoke. It was a haven for the counterculture and it was never quite respectable. Fans threw reefers onto the stage and once a woman opened her blouse so that Fats Domino could autograph her left breast. Holding the breast steady with one hand, he signed with the other. Afterward they both said, "Thanks."[117] Jim Franklin, who pioneered poster art in Austin, covered the walls with murals of life-like armadillos in surreal settings. "I used the armadillo," he said, "because I was visualizing the club's audience. They were celebrating the freedom of being odd."[118]

The Armadillo World Headquarters was run by naivete, absurdity, spontaneity, a staff that lived there to avoid paying rent, and countless hippie volunteers. It careened along from performance to performance with decisions made by consensus and plagued by problems of rent, telephones, booking, heating and cooling, and a bankruptcy in 1976. Eddie Wilson resigned and Hank Aldrich, one of those who lived at the Armadillo, invested his life savings and took over. Surprisingly, he turned a profit, but in 1980 the landowner sold the property to a real estate developer for $8 million. Aldrich choose not to relocate, the magic was gone, and there was a final all-night show on December 31, 1980, that ended with the audience singing "Goodnight Irene," a song popularized by Huddie "Leadbelly" Ledbetter.[119] Thus, the Armadillo World Headquarters ended, like a meteor that burned itself out in an arc across the dark Texas sky. One Texas Center, a pristine office building, now occupies the space, but every once in a while someone will leave the carcass of a roadkill armadillo on its doorstep.[120]

"Onward: Thru the Fog"

In the 1970s Oat Willie's, a hippie store in Austin, sold bumper stickers with its motto, "Onward: Thru the Fog." This slogan expressed various sentiments: frustration with the Vietnam War, support for a drug-addled existence, and courage for humanity to face an uncertain future. What it meant was determined by personal viewpoint. Although the past may be fairly clear, no one ever knows precisely what the future will bring. Drinking, nevertheless, has run more than a full circle from the open saloons of the nineteenth century to Prohibition to liquor by the drink. There remain from the past some residual restrictions based upon age, county preference, and Sunday blue laws. And there are some differences in contemporary bars with less racism, the presence of bar stools, a greater variety of products, knowledge of cocktails, and the acceptance of women without the assumption that they are prostitutes. In the 1970s, in addition, there appeared the first gay and lesbian bars in the large Texas cities, where a homosexual looking for a dance partner could go up to a table and ask, "Are you butch or fluff?" The butch played the male role, the fluff assumed the female role.[121]

Saloons, however, as of old remained places of refuge. As Louie Canelukes of Louie's in Dallas, a bar for authors and athletes, said, "I know nothing, I hear nothing, I see nothing. . . . You're not here even if you are. Nobody's here, unless they say they are."[122] Alcohol has once more become an accepted drug, except in excess. The big drug fight now concerns other mind-altering substances, particularly the hard drugs of cocaine, heroin, and methamphetamine. There is also a small drug fight that involves the corrupting influence of body-altering substances such as anabolic steroids upon athletes. How this will be sorted out remains in the future.

Unlike drinking, gambling is still illegal in Texas . . . somewhat. For income purposes, Texas installed a lottery in 1991 that brings in almost one billion tax dollars each year. Some one thousand illegal bookies ply their trade in Texas, but the police and the public are apathetic. Who worries about football bets? The state established a racing commission in 1986 and, although not particularly successful, both dog and horse racing tracks appeared.[123] Ironically, the Maceo gambling empire was crushed in the 1950s in part for taking horse racing bets by telephone.

With their spines stiffened by religious groups, both Governors Ann Richards and George W. Bush, however, successfully resisted the efforts of Tigua Indians in El Paso, the Alabama-Coushatta Indians in Polk County, and, less successfully, the Kickapoo Indians in Eagle Pass to install casino gambling, still prohibited under Texas law.[124] The Tiguas and Alabama-Coushattas became entangled in an infamous fraud scandal from 2002–2006 in which Jack Abramoff and Michael Scanlon worked to shut down the Indian casinos by rousing religious opposition. The Washington, D.C., operatives then turned around to accept Indian money to reopen the casinos through their lobbying efforts. Scanlon had to pay restitution and Abramoff went to jail.[125]

Apparently extensive but uncounted, moreover, was Internet gambling through offshore betting services. As a University of Texas student explained about e-gaming, "It's right click, right click, and you've got a bet down. It's that easy."[126] This activity was shut down late in 2006, however, by enforcement of the federal law prohibiting the transport of wagers over telephone lines. Effective Methodist, Baptist, and Roman Catholic church opposition to gaming has followed the same anti-drinking line that runs from El Paso to Orange. With the exception of the large cities, counties have blocked gaming in North and West Texas.[127] Texans who wished to gamble, consequently, traveled to Las Vegas and carried with them a variation of seven-card stud called "Texas Hold'em." It was a poker game that originated in the private Elks Club of Waco in the 1940s.[128] The wall against gambling thus has eroded, but not crumbled, and gamblers have been hindered, but not stopped.

From a time of wide-open gaming, drinking, and prostitution in the nineteenth century through the purity period that suppressed one aspect or another of the vices in the twentieth century, the most salient feature of the triad has been its persistence. Drinking, gambling, and whoring, whether licit or illicit, have remained a part of Texan and American society. Moralizing and preaching did not kill the triad, and laws only channeled it to a temporary acceptable point. The history indicates that these recreational activities, despite opposition, have been a vital part of Texas life. Participation certainly reflects human desires, and for better or worse, also reveal an aspect of Texan character that should be recognized and studied.

CHAPTER 2

Parks and Other Public Spaces

Recreational land set aside for private use is not new—it is as old as monarchy—but the idea of recreational land designated for public use is comparatively recent. Hyde Park, for example, characterized as the "Lungs of London" by English politician William Pitt the Elder (1708–1778), began as a hunting ground for Henry VIII in 1536 and evolved into a public park one hundred years later. The lower classes constantly encroached onto royal lands and reserves to such an extent that it became dangerous to exclude them.

When George I (1660–1727), for example, came from Hanover to take over the English throne in 1714, he was told by his new servants at St. James' Palace that the nearby park with its walks and canal belonged to him. The next day his chief ranger sent him a brace of carp, and the king complained to his secretary of state, "I was told I must give five guineas to Lord Chetwynd's man for bringing my own carp, out of my own canal, in my own park." George asked how much it would cost to close St. James' Park to the public, plow it over, and grow turnips. Lord Townshend wisely replied, "Only three crowns, Sir." Although the "crown" was a coin of some value, his secretary's double meanings warned of the riotous nature of London's populace, the unstable condition of the new Hanoverian rule, and the price of George's own crown that was being made. At the time, Parliament was slowly limiting royal power and democracy was on the rise. The park remained.[1]

English immigrants carried the idea of public land across the Atlantic into the colonial settlements. Boston Common, now the nation's most venerated urban park, began with the founding of the city in 1630. William Penn in his effort to build Philadelphia (1682) as a "green country town" placed evenly spaced parks on his initial gridiron layout, and James Oglethorpe designed house lots oriented around open squares for his new town of Savannah (1733).[2] Travelers and migrants poured through these ports and conveyed what they had seen and experienced into the planning and establishment of the newer towns of the frontier country. For Spanish America, the Laws of the Indies (1573) actually instructed founders to build their towns around a central public square. Today, the effect of this command can be seen most dramatically in downtown Santa Fe, New Mexico, but also in the remnants of the Alamo, Main, and Military Plazas of San Antonio. Thus, it was from the English and Spanish forebears that the idea of publicly owned parks originated and endured in America. It was also in their crowded towns where the open spaces were most needed for recreation.

MUNICIPAL PARKS IN TEXAS

Most urban parks in Texas started with the quiet generosity of older local philanthropists. In Houston, George H. Hermann (1843–1914) bequeathed land for Hermann Park; in San Antonio, George W. Brackenridge (1832–1920) donated the riverfront property that became Brackenridge Park; in Dallas, William H. Gaston (1840–1927) provided land for the Dallas State Fair; and in 1876 the obscure James (or John) J. Eakins gave the ten acres at Browder's Springs in Dallas that eventually became Old City Park. Cities bought land on their own, of course, such as Houston's purchase of Sam Houston Park in the center of town in 1899 and Memorial Park in 1924. Both Sam Houston Park and Old City Park eventually became places to display historic homes and structures that were moved to the sites.

Inspired by the City Beautiful movement of the early twentieth century to improve the appearance of their cities, urban leaders in Dallas, Houston, San Antonio, and El Paso hired George E. Kessler (1862–1923) of Dallas, a nationally known landscape architect, to help plan their cities with parks and thoroughfares. Although politicians did not always follow Kessler's suggestions, this effort, as well as the early establishment of boards of park commissioners in Dallas (1905), Fort Worth (1909), and Houston (1910) marks a Texas recognition of the significance of public open space in the totality of urban life.

San Antonio: Plazas and Parks

Although such places as San Augustine (1833), Nacogdoches (1779), Gonzales (1827), San Felipe (1824), and El Paso (1859) provided for town squares, San Antonio (1731) was the most impressive.[3] All of these towns had Spanish antecedents and the founding dates can be argued, but regardless, fifty-five Canary Island settlers arrived in 1731 to establish the villa of San Fernando de Bexar that later became known as San Antonio. On the west side of an unpaved Main Plaza, they completed a church in 1758 that was rebuilt as San Fernando Cathedral in 1873. Meanwhile, Main Plaza, defined by a perimeter of low, flat-roofed stone buildings, became a place for wagon trains, religious celebrations, and various ceremonies, such as a Spanish peace with the Apaches in 1749. After holding hands and dancing, the Indians, padres, and government officials buried a lance, a tomahawk, six arrows, and a live horse in a large hole in the plaza. The peace did not last. Later, Santa Anna established his headquarters on the north side of the plaza and flew his red flag of no mercy from the church during the 1836 siege of the Alamo.

This public square—when San Antonio was a town of about one thousand people—was also the site of the infamous Council House Fight in 1840 that exploded on the east side of the plaza. In order to strengthen a peace treaty, twelve Penetaka Comanche chiefs, brightly painted and clothed, along with fifty-three men, women, and children rode into the square under the protection of a truce to meet with officials of the Republic of Texas. It had been agreed that the Indians would turn over all their captives, but they offered only a Mexican boy and a sixteen-year-old Anglo girl, Matilda Lockhart. The girl had been severely abused as a slave for two years, and her captors had burned her nose off to the bone. She informed her rescuers that the Comanches held other prisoners.

The Texan negotiators again demanded all the captives. The Penetakas explained that the two were all their tribe possessed and that the Texans would have to bargain with other Comanche groups for the rest. The Anglos did not understand the independent nature of the various tribes and decided to hold the Penetakas at the Council House as hostages to exchange for all captives. The interpreter hesitated to relay this information that violated the truce, but then informed the chiefs and fled the room. Armed Texas Rangers entered as others surrounded the building. The surprised and angry Indians leaped for their weapons and one of them plunged his knife into the Ranger blocking the door.

With war screams, slashing knives, blood, shrieks, the swish of arrows, powder smoke, and the sharp report of firearms, the fight spilled into the dirt square as the Indians tried to break for the river. In the melee all twelve chiefs died along with eighteen other Indians. Six Texans also died and ten were wounded. The soldiers captured the remaining Indians, put them in a jail, and sent an Indian woman on horseback to the tribal camp with the message that the imprisoned Penetakas would be exchanged for the remaining captives. It did not work, and the bloody Council House Fight produced long-lasting consequences.

In a frenzy of mourning at their camp, the Comanches sacrificed horses and killed thirteen prisoners, some by roasting. Then shortly, young Chief Isimanica ("Hears the Wolf") rode into the Main Plaza at San Antonio, circled, shook his fist, cursed, and screamed challenges to battle. This marked the beginning of an unceasing, brutal Texan-Comanche war, fired by hatred that did not end until the winter campaign against the followers of Quanah Parker at Palo Duro Canyon in 1874.[4] What had happened at Main Plaza was important.

For the most part, however, Main Plaza was peaceful, a place for commercial activity—horses, cattle, and oxen trains from the coast—for the religious exercises of San Fernando Cathedral, and for entertainment. The infamous Jack Harris' Vaudeville Saloon and Theatre stood near its northeast corner. Much of this varied activity ended when the city placed the Bexar County Courthouse in the center of the plaza in 1896. After this, the block devolved into a pleasant urban green space crisscrossed by streets.[5]

More blood-drenched was Alamo Plaza because of the fighting that swirled around it during the Texas Revolution. The often-told tale describes the desperate, outnumbered Texans who were defeated and killed by the Mexican forces of Santa Anna in 1836. The fighting left the old San Antonio de Valerio Mission (1724–1793) and its compound in ruins. In 1841 the Republic of Texas gave this property, known as the Alamo, to the Catholic Church; after annexation to the United States in 1845, the property went to the federal government; the Confederate States of America used it during the Civil War; the United States took it back after the war; and in 1883 the Texas legislature bought the Alamo Chapel and gave it to the City of San Antonio. By this time, historic consciousness and tourism made possible by the railroad brought the battle place to public attention.

Philanthropist and cattlewoman Clara Driscoll (1881–1945) bought the Long Barracks area, part of the ruined compound, in 1903 to prevent the construction of a hotel on the land. Educated in Europe, she acquired a deep respect for history and upon returning in 1899 was shocked at the dilapidated condition of the Alamo. "How can we expect others to attach the importance to it that it so well deserves, when we Texans who live within its shadow, are so careless of its existence?" she asked newspaper readers.[6] So, at age twenty-two she became the state's earliest historic preservationist and hoped to persuade others to follow her lead. In 1905 the Texas legislature purchased the Driscoll land and turned it all over to the Daughters of the Republic of Texas for care. Driscoll became known as "the Savior of the Alamo." Various restorations, especially during the Texas Centennial, occurred, but roads and businesses already had intruded onto the location. The Alamo and its surroundings with its current small plaza, a former courtyard, nonetheless became a shrine for Texas independence.

Military Plaza experienced a somewhat less bloody history. Originally, it was the presidio, or fortress, of the town with a parade ground and captain's headquarters (Spanish Governor's Palace). Begun in 1722 and separated from Main Plaza by the church, it was the preferred place for executions and lynchings. A particular vigilante was memorialized in verse: "The law of Mondragon/ All Texans will endorse/ That here in San Antone/ You must not steal a horse."[7] In the 1840s city officials cleared the area of corrals and clutter and in the 1850s constructed a courthouse nicknamed the "Bat Cave" on the perimeter. The resultant Military Plaza became a city market with vendors selling eggs, poultry, corn, beans, honey, pecans, wool, hides, and canaries in wicker cages. On the west side Billy Simms established the Fashion Theatre (1885–1890) after the notorious killing of Ben Thompson made Jack Harris' Vaudeville Saloon and Theatre unpopular.

The most memorable activity at Military Plaza was the nightly banter of flirtatious chili queens. These young women sold their parents' savory dishes from heated clay pots at open-air tables under the light of hand-hammered tin lanterns. Here could be felt the pulse beat of the city—it was the place to go for chili, tamales, tacos, boiled coffee, dancing, accordion music, and cockfights. All colors and diversity of humanity sat at the same long tables with no conflict. But it all faded away when people began to worry about food cleanliness and San Antonio officials plopped their new city hall in the middle of the plaza in 1891.[8]

Beyond the city center to the northwest, San Antonio citizens enjoyed what is probably the first amusement park in the state. From a white rocky hill burst forth a stream of crystalline water called San Pedro Springs that formed a small lake that emptied into the San Antonio River. The spring was the major source of fresh water for the early town, and its 46-acre area had been declared public land in the earliest Spanish proclamations about Bexar in 1718. Later, in 1851 the city council reconfirmed it as a public square. As a young man, Frederick Law Olmsted, the intrepid traveler from New York, found a beer garden and restaurant there in 1854.[9] The city allowed J. J. Duerler from Switzerland to build a house on the land, and in 1864 he leased the reserve to develop an amusement park. Poet Sidney Lanier who came to San Antonio seeking a cure for tuberculosis described the park in 1872:

> With spreading water-oaks, rustic pleasure buildings, promenades along smooth shaded avenues between concentric artificial lakes, a race-course, an aviary, a fine Mexican lion, a bear pit in which are an emerald-eyed blind cinnamon bear, a large black bear, a wolf, and a coyote, and other attractions, this is a very green spot indeed on the prairies.[10]

Duerler died from a fall in 1874, but the public park continued, and in 1878 a streetcar pulled by mules began to transport visitors to the site from Alamo Plaza. Successive managers installed a museum of natural history, electric lights, a bandstand placed over the abandoned bear pit, a swimming pool, a playhouse theater, and a public library. In the 1940s the spring dribbled out, a victim of urban water wells, and the pool had to be closed. In 1954, through a grant from grocery store magnate Howard E. Butt, the park was refashioned to accommodate tennis courts and softball diamonds. In 2000 the city reworked the park and revived the swimming pool at the site of the abandoned spring. San Pedro thus became a park for the enjoyment of the neighborhood and the across-the-street students of San Antonio College.[11] Behind Boston Commons, it is the second oldest public park in the United States.

Austin: Barton Springs

The urbanization that dried up the spring at San Pedro also threatened the most famous spring-fed pool in Texas at Austin's Zilker Park. In the public-conscious capital, however, the threat was met with an angry citizen outburst. Politician Andrew Zilker, the first Coca-Cola bottler in Austin, bought land to the south of the city in 1901 and gave 42 acres for a park in 1918. He added 313 more acres in 1932–1934 during a period of park development in the city.

The Zilker land included Barton Springs, a rocky extension of Barton Creek that arises in the Hill Country near Dripping Springs fifty miles away. The creek drops one thousand feet in elevation, moves eastward toward the Colorado River, and disappears as it trickles water into the shallow limestone fissures of the Edwards Aquifer. There it mixes its water with other underground sources and brings it all to the surface again several hundred yards away at Barton Springs, clear and cold as a mountain lake. The springs draw water from a watershed of 157 square miles. Comanche Indians had camped near the water, and pioneer William "Uncle Billy" Barton, who built a cabin close by in 1837, gave his name to the waters.

In the 1920s the city built a bathhouse and a small dam to form a pool. It eventually became a rough rectangular area with a limestone bottom 1,000 feet long, 150 feet wide, and 15 feet deep at the diving board. The spring water burbles forth at one end at a frigid temperature of sixty-eight degrees. With a tree-lined and grassy bank, Barton Springs thus became "Austin's Eden," a retreat that in recent times attracts about 750,000 visits per year. It is a place for picnics, weddings, and sunbathing. Although it is illegal to skinny dip, in the 1970s it became clear that no one would punish the women who chose to leave their bathing suit tops at home.

Nature writer Roy Bedichek, who reserved a space on "Bidi's Rock" under a cottonwood tree at the mouth of the main spring, said, "I go to Barton's every afternoon and have a delightful cooling off. What a poem that place is!"[12] In 1994 local literati commissioned a bronze statue by Glenna Goodacre of the mid-century Texas intellectual triumvirate of J. Frank Dobie, Roy Bedichek, and Walter Prescott Webb, all barefooted and pants rolled up, arguing their points at the edge of the spring. Kids today scramble over the statue, hippies put flowers in Bedichek's hand, and jokesters put baseball caps on the bald head of dour Dr. Webb.[13] All in all, Barton Springs became a very special place for the city.

Land development in southwest Austin during the 1980s, however, brought a threat. The water quality of the springs began to deteriorate, and the pool had to be closed at times because of contamination. The shallow aquifer possessed little filtration ability, and the water at the springs quickly registered pollution—pesticides, herbicides, fertilizer, dirt, and sewage—within twenty-four hours of rain storms. In 1981, for example, silt from the construction of a mall two miles away closed the springs for thirty-two days. As environmentalists became nervous, the Austin City Council recognized the delicate nature of the springs and passed ordinances in 1980 and 1986 in an effort to regulate, but not halt, land development on the watershed. Raymond Slade, a hydrologist for the U.S. Geological Survey, commented, "If I wanted to be a real villain, I could pick a couple of spots over the aquifer, drill a well with a 9-inch or so pipe and a turbine engine, and probably stop the flow of Barton Springs."[14] Such had been the fate of San Pedro Springs in San Antonio forty years earlier.

In the expanding capital city, the recharge zone for Barton Springs tempted suburban developers who kept nudging the planning department for streets, water, and sewers. The situation boiled over in 1990 when Jim Bob Moffett, a millionaire developer from New Orleans with Freeport McMoRan, sought approval for 2,538 houses, 1,900 apartments, 3.3 million square feet of shopping and offices, and four golf courses along Barton Creek. The current ordinance required open space in developments and Moffett wanted his golf courses to count as the open space. He said that his project would not affect the springs, but worried citizens thought otherwise. Some seven hundred environmentalists packed an all-night session of the City Council to jeer Moffett's presentation and offer contrary testimony. The council unanimously rejected the Freeport proposal, declared a moratorium on building, and then later passed a new ordinance that allowed construction with catchment and diversion of water runoff. This was not good enough for the conservationists and a coalition of environmental groups called "Save Our Springs" (SOS) took to the streets.[15]

There were angry talk shows on the radio, a silent vigil at Barton Springs with a trumpeter playing "Taps," negative phone calls at a rate of 30:1 to the City Council representatives, and, most importantly, a collection of thirty-five thousand signatures to force a more restrictive ordinance.[16] "The only way to save the spring is to stay off the aquifer," said environmentalist Bill Bunch of the Hill Country Foundation. "Nobody has the constitutional right to pollute Barton Springs," he continued. "Government institutions have the responsibility to protect the public's right to clean water."[17] The Austin Chamber of Commerce argued in an opposition campaign led by Karl Rove, Republican Party strategist, that the restrictive SOS ordinance would stop city growth and make Barton Creek property worthless. Jim Bob Moffett moaned, "I keep thinking about that guy up on the cross. I tell myself, 'Forgive them for they know not what they do.'"[18] Brigid Shea, the director of SOS, countered, "The fundamental question before this community is whether or not the citizens of Austin have the right to control their own water quality or if it will be dictated by development interests."[19]

The people voted 2:1 in favor of the SOS ordinance in 1992 and elected Shea to the City Council in 1994. The courts sustained the law after a four-year fight and the developers were mollified, somewhat, when voters approved bond issues to purchase their land in the recharge zone.[20] Barton Springs thus survived through the righteous outrage and political power of active citizens. In addition, the fight left a legacy. SOS remains as a permanent watchdog organization to combat the various companies that had rushed to purchase land and file for development while the ordinance was being installed, and to stimulate broad awareness of the importance of the Edwards Aquifer from Del Rio to Salado, Texas. The city government was also sensitized. For example, when the small town of Dripping Springs, near the headwaters of Barton Creek, proposed a shopping center in 2006 the Austin politicians quickly demanded a review of the plans to ascertain how Austin's water interests might be affected.[21] Barton Springs, a beloved place of recreation, required vigilance. It was a special place.

Galveston: Stewart Beach

In Galveston, the Gulf Coast beachfront dictated a different history and offered an unofficial natural public space from the start of Texas history. Early visitors such as Francis C. Sheridan, Mrs. M. C. Houstoun, and Ferdinand Von Roemer praised the shoreline. "To drive along the beach in the evening in a light cabriolet drawn by a spirited horse and fanned by a cooling breeze usually coming from the south, affords the inhabitants of Galveston much pleasure," observed Roemer in the 1840s. "This pleasure," he continued, "is enhanced by the beautiful view of the Gulf where the waves, rolling in ceaselessly, tumble over each other in a broad, white foaming surf. A bath in the rolling surf is equally refreshing."[22] The local folk used the attractive, light brown beach for picnics, parties, and swimming with and without clothing. They built roads and a street railway to the shore and, after the horrendous 1900 hurricane, constructed a seawall with bathhouses, hotels, and shops along the Gulf edge. The city's coastline was a continual source of recreation for its citizens and included a segregated portion called "Brown Beach" for African-Americans—as if the ocean would care.[23]

In 1941 real estate developer Maco Stewart Jr. gave twelve blocks of frontage to the city in memory of his father, and with the labor supplied by the Works Projects Administration and the money from Galveston revenue bonds, the city built Stewart Beach. Inspired by beach parks elsewhere in the country, such as Atlantic City, Galveston officials installed a boardwalk, pavilion, gift shop, snack bar, roller skating rink, umbrellas, and bathhouse. The city provided lifeguards and workmen who regularly cleaned the sand. The bonds were paid off eight months early and local journalist Lilian E. Herz commented, "Perhaps no political entity established by the city has been more successful than Stewart Beach, nor has any other municipal venture afforded more pleasure and recreation to residents and visitors alike."[24]

During the first half of the twentieth century when Galveston evolved as a resort, the state built roads and entrepreneurs provided interurban service from Houston, its muscular neighbor to the north. In 1952 the Gulf Freeway opened as a straight, four-lane, fifty-mile link between the two cities. When the freeway became a part of I-45, automobile drivers from North Texas could head south, thread through Dallas and Houston, drop onto the coastal plain, go over a causeway, funnel onto the main street of Galveston, and terminate their trip in the waters of the Gulf of Mexico at Stewart Beach, the first municipal beach park in the state.

Stewart Beach thus became a destination for family recreation and for such springtime revelries as Splash Day (1916–1965) and the regional reunions of the black fraternity Kappa Alpha Psi (1983–2000). Officials had to end these festivities eventually because they grew beyond the law and order capability of the island. The beach park, in addition, became a focal point for racial integration in Galveston. Blacks could use the old segregated block of the beachfront—their only access in Texas—but their taxes supported Stewart Beach as well as other white-only facilities. As part of the national movement to break barriers, local African-Americans began to play golf on the municipal course in 1958 and twenty-five students made an attempt to use Stewart Beach in July 1960. There was no violence, just nervous discussion, and after some equivocating segregation ended. In May 1962 the Board of Managers of Stewart Beach declared the park open to all regardless of "race, creed, or political affiliation."[25] Recreation in an urban park, thus, played a role in the struggle for social justice.

ZOOS

Citizens have used their parks for all sorts of activity—picnics, sports, playgrounds for kids, sleeping, meditating, kite flying, walking, cooling off in the summer, concerts. Parks offer relief from the hustle and the jarring stress of the city. Frederick Law Olmsted, who early in his life had seen San Pedro Springs in San Antonio and later became the greatest of the nineteenth-century American landscape designers, viewed parks as the rural antithesis of urban life, a counterpoint to the noise and confusion of the town.[26] Parks thus became places for the quiet beauty of horticultural display and the entertaining distraction of zoos. Both uses date back to the Hanging Gardens of Babylon where Nebuchadnezzar II planted trees on the terraces of his palace and where Assurbanipal, the king of Assyria, kept captive lions for hunting purposes.

However, even before then, around 1150 BCE, Emperor Wen Wang of China maintained a 900-acre zoological park and Queen Hatshepsut (1540–1481? BCE) of Egypt sent out expeditions to collect monkeys, leopard, giraffes, and birds. King Solomon was known to keep lions, apes, and peacocks; Marco Polo described the menagerie of Kublai Khan; Cortez noted the aviary, captive wild animals, and gardens of Montezuma II in Mexico; and Pope Leo X in the sixteenth century kept exotic animals at the Vatican. Zoological parks were nothing new, but they were for the wealthy and ruling class.[27]

The first public zoo resulted from the French Revolution. Louis XIV had built Europe's initial zoological gardens at Versailles, and when overrun by revolutionaries some 125 years later, the animals were taken to Paris where they became a part of the Museum of Natural History and the first national zoo.[28] Natural history museums resulted from the European scientific exploration of the world in the eighteenth and nineteenth centuries. It was easier to bring home the bones and skins of animals, or specimens dried, pickled, or pressed rather than something alive and breathing. To capture and transport a living sample and keep it viable, however, represented a triumph over nature. A live collection of animals from around the British Empire, for instance, started in London in 1828 as a symbol of global domination.[29] It was more than an idle gesture, therefore, when Meriwether Lewis presented two grizzly bear cubs to President Thomas Jefferson at the completion of the Lewis and Clark exploration of the American West. The cubs lived in a stone bear pit on the White House lawn and were more than a curiosity. They were a living symbol of conquest.

In the nineteenth century the zoo became a mark of urban sophistication, like an art museum or a stadium. After the glass tank was perfected, aquariums joined in with special aqueous "cages" for exotic, swimming creatures. Such facilities became places of public entertainment and education. To be able to see an animal in motion—and perhaps hear, smell, and touch—conveyed a meaning and understanding that stationary exhibits in natural history museums could not match. The experience illustrated the rank of human beings, mentally and physically, in the global animal kingdom. Zoos thus appeared in Amsterdam (1839), Berlin (1844), Philadelphia (1874), and Washington, D.C. (1889). The first aquarium opened in 1853 at Regent's Park in

London. As nations became more urban and the memory of the wilderness faded, a zoo became a place to satisfy curiosity, a place where someone could safely meet a real lion, tiger, shark, or bear. These special parks, expensive and sometimes controversial, became beloved by the public.

Texas Zoos

By 1900 there were thirty-two zoos in the United States, mainly in the eastern cities, but also in San Francisco and Denver. Shortly after the turn of the century, Texans began to establish their public zoos—Fort Worth (1909), Dallas (1912), Houston (1923), El Paso (1925), and San Antonio (1928). Later zoos appeared in Austin, Tyler, Waco, Gainesville, Abilene, Lufkin, Amarillo, Victoria, and Brownsville. The first animals, acquired from dealers, donors, or traveling shows, were initially displayed in rows of separate, bare cages placed in city parks arranged by species—all the cats side by side, all of the monkeys, and so forth. In time, Texas zoos, like those elsewhere in the world, endeavored to remove the cages and to display the animals without the obstruction of bars or wires. This was accomplished with the use of moats and windows. In the process, there was an effort to give the animals expanded space and a semblance of their natural habitat.

These ideas came largely from Carl Hagenbeck (1844–1913), a wild animal dealer and circus owner who built a *tierpark*, or zoo, near Hamburg, Germany, in 1902–1907. He constructed an African exhibit with an artificial mountain in back and a pond in front. Zebras, antelope, and ostriches were displayed together, then lions restricted by a moat concealed by vegetation, and then goats on the far mountain separated from the lions by another concealed moat. Visitors could stand at one end and look at the entire panorama or see the various parts from closer walkways. Important design concepts included the removal of cages, the suggestion of habitat, the mixing of compatible animals, and the ease of viewing. Hagenbeck displayed his ideas at international fairs in Berlin (1896) and St. Louis (1904), and his legacy was carried on by his sons, Heinrich and Lorenz, who became zoo consultants and designers. Lorenz is given credit for the popular idea of an island for monkeys created by a circular moat filled with water.[30]

FORT WORTH ZOO

The oldest operating zoo in Texas was started during this Hagenbeck era by the newly formed park commission in Fort Worth. In 1909 the commission bought a lion, two bears, an alligator, a coyote, a peacock, and a few rabbits from a traveling circus that had broken down at Trinity Park. Shortly thereafter, the collection drowned in a flood of the Trinity River. However, the commission refused to give up, asked for donations of animals, and bought land in Forest Park where the zoo is now located. The land was far from the center of town, but in a beautiful setting. Texas Christian University moved in next door in 1911 and the location developed into an upper-class neighborhood. For the close neighbors, the Fort Worth Zoo became *their* zoo.

In 1913 city officials tried to eliminate the zoo because it cost too much—$27.50 per month—and replace it with a cheap, simple playground. This suggestion brought about hot citizen opposition, and the dispute was finally settled in favor of the zoo. The main proponent for the playground, attorney Q. T. Moreland, tactlessly argued that the facility was of little use and that the animals should be given to Dallas. That did it, for even then there was rivalry between the two cities. The zoo, thereafter, was an integral, permanent part of Fort Worth life.[31]

What Moreland failed to recognize was the deep affection that people develop for their zoos. These are family places where parents go with their young children, and the simple joy of watching the animals is long remembered. Particular animals, moreover, often become local personalities that are celebrated in the newspapers. In 1923, for example, Fort Worth was able to use $3,500 in donations to buy a three-year-old Ceylonese elephant from a circus. After a "Name the Elephant" contest, she was christened Queen Tut and every year the city celebrated her birthday. When she was eighteen, some ten thousand people turned out to sing "Happy Birthday" and share her 1,100-pound cake. Queen Tut, moreover, became a hero two years later in 1940 when another elephant, Sugar, attacked Jim Brown, an attendant. Tossing him about like a rag doll, Sugar rendered to Brown two broken collarbones, a concussion, and ribs cracked in thirty-two places. Queen Tut stopped the assault by straddling Brown's broken body and fending off Sugar until keepers could effect a rescue. Brown recovered, Sugar was shot, and Queen Tut lived in honor until her death in 1964.[32]

The Fort Worth Zoo is also noted for the "hiss heard 'round the world" after Pete the Python escaped in mid-September 1954. He was eighteen feet long and one foot wide, and keepers said he was not dangerous unless stepped upon. He had not eaten in seven weeks, however, and, of course, everyone else thought Pete was ready to coil around children and yappy spaniels. A Keystone Kops panic occurred as the zoo was cleared and the city assigned nine police cars, the motorcycle patrol, and twenty-five workers to recapture the python. They scoured the park grounds, Pete remained at large, and rumors began to circulate. A woman in Monroe, Louisiana, with the aid of a Ouija board said that Pete could be found at Jack's Bar near Forest Park. The police could locate neither the saloon nor the snake. A jokester caused alarm by floating a long inner tube down the Trinity River and a local restaurant sold Peteburgers. Weeks passed and still no Pete. Then at 4:00 a.m. in early October, a security guard heard the monkeys in a raucous uproar led by Al the Chimp who was screaming loudest of all. A flashlight revealed the python nearby and he was retaken. Returned to his glass case, Pete coiled up, laid a clutch of infertile eggs, and thereafter was known as Patricia.[33]

In 1939 a zoological society formed to solicit money for the zoo and in 1950 the group evolved into the Fort Worth Zoological Association, a corporation. Anyone could join by paying a $5 fee, but it was mainly to interest rich people to make large donations for the zoo. The association quietly enhanced the animal collection, managed the concession stands, and convinced the park board to open the zoo to African-Americans. In 1991 the city authorized the association to take over the management and budget of the facility while the city retained possession of the land and buildings. This was similar to other private-public arrangements such as that of the famous San Diego Zoo and a pattern followed by most Texas zoos. The association doubled the budget to $8 million and aggressively pursued wealthy donors, public and private. During the decade of the 1990s the association rebuilt the zoo to make it appealing to the public and comfortable for the animals.

Frequent restrooms, brand-name fast food restaurants, shade, benches, mist-making machines for hot days, and short walks between exhibit areas were installed for the comfort of visitors. "Even the textures of sidewalks are different," said planner Kenneth Sims. "We go from concrete to a more natural granite path, trying to make every element right, so when you visit our zoo we put you in a special place, just like being in Asia or Africa."[34]

The zoo became more like a theme park, with officials promoting celebrations such as the "Zoobilee of Lights" at Christmas and "Boo at the Zoo" at Halloween. They took advantage of traveling exhibits and current fads such as the interest in meerkats prompted by the Walt Disney movie, *The Lion King*. Indigenous to South Africa, these beady-eyed, mongoose-like, carnivorous, over-sexed mammals would wreak havoc on the Texas landscape if they escaped. They are dedicated excavators of tunnels. "It's kind of a hippie-commune life with an egalitarian work-share ethic," a zoo curator explained. "Everyone trades off guard duty, minding the babies and the ubiquitous digging. At night everyone sleeps together in a big, floppy pile." The curators, therefore, gave them lots of dirt encased in a concrete shell as a home for the zoo's most popular animal of 1997.[35]

Attendance at the Fort Worth Zoo increased four times in five years during the mid-1990s, reaching over one million people per year. Director Gregg Hudson commented, "When you walk through our zoo, you feel safe. The people are friendly. The animals are happy. It's a great place to be."[36] The Fort Worth Zoo became both the most visited zoo in Texas and the most important tourist facility for the city. It attracts, according to its Web site, an estimated $100 million per year.

DALLAS ZOO

Next door in Dallas, where the factor of public entertainment was downplayed, the situation was not so happy. As early as 1888, the city began collecting a hodgepodge menagerie—deer, bears, wolves, and birds—at Old City Park. City officials shortly wanted to be rid of them, but the public resisted. The officials responded by simply refusing to replace the animals when they died and in 1909 merged the remainder with a menagerie that had become a part of the State Fair. A subscription campaign established the present zoo at Marsalis Park, and the surviving animals were moved to that site in 1912. This was a 36-acre tract, hilly and wooded, that the city had bought in 1909 in Oak Cliff, south of the Trinity River that bisected Dallas. In terms of urban geography, this was significant because the Trinity River also divided the city between the rich north and the not-so-rich south. In comparison to Fort Worth, the Dallas zoo was in the wrong place. It should have been placed next to Southern Methodist

University and the wealthy Highland Park suburb in the north in order to achieve the same sort of concern and support found in Fort Worth.

In the early 1920s, under contract with the city, Frank "Bring 'Em Back Alive" Buck (1884–1950), who had begun his career as a wild animal dealer trapping wildlife along Dallas' Turtle Creek, furnished the zoo with captured wild animals shipped in bamboo cages from around the world. He once formally presented to the zoo a baby orangutan that he cradled under his overcoat. Buck represents the last of the wild game collectors. After this, there was increasing emphasis upon breeding programs between zoos.[37] Planners, meanwhile, placed an aquarium—often a part of a zoo complex—at Fair Park for the Texas Centennial in 1936 as a complement to the Museum of Natural History. It has remained separated from the Marsalis location, of course, but has been managed as a part of the zoo.[38] This aquarium was the best in the state until the construction of the Texas State Aquarium in Corpus Christi in 1990.

The zoo expanded after World War II and the Dallas Zoological Society formed in 1955 to create elite support for the institution. The number of species displayed doubled to more than five hundred in 1966. A shift in attitude in the 1980s, however, sent the zoo along a different and unprofitable path. In response to increasing criticism about the ethical treatment of animals, the American Association of Zoological Parks and Aquariums (AAZPA) began to emphasize a role of zoos in saving endangered species with a program of breeding in captivity and improving zoo habitat. This required a focus on fewer species and the loaning of breeding stock. This was also a part of a historical progression toward science and the humane treatment of animals. Dallas cooperated with the program and was accredited by the AAZPA in 1985.[39] During this interval, in 1984, Warren J. Iliff, a personable businessman with experience at the zoos in Portland and Washington, D.C., took over as director. He settled a rivalry among three competing volunteer organizations, promised a world-class installation, and completed a planned Wilds of Africa exhibit area.

Herbert W. Riemer, a New York architect, had designed an expansion of the zoo in 1983 with the idea of an open "zoogeographic grouping" of African animals. Visitors could observe the animals from a slow-moving monorail as if on a safari. The exhibit of mainly unpopular hoofed animals would also be used as an open research area. At the insistence of the park board, Riemer modified the 55-acre project to include walkways to bring people closer to the animals. Two bond drives, amounting to $30.4 million, financed the expansion.[40]

The Wilds of Africa exhibit opened in 1991, but the recession of the Texas economy stalled further renovation. Many of the animals remained in cages. After spending almost twice the amount of money, Dallas attracted only one-half as many visitors to their facility as did the Fort Worth zoo, thus reinforcing the old joke, "How do you entertain visitors when they come to Dallas?" Answer: "Take them to Fort Worth." Compared to its rival, the Dallas Zoo never gained enough elite funding and had to be supported by tax money and bond issues rather than by donations. It was whispered that the problem was that the zoo was located in a poor section of town, a question of class and racial prejudice.[41] To a greater extent, it was a poor balance between showmanship and science.

Visitors were treated in an almost hostile manner by the design of the zoo: long expanses of summer-hot concrete, little shade, few refreshment stands, a monorail frequently out of service, and animals that were difficult to see. Furthermore, the big cats were left pacing in cramped cages. The cats were given some breathing room with the opening in 1999 of the $4.5 million ExxonMobil Endangered Tiger Habitat. But in 2004 the zoo experienced a horrifying event that made nation-wide news. Jabari, a 340-pound gorilla escaped, apparently by leaping a 12-foot moat and climbing a 14-foot-high wall. It was a seemingly impossible feat, and no one saw it. He went on a rampage for forty minutes, snatched a toddler in his teeth, injured three others, and charged within fifteen feet of the police before he was shot to death.[42] It was the sort of primordial nightmare that all zoos sought to prevent; it was the sort of event that fed the damning criticism of anti-zoo constituents.

HOUSTON ZOO

Carl Hagenbeck in his early Hamburg zoo had tested the vertical and horizontal leaps of big cats by putting a stuffed pigeon on a branch over a pen. He then built his moats large enough to protect the observers.[43] After all, these wild animals retained their ferocity even in captivity and almost all zoos experienced difficulty in spite of precautions. In Houston in 1988, for example, zoo attendant Ricardo Tovor was working alone at night in the corridor behind a new large cat exhibit. Miguel, a 450-pound Siberian tiger noted for his snarls and growls, broke through an 18-inch by 24-inch wire-reinforced window, grabbed Tovor, who was apparently looking through the window, and pulled him inside.

At daybreak a supervisor saw Miguel picking up the limp Tovor by the head in the outside exhibit area. The keeper, a former combat Marine in Korea, knew the worker was dead, but fired three shots to make the tiger back away. Miguel was forced into a cage by spraying a fire extinguisher and the body recovered. Tovor had died of a broken neck and crushed chest. The zoo director, John Werler, decided against killing Miguel in spite of insistent phone calls that demanded an execution.[44] Ferocity was in the nature of tigers and should be expected. Interestingly, two weeks later a twenty-seven-year-old man climbed on top of the artificial rock above the tiger area, beat his hands on his bare chest, and traded growls with the Bengal tigers twenty feet below. According to the police, the man was "incoherent, appeared intoxicated, and gave no explanation for his action."[45] Cages and moats are also needed to protect the captive animals from humanity.

In the visible claws, fangs, and attitude of tigers, bears, lions, and alligators, danger is apparent. It is not so obvious with the ungainly elephants, although with an average of nine deaths per year, they are the greatest killers of zoo personnel. Handlers and the public develop affection for these large animals that are so notably easy to train, sociable, and docile most of the time. It is easy, therefore, to become anthropomorphic about elephants. This largest of all land mammals possesses the power to touch the human heart. As elephant protectionist John Kay commented, "Once one of those trunks finds its way into your pocket, you're immediately engaged with that creature. It's a bond that lasts a lifetime."[46]

All of Houston mourned, for example, when Nellie died at age fifty-six in 1941. Banker William S. Patton had led a fund drive to buy an elephant for the new Houston zoo shortly after it opened in 1923. It seems that zoos gain respectability only after they obtain their first elephant.[47] Patton was able to purchase Nellie from the Ringling Brothers Circus when it passed through San Antonio, and along with Hans Nagel, the zoo director, he brought the elephant to Houston on a train. When Nellie saw the circus leave without her, she trumpeted and cried. Nagel and Patton spoke softly to her, gave her an apple, and stayed with her on the ride to Houston. They led her on foot through the early morning streets to Hermann Park where in the years to come she became the delight of the children of the city. When she grew old and sick, Nagel kept a deathwatch over her as her legs gave out and she rolled on her side. At 2:30 a.m. Nellie looked at Nagel, groaned, and died. The city wept.[48]

In El Paso the longtime favorite was a 6-ton elephant named Mona. The zoo acquired her in 1956 and in 1985 began celebrating her birthday as a fundraiser called "Cocktails with Mona." The keepers dressed in tuxedos and gave their elephants watermelon stuffed with fruit. Mona usually stomped her watermelons flat and ate them all at once. For seventeen years Mona was alone, but in 1997 the zoo purchased Savannah to keep her company. It took Mona awhile to realize that she was bigger and did not have to put up with the bossiness of the younger elephant. The zoo built them a large open compound with a pool in 1995 to show off their most celebrated creatures.[49]

SAN ANTONIO ZOO

The most impressive early effort to go without bars occurred with the construction of the San Antonio Zoo in 1928–1929. Animal-keeping in the town had begun with a menagerie at San Pedro Park, but in 1928 the San Antonio Zoological Society formed and entered into an agreement with the city to provide animals for a zoo. The facility was constructed on city property at an abandoned stone quarry in a conglomeration of donated land that became known as Brackenridge Park. Although barren, the chiseled limestone walls made a dramatic backdrop for the barless exhibits of bears, lions, and others. The zoo opened in 1929, the Works Progress Administration added artificial stone to some exhibit areas during the Depression, and the Zoological Society eventually took over the complete management of the park. The facility demonstrated Hagenbeck ideas for Texas and became one of the enduring tourist sites for the Alamo City.[50]

BROWNSVILLE AND THE GLADYS PORTER ZOO

A more recent example of a Texas zoo that incorporated most of the principles of successful design is the Gladys Porter Zoo in Brownsville. The Earl C. Sams Foundation built, stocked, and equipped the zoo for $7 million in 1968–1971 in a slum area of the town. Sams had been president of J. C. Penney department stores and the zoo was named for his daughter. The design used freshwater moats and river water streams to isolate the animals on small islands. Fences were used only to keep visitors on elevated wooden walkways. From the start, the zoo was managed by the Valley Zoological Society, which worked to build an endowment so that the installation became nearly self-sufficient. Gladys Porter (1910–1980), who had lived in Brownsville and who had traveled extensively in Africa, was vitally concerned about endangered wildlife. Consequently, the zoo from the outset embraced a "Noah's Ark" policy and made an effort to use its facilities for breeding and repopulation.[51]

It was successful in hatching tortoises and reproducing white rhinos. In 1992 the zoo received the prestigious Edward H. Bean Award from the Association of Zoos and Aquariums (AZA) for success in breeding Philippine crocodiles. The numbers of these fearless, aggressive reptiles had been reduced to about one hundred in the wild. Nasty in temper, they fought with each other and attacked humans, so zoo personnel had to be careful. The crocodile hatchlings were sent to the Philippines for release into the wilderness.[52] At the same time that the zoo aided endangered species, it did not forget its obligation to public education, one of the fundamental reasons for zoo existence. Don Farst, the former director, commented, "Our animals do serve as ambassadors for a rapidly shrinking natural world, and it is our responsibility to appreciate this and to utilize them to help us teach our growing populations how to take better care of the planet."[53] John Werler, director of the Houston Zoo for thirty-six years, added, "If you had all the money in the world, and the rest of your life to spend to travel the world, you still would not see nearly the number of animals you see in a large zoo park collection."[54]

For children, the zoo is often their first introduction to a broader environment. Barbara Stanush, a writer for the *San Antonio Express-News,* observed this poignant example at Brackenridge Park in 1989:

> As I neared the polar bear flats a group of deaf children made signs with their hands. A little boy with thick glasses looked from the polar bears to his teacher with a quizzical look. She crossed her arms over her chest and curved her fingers into claws. The child's face lit up. Turning back to the animals, he too crossed his arms and curved his fingers, making the sign for "bear."[55]

ZOO PROTESTS AND ARGUMENTS

In spite of the conservation and education provided by zoos there have been voices of protest. The most extreme critics advocate an acknowledgment of the human oppression of other species and demand a new ethic that would eliminate zoos. Human beings, so the argument goes, have no right to seize or harm another animal. No animal ever voluntarily walked into captivity and they deserve as much freedom as humans.[56] Supporting such an ethic is the long-standing land conservation movement in the United States and also such laws as the Marine Mammal Protection Act (1972) and the Endangered Species Act (1973). These enactments emphasized a preservation attitude toward wildlife, brought about a decline in the capture of wild animals to supply zoos, placed emphasis on wildlife preserves, and, paradoxically, gave places such as the Gladys Porter Zoo a role in protecting exotic species.[57]

Less extreme have been the critics demanding better treatment of animals. This reaches back at least to the founding of the Society for the Prevention of Cruelty to Animals in London in 1824 and to the United States counterpart, the American Society for the Prevention of Cruelty to Animals in 1866. In Texas there has been scattered criticism. Journalist Skip Hollandsworth, for example, scolded the Dallas Zoo in 1982 for the death of Shamba, an aged lowland gorilla who was the equivalent age of a 50-year-old human. A Dallas favorite, she died in childbirth after mating with a borrowed male named Fubo who was half her age. "What other place sticks a 50-year-old female in a concrete box with iron bars just to get her impregnated by Fubo the Magnificent?" he asked.[58] The year before, the United States Department of Agriculture, with its authority under the Animal Welfare Act (1966), denied Dallas the permits necessary to keep their polar bears and sea lions because of "jail-like" enclosures.[59] In 2000 the zoo was fined $25,000 under the federal law because of poor housing, pest control, a gorilla that had to be tranquilized after attacking a worker cleaning a cage, and the extreme overgrowth of a giraffe's hoof.[60]

A group called Voice for Animals accused the San Antonio Zoological Society in 1992 of selling exotic animals for hunting on private ranches. This was unproven.[61] *U.S. News and World Report* published an exposé in 2002 about the cruel dumping of old zoo animals at marginal facilities such as a failed New Braunfels Zoo.[62] Peter Batten, a director of the San Jose Zoo of California, was inspired to write a book about zoos after sending twenty-four animals to the Gladys Porter Zoo in 1973. He had been assured that the animals were doing well, but upon investigation he discovered that five were dead, six had been injured, and two had been traded away. In his book, *Living Trophies* (1976), which has become a classic of zoo criticism, Batten pointed out that zoos do not report mortality, and he estimated that half of the specimens die before being exhibited. He recognized, however, that zoo animals simply could not be turned loose and so he recommended closer surveillance for their welfare.[63]

The defenders of contemporary zoos point out that most of their specimens, about 97 percent, now come from other zoos through breeding in captivity. The concept of freedom, they continue, is a human idea that does not exist in nature because of restrictions of food supply, enemies, and disease. Zoo animals live a comfortable existence free from predators and danger. "Freedom," according to zoo veterinarian Kenneth Fletcher of San Antonio, "is just another word for being eaten alive."[64]

The defense of Texas zoos and others ultimately rests upon the historic purposes of entertainment as with Fort Worth, education as with San Antonio, research as with Dallas and Houston, and preservation as with Brownsville. In an age of global warming, the zoos may be the last refuge for some species, such as polar bears. Zoos are, above everything else, places of inexpensive recreation embedded for a century in the cultural infrastructure of the cities. In the United States, 142 million people visit zoos every year, more than go to all the professional football, baseball, and basketball games combined. It seems unlikely that the people of the nation or Texas will ever give up their zoological parks.

THE RURAL PARKS

It was the cities of Texas that led the way in the establishment of parks, and it was changes in transportation that spread the movement to the countryside. Railroads connected town to town and made possible a visit to the Alamo or to Stewart Beach, and, with effort, a horse and wagon could reach the first state historical property in 1883 at the San Jacinto Battleground. It was the automobile, however, that opened the door for the organization of rural parks. In Texas, as elsewhere, the number of automobiles increased precipitously as the ultimate vehicle for personal transportation. People could go wherever and whenever they wished so long as roads and fuel were available. Preceded by swarms of recreational bicyclists, automobile drivers from the cities demanded improvements in the rutted, dirt wagon roads.

The state established the Texas Highway Department in 1917, which then registered and presented the first license plates to an astonishing 195,000 vehicles. In 1930 the number of registered vehicles reached almost 1.5 million. By that time, the state highway system embraced 96 miles of concrete; 1,060 miles of asphalt; 5,000 miles of gravel or shell; and 10,000 miles of dirt roads. The motorized invasion that swept over Texas and remained to transform urban and country life prompted the establishment of state parks, historic sites, federal parks, and other places of public retreat. A technological revolution thus created a recreational opportunity.

The Texas State Parks

The Texas state system began with the "headache" of Stephen T. Mather, the first director of the newly created National Park Service (1915). National parks, beginning with Yellowstone National Park in 1872, had been established to protect the outstanding scenic places of the nation. There were five national parks with more to come by 1900; President Theodore Roosevelt, who enthusiastically supported the idea of parks, designated sixteen national monuments in two years; and Congress approved a parks board to administer to the growing public properties. Mather's vexation came from the many congressmen who badgered him for a prestigious national park where no scenic value could be demonstrated. But Mather found a way to deflect the problem and relieve his headache.

After brainstorming with advisors, he called for a national conference in Des Moines, Iowa, in January 1921. Two hundred delegates met for a three-day meeting, and Mather encouraged the conference members to set up state parks that could meet the public need for outdoor recreation. These could stand between the cities and the national parks and, coincidentally, solve his problem. The idea of state parks appealed to the politicians for the purposes of preservation and tourism. The mantra of a state park every hundred miles came from this meeting, and as a southerner later said, "Every tourist is worth a bale of cotton, and he is twice as easy to pick."[65]

Governor Pat M. Neff (1871–1952) of Texas readily took up the challenge of establishing state parks. In 1920, wearing a string tie and frock coat, he had campaigned six thousand miles across rutted, dusty Texas roads in his Model T Ford. The thought of a park every hundred miles appealed to him, and, moreover, his mother, who died shortly after he took over leadership of the state, donated ten acres of family land along the Leon River for what would become Mother Neff State Park. The pioneering Neff family grew the first cotton on this land and Isabella Neff said, "We got the title to that place from the governor of Texas and I don't see why I shouldn't just deed it back."[66] Governor Neff took up the issue of state parks in his 1922 campaign, created a State Parks Board in 1923, and then toured Texas to solicit donations of land. "Nothing is more conducive to the happiness of a people," he said repeatedly in speeches, "than for them to go back to nature where the bees hum, the birds sing, the brooks ripple, the breezes blow, the flowers bloom, and the bass bite."[67]

The Parks Board with no office, little budget, and volunteer members bumped along through the 1920s, burdened with a legislative policy that park lands had to be donated and self-supporting. The legislature approved twenty-three unimproved sites in 1927 and appropriated no money for development. The distress of the Great Depression that paralyzed the state budget brought opportunity with the federal New Deal programs. Before helping a state improve facilities, however, the national government required money for maintenance. The Texas legislature refused, but Governor Miriam Ferguson authorized emergency funds in order to bring the Civilian Conservation Corps (CCC) to Texas in 1933. She also appointed former governor Pat Neff to energize the State Parks Board. Money and labor, consequently, flowed into Texas to combine with land donations and purchases to produce a state parks system. The New Deal allocated $20 million for the state parks out of the $750 million expended in Texas. Left behind as a visual legacy of the Depression-era projects are the four hundred buildings and structures built by the CCC that presently remain in the 124 Texas parks.[68]

PALO DURO CANYON

Places such as Bastrop State Park, Davis Mountains State Park, Longhorn Cavern State Park, Mother Neff State Park, and Washington-on-the-Brazos State Park all benefited, but the most important CCC project was Palo Duro Canyon State Park in the dry Panhandle of Texas. Just south of Amarillo, the Prairie Dog Town Fork of the Red River had cut a 60-mile canyon into the escarpment of the eastern High Plains. In places there were 800-foot walls exposing layers of orange-red, lavender, gray, brown, and yellow rock. Characteristic was a flat-topped pinnacle, later called the "Lighthouse," that had hard caprock on top and softer worn layers underneath. The canyon represents some 230 million years of geologic history and is reminiscent of the Grand Canyon of Arizona. It is spectacular.

The Spanish named it "Palo Duro," meaning "hard wood," for the juniper that remains even yet in the chasm. Various groups of Indians had used the canyon with its grassy floor and wooded stream for some one thousand years. The canyon provided a shelter from the sweeping winter wind of the plains and a camping ground hidden from enemies, who thought their quarry had simply vanished into the limitless prairie grass.

Possibly, this was the place where Coronado in 1541 split his wandering *entrada* and sent the main party back toward Mexico while he took a smaller group in search of an illusionary city of gold in what is now Kansas. Various Spanish explorers crossed the Panhandle area in the eighteenth and early nineteenth centuries, and the effort of Randolph B. Marcy (1812–1887) to find the headwaters of the Red River took him into Palo Duro Canyon in 1852. "The magnificence of the views that presented themselves to our eyes as we approached the head of the river, exceeding anything I had ever beheld. . . . We all, with one accord, stopped and gazed with wonder and admiration upon a panorama which was now for the first time exhibited to the eyes of civilized man," he wrote.[69] This astonishment is still experienced by travelers on I-27 when they leave the relentless prairies south of Amarillo to visit the park. It is such a surprise. Who could have suspected? The ground just drops away from the flat land in a broad, sharp gash. "It was as if it had been designed and executed by the Almighty artist as the presiding genius of these dismal solitudes," said Marcy.[70]

It was not such a surprise for Colonel Ranald Mackenzie (1840–1889), the leader of the Fourth Cavalry during the Red River Campaign of 1874, a concerted effort to force the rampaging Plains Indians onto the reservations. Two years earlier, he had learned about the Palo Duro area while in pursuit of Comanches and, consequently, established his base at the head of Tule Canyon, which connected with Palo Duro. Scouts brought news of a huge Indian winter encampment of Comanches, Kiowas, and Cheyennes in the neighboring canyon, and Mackenzie led his men to the rim of the chasm for a surprise dawn assault. The bluecoats found a winding trail to the bottom, formed a line, and attacked the various villages. The Indians fled up the walls of the canyon and only three were killed.

The soldiers, however, methodically destroyed the lodges, clothing, robes, new repeating rifles, ammunition, and food supplies before retreating with the entire herd of Indian horses. Mackenzie had prior experience with the ability of Indians to steal back their horses, and so after keeping some for his own men, he ordered the remaining herd of 1,050 ponies shot and killed in Tule Canyon. This action in late September left the Indians bereft of food, shelter, clothing, weapons, and transport to face the coming winter. In June 1875, after a season of starvation, Quanah Parker (1845–1911), the last of the Comanche war chiefs, led his followers into peaceful surrender. The war was over.

CHARLES AND MOLLIE GOODNIGHT

Palo Duro Canyon then remained empty until Charles Goodnight (1836–1929), following the vague lead of a Mexican mustanger, led his cattle herd to the very brink of the canyon. Seven hundred feet below in the broad valley were thousands of buffalo. The cowboys moved the herd single file down an ancient trace, descended with their supplies and dismantled chuck wagon on mule back, and stampeded the buffalo down the valley to make room for the cattle. It was a perfect place for a ranch—water, grass, shelter, and no need for a fence. Goodnight was an experienced drover who had helped to establish the north-leading Goodnight-Loving cattle trail shortly after the Civil War. He acquired cattle of his own and his search for a ranch site brought him to Palo Duro in October 1876.

With a financial partner, John G. Adair of Denver, Goodnight bought title to the canyon from land speculators and established the JA Ranch that by 1885 embraced 1.35 million acres and 100,000 head of cattle. He tried to keep his cowboys from drinking, fighting, and gambling; experimented with barbed wire fencing; improved his herd with Hereford bulls; preserved a small herd of buffalo; made an agreement with Quanah Parker to supply two beeves every other day to prevent theft from Indians; became the first president of the Panhandle Stock Association; invented a comfortable sidesaddle for women; and experienced one of the heart-warming love affairs of Texas.

He first met Mary Ann (Mollie) Dyer (1839–1926) at Fort Belknap about 1864 and maintained the friendship between cattle drives after she moved to Weatherford, Texas, to teach. They married in 1870—an interesting match between a dour, straight-talking, largely unlettered, humorless cattleman and a lively, winsome, strong-willed schoolmarm. They started out life together in Pueblo, Colorado, a place that left a bad impression with Mollie. It was a shock for her to learn on the morning after their arrival that two outlaws had been lynched on a nearby telegraph pole. It did not help any when her new husband, searching for something to say that might soothe her, said, "Well, I don't think it hurt the telegraph pole."[71]

Mollie wanted to go back to Texas and leave such a barbaric place. Drought and the financial panic of 1873 ruined their business in Pueblo and Goodnight had to start over, which eventually led him to Palo Duro Canyon. Left alone as her husband rode back and forth across the plains arranging business, the indignant Mollie called for a showdown and wrote, "Leave the Panhandle and come out to civilization." They met in Denver and Goodnight explained that he could not honorably leave the partnership he had arranged for the Palo Duro ranch. Mollie replied, "Very well, I will go home with you."[72]

With John Adair and his wife, cowboys, horses, four wagons of supplies, and a herd of one hundred Durham bulls, the Goodnights left for the Panhandle. Mollie drove one of the wagons while the cowboys teased her about starting a ranch with a herd of bulls. They arrived at the canyon, joined the earlier group, the Adairs returned home, and Mollie settled in to spend the second winter with the Goodnight ranch hands. She patched clothes, sewed on buttons, listened to woes, sent cobblers to the line camps, and nursed the needy—"coal-oil for lice, prickly pear for wounds, salt and buffalo tallow for piles, mud for inflammation and fevers, and buffalo meat broth for a general tonic."[73]

According to her husband, "Aunt Mollie," as the cowboys called her, claimed that this was the happiest time of her life, although she lived in distant separation from other ranch wives. Maybe. A cowhand brought her a gift of three chickens that she turned into pets. "They were someone I could talk to. They would run to me when I called them and followed me everywhere I went. They knew me and tried to talk to me in their language. If there had been no outside dangers the loneliness would not have been so bad," she said. Her sympathetic husband later presented her with a grandfather clock that had an engraved plaque. It read in part, "She met isolation and hardship with a cheerful smile, and danger with undaunted courage. With unfailing optimism, she took life's varied gifts, and made her home a house of joy."[74]

The death of partner John Adair in 1885 led to the division of the JA Ranch and the sale of the property. Charles and Mary Ann Goodnight moved into northeastern Armstrong County and established a new ranch that included Goodnight, Texas, a station point on the Fort Worth and Denver Railroad. Ownership of Palo Duro Canyon splintered, but its haunting beauty remained. Local folks used the head of the canyon for gatherings and one of the first actions of the newly organized Canyon City Commercial Club in 1906 was to request that the area be made into a national park. Local politicians in 1908, 1911, and 1915 carried forward proposals for such a park to Congress with no success. The major obstacle was that the land was private property and would have to be purchased.[75] National parks generally came from donated land or from the public domain.

PALO DURO CANYON STATE PARK

After much negotiation, sympathetic owner Fred A. Emery of Chicago in 1933 allowed the Texas State Parks Board to take over fifteen thousand acres and to pay for canyon land with gate receipts from tourists. The CCC then established a tent city on the northwest rim for six hundred men under the direction of the U.S. Army. It was the largest CCC project in the United States. With picks, shovels, wheelbarrows, and dynamite, the CCC built a switchback road to the bottom and worked on hiking trails, low-water stream crossings, and a lodge of rustic design. The park opened on July 4, 1934, as work continued. The brief use of an all-black CCC unit prompted a visit by the Ku Klux Klan to the nearby city of Canyon in 1935, but the main problem concerned financing. The dust storms of the 1930s and the gasoline rationing of World War II curbed the tourism, which in turn affected the payment of debt to Emery. After a hint of foreclosure from Emery, the lack of regional interest in private revenue bonds, and a threat of public auction, the Texas legislature finally sold $300,000 in bonds to pay for Palo Duro Park in 1946.[76]

Promoter John McCarty of Amarillo who took over the concessions from 1949–1954 rebuilt the tourism with travel promotions, publicity, and displays of live buffalo, longhorns, and deer. After constructing an amphitheater on the basin floor in 1963, the Texas Panhandle Heritage Foundation began to experiment with summertime sunset productions that culminated with the music and dance of *Texas*, a show by playwright Paul Green, in 1966. This was a memorable year for the park. Tourist income paid off all the bonds sixteen years ahead of schedule, and *Texas*, a tale of early settlement, began a run that continues to the present day.[77] Palo Duro Canyon State Park thus became the crown jewel of the state park system.

The history of Palo Duro traces a successful evolution of a park, but it was accomplished over a 40-year period and with a great deal of self-sacrifice and frustration by the people who pursued the vision. This was often the case. As an example, Governor Pat Neff appointed David E. Colp, a good roads advocate from San Antonio, to the unpaid position of State Parks Board chairman in 1923. Colp served for twelve years with almost no budget, but among other achievements befriended Fred Emery and worked out the initial land purchases for Palo Duro Canyon. In trying to gain broad tax support for parks with a driver's license tax, Colp wrote in 1930 to the secretary of the Palo Duro Park Association in Amarillo, "I have been working with this matter for seven years, paying all expences [sic], even furnishing my own stationery and postage and I just feel like I cannot afford to keep this up indefinitely and I am very anxious to do everything possible to insure the passage of this Legislation [sic]."[78] He failed to get the tax support; it was not easy work to create public space for people in Texas.

National Parks

In the same time frame that it took to establish Palo Duro Canyon State Park, interest developed in the great southern arch of the Rio Grande in southwest Texas, the Big Bend. More isolated than Palo Duro, Big Bend is just as spectacular. The Chisos Mountains, with peaks as high as 7,800 feet, dominate the arid landscape of the northern Chihuahuan Desert. It is inhabited by jackrabbits, javelinas, mice, gray fox, coyotes, badgers, mountain lions, bobcats, raccoons, roadrunners, white-tailed deer, bats, skunks, golden eagles, four kinds of rattlesnakes, and eleven species of scorpions. There are cacti, bluebonnets, thistles, agave, nettles, ponderosa pine, and Douglas fir that vary with the elevation of the mountains. Over one-half of the bird species of the United States can be spotted in the area. The river carved canyons through the mountains, including Santa Elena Canyon where tilted limestone layers give an illusion of water flowing uphill.[79] Big Bend is blazing hot in the summer. For living beings, including humans, it is a place, as has been said, that stuck, stung, stank, or bit. It is forbidding country. A photographer in 1916 observed, "The country isn't bad. It's just worse. Worse the moment you set foot from the train, and then, after that, just worser and worser."[80]

In addition, there is an uneasy feeling to the land. The mountains glow with phosphorescent light after a rain, and the sharp peaks, sometimes clad in wisps of mist, are gray in the moonlight. They seem to float. This may have inspired one of the explanations for the name, that "chisos" meant "ghosts" and that the mountains were haunted by long dead Indians and Spaniards.

The country was the final Texas stronghold for the Apaches as the Comanches pushed them westward into Mexico and New Mexico. The Comanches cut a war trail through the Big Bend, where their raiding parties captured Mexican slaves, cattle, and horses. The feared forays subsided with the annexation of Texas, flared again during the Civil War, and ended with the defeat of Quanah Parker.[81] In the Big Bend there echoed tales of lost treasure, the ghost of a betrayed Apache warrior, the cry of a sacrificed ill-born Indian baby, and the vengeful scream of a captured Mexican girl who drowned herself in a pool to escape rape by bandits.

The spookiest story, and one grounded in fact, involved an argument over the ownership of a year-old maverick bull at a roundup about thirty miles east of Fort Davis. Finus Gilliland gunned down one-armed Henry Powe and fled to the Glass Mountains near Marathon, Texas, where law officers finally hunted him down and shot off his head. Meanwhile, the cowboys at the roundup branded the young, brindle bull with the words "MURDER" on one side from jaw to tail and "JAN 28 91" on the other. They set the bull free to wander the range as a wraith. Occasionally, people would report seeing the lone bull and, supposedly, he would appear and then disappear when murder would occur in the Big Bend. The truth, apparently, is that, at the request of Powe's son, in 1896 the bull was driven northward with a herd and out of the country.[82]

The Big Bend lawlessness of the nineteenth century, however, attracted the worst rakehell in Texas history, John J. Glanton (1819–1850). He was a person who meant trouble. Although he fought in the Texas War for Independence and the War with Mexico, he was banished by both Sam Houston and Zachary Taylor. Houston dismissed him for reasons unknown, and Taylor tried to arrest him during the Mexican War after Glanton killed a man in order to steal his horse. This was the same short, stout, bearded man mentioned in Chapter 1 who, in a San Antonio saloon squabble, partially decapitated a Ranger, wiped his bloody knife on his sleeve, stepped over the body, and calmly took a drink at the bar.

In 1849 Glanton formed a band of bloodthirsty riffraff, contracted with Chihuahuan authorities for a scalp bounty of $200 each—a scalp with the hair, skin, and right ear attached—and began to hunt Indians. He circled back and forth through the Big Bend, and near Santa Elena Canyon the gang found Apaches. Glanton and his men scattered their village, hunted them down individually, and harvested 250 scalps. In their cutting and ripping violence, they killed men, women, and children; they looted; they got drunk; they disguised themselves as Indians and slaughtered Mexicans; and they cashed in wagonloads of scalps. On his way westward in the mid-1850s, a tribe of abused Yuma Indians wielding stone axes surrounded and wiped out Glanton and his men. With proper justice the Indians scalped Glanton.[83]

After the Indians and outlaws were gone from Big Bend, the land remained largely uninhabited. In 1859 Lieutenant Edward L. Hartz led twenty-three U.S. pack camels on a trek from Fort Davis into the Big Bend along the Comanche War Trail to the Rio Grande and then eastward to Camp Hudson. Although his horses and mules suffered from lack of water, the camels appeared unbothered by this boring and uneventful march.[84] In 1885 ranchers led by the Estacado Land & Cattle Company began to move livestock onto the grassy areas that encircled the Chisos. It was still desert country, of course, so life was not easy. There was drought, there were nature's own predators, and there were border troubles.

The shallow, rock-bottom river crossing of the old Comanche raiding trail at Lajitas remained ideal for illegal, cross-border forays. General John J. Pershing established a cavalry post at that point in 1916 during his fruitless search for Pancho Villa. Nearby Terlingua, Texas, experienced a quicksilver boom that lasted for fifty years before it returned to sand. When historian Kenneth Ragsdale asked Mary Daniels—a border storekeeper, rancher, and midwife who carried a .38 revolver in her purse—about her life she replied, "Nobody down here has a completely clean skirt. We don't do anything criminal you understand, but people on one side of this river can't live without those on the other, and we do what we do . . . we ranched a little, we farmed, and we smuggled."[85]

Big Bend thus has remained forbidding, distant, mysterious, lawless, and alluring with aching beauty. Journalists and intellectuals slowly began to take notice of it. At the very end of the nineteenth century, geologist Robert T. Hill floated 350 miles down the river and through the canyons from Presidio to Langtry, Texas. He found the Big Bend "weird," "strange," and "unfamiliar." He froze in the night and roasted in the day. From the top of the great perpendicular cliffs of the narrow chasms he could not see the river far below. "Nature became tired of making this country before turning on the water," wrote Hill.[86] J. Frank Dobie pursued his folklore into the Big Bend and wrote about lost treasure and a bull branded with the word "MURDER." In the December 1930 issue of *Nature Magazine*, Dobie lamented the lack of Texas parks and argued that places such as Big Bend should be saved. Later, his intellectual companion at the University of Texas, Walter Prescott Webb, repeated Hill's float trip through the canyons, and commented that it was "the finest example of earth-wreckage in Texas."[87] Even contemporary historians Kenneth Ragsdale and Ron Tyler have been drawn by the siren call of this remote land.

But, why would anyone want to visit, much less live, in such a godforsaken place? An often-repeated anecdote hints at an answer. According to Frank X. Tolbert, a mid-century columnist for the *Dallas Morning News*, Don Milton Faver (1822?–1889), the first cattle baron in Presidio County near Fort Davis, once asked a cowboy for directions to Big Bend. The anonymous cowhand replied: "You go south from Fort Davis and come to the place where rainbows wait for the rain. And the Big River is kept in a stone box. And water runs uphill. And the mountains float in the air, except at night when they go away to play with other mountains."[88] Tolbert used the story frequently in his columns to promote and publicize Big Bend. Others picked up and used the anecdote, such as Ragsdale for his book, *Big Bend Country* (1998), and historian Joe B. Frantz in 1966 on a float trip when he introduced Lady Bird Johnson and her entourage to the romance of Big Bend National Park.

BIG BEND NATIONAL PARK

Everett Ewing Townsend (1871–1948), Texas Ranger, cattleman, sheriff, and Texas legislative representative from Brewster County in 1932, is known as the "father of Big Bend National Park." His wanderings had acquainted him with the area that was largely in his legislative district. When he first viewed the 1,000-foot uplift of Bandera Mesa at Big Bend, Townsend wrote that he saw God as never before and wished he could create a personal hunting preserve there that he later would donate to the state.[89] One of Townsend's legislative colleagues, Robert M. Wagstaff (1892–1973) of Abilene meanwhile read Dobie's account of the Big Bend in *Nature Magazine* and investigated the land holdings of the area. He gave Hill's article about floating the Rio Grande to Townsend who confirmed the descriptions. Wagstaff then conspired with Townsend to pass a bill to purchase the unsold school lands of the region and to form a park. This bill and several supplements passed to establish Big Bend State Park in 1933 on 150,000 acres bought at one cent per acre.[90]

Townsend then campaigned to turn Big Bend into a national park. He prodded Congressman R. Ewing Tomason from El Paso to come see the land with letters, telegrams, phone calls, and a warning, "Ewing, you're going to if I have to threaten you with your constituency or a six-shooter."[91] Tomason took a look and, along with the Texas Senators Tom Connally and Morris Sheppard, became a champion of the park. The CCC set up a camp (1934–1937) in the Chisos Mountains; a pack trip by the National Park Service resulted in an enthusiastic endorsement; Walter Prescott Webb floated through Santa Elena Canyon for park publicity; and President Franklin D. Roosevelt approved an enabling act in 1935 that required a free and clear donation of the land. Roosevelt was particularly interested in a possibility of extending the preserve across the Rio Grande and setting up an international park with Mexico. This was an idea that was explored, but never fulfilled. In 1937 Governor James V. Allred, however, vetoed a bill to purchase more Big Bend land on the basis that the state did not have the money. The momentum to establish the park temporarily stalled.

Promoted by the *Fort Worth Star-Telegram*, a Big Bend Park Association, chaired by publisher Amon Carter, began a statewide campaign to raise money. It collected only $8,347 in private contributions, but won $1.5 million with a legislative enactment in 1941. Land prices subsequently jumped and stockowners overgrazed the range in an effort to eat up the last morsel before they sold out. There were more than three thousand owners although only fifty-five actually lived in Big Bend, and twenty owned more than half the desired parkland. Purchasing proceeded during World War II and Amon Carter presented the deed for 708,000 acres to President Roosevelt in July 1944. Later additions brought the park possessions to 801,000 acres. Secretary of Interior Douglas McKay officially dedicated the park in 1955, construction for better accessibility came in the next decade, and in 1966 historian Joe B. Frantz of the University of Texas celebrated the completion and rededication by telling Lady Bird Johnson about the place where the rainbows wait for the rain and a big river is kept in a stone box.[92]

Considering the remote location and the sparse population, you would not think that Big Bend would create much controversy, but it did. The National Park Service gradually ended grazing rights in 1944–1946 so that the countryside could revert to a natural state. Free-ranging cattle would drift into the park and the rangers dutifully would round them up and then charge the neighboring ranches $18 per head for their return. When hoof-and-mouth disease came north from Mexico in 1947, the rangers shot the cattle and charged $18 per head for the return of the mules, horses, and donkeys that did not carry the ailment. The ranchers thought that the Park Service should fence the park, and the Park Service thought that ranchers should fence their land.

The ranchers also complained that the park was a refuge for predators—such as mountain lions, wildcats, coyotes, wolves, and eagles—that would kill outside the park and then retreat to a sanctuary where they could not be hunted. Ranchers wanted the right of "hot pursuit" onto park land, which of course was denied, but they shot golden eagles in flight from small airplanes. A study by the Fish and Wildlife Department, however, indicated that the predator problem was practically nonexistent. Ten times the number of coyotes lived outside the park and the last wolf had been killed in the early twentieth century. The real issue was that the cattlemen could not freely graze their livestock in the park and so the grumbling continued.[93]

The worst recent difficulty was a white haze of air pollution that obscured the scenic views. It began to gather about twenty years ago and could be traced to power plants more than 125 miles distant in both Texas and Mexico. Since there no longer existed any truly clean air anywhere in the United States, this remained an intractable loss for Big Bend.[94] Ross A. Maxwell, the first superintendent of the park in the 1940s, recalled an incident to historian Ron Tyler in which an awestruck visitor to Big Bend simply stood outside his car looking and taking deep breaths of "sweet air." His wife, however, never got out and shouted for the man to get back in and "Get me out of this place!"[95] Life has never been easy in the Big Bend.

THE DESOLATE SHORE

Although Big Bend National Park was the first, the federal government and the National Park Service have been involved in other Texas public places, such as the Fort Davis National Historic Site (1963), Chamizal National Memorial (1963), Guadalupe Mountains National Park (1972), and Big Thicket National Preserve (1974). The most unusual, however, is Padre Island National Seashore, established in 1968. Curving southward parallel to the Texas coastline from Corpus Christi Bay almost to the mouth of the Rio Grande for 130 miles, Padre Island is the longest sand barrier island in the world. It is about three miles wide with thirty-five-foot dunes and, like other sand barrier islands, is unstable and moves in slow motion toward the main shoreline across a two-mile-wide lagoon. The island with its light, brown sugar-colored sand is bright hot with no shade and windswept. There are almost no trees or shrubs. The island is a type of desert of scant use for agriculture; it is a thin border strip between land and sea that early settlers quickly discarded for the rich alluvial land of the Texas river valleys.

In such a harsh environment laced with salty air, most plants hug the ground or expose only wiry stems and tough leaves to the corrosive atmosphere. Beach morning glory, goatweed, sunflowers, dove weeds, and various salt grasses thus provide some stability to the restless dunes and offer sustenance to various animals such as lizards, ghost crabs, gophers, grasshoppers, rabbits, deer, and rattlesnakes. Seagulls rule the surfline, and ducks dominate the lagoon. In this punishing borderland, primitive Karankawa Indians would go to hunt, but not to stay. About midway on the island is an area called "Big Shell" where a curve and turbulent offshore currents combine to cast seashells onto the shore and to create havoc for close-sailing ships of wood and canvas.

In 1554 a storm caught a fleet of four Spanish ships carrying gold, silver, red dye, cowhides, and 410 people traveling from Veracruz to Spain. Three of the vessels—*Santa Maria de Yclar*, *Espiritu Santo*, and *San Esteban*—ran aground at Big Shell and burst apart; the other escaped to Havana. The majority of the passengers, probably around two hundred, along with floating crates of meat, biscuits, and fruit jelly made it to shore. A small boat with some of the survivors may have sailed back to Veracruz, but the rest—men, women, and children—were left to walk back along the coast. On the way, their clothes and shoes wore out, they lost their crossbows in a stream, they ran short of food, and Indian bands preyed upon the stragglers. Only two Spaniards survived, one who returned to the wreck and Fray Marcos, who was wounded and abandoned in a shallow grave with his face exposed. He revived, arose from his premature grave, avoided the Indians, and with maggots in his wounds made it to the village of Tampico. He lived for thirty more years with arrow points that could be felt beneath his skin and told the story.[96]

Spanish salvage crews recovered about 40 percent of the treasure, abandoned the remainder, and forgot about the wreck. Three centuries later, recreational shell hunters on Padre Island occasionally found encrusted coins in the sand, and in the early 1960s engineers digging a cut for a ship channel dredged straight through the wreckage of the *Santa Maria de Yclar*. Not much was left, but this located the point of the disaster, and in 1967 Platero, a treasure hunting company from Indiana, began to extract the wealth of the *Espiritu Santo* from shallow water—silver, gold, astrolabes, coins, and ships' parts. Since they were scavenging in the state-owned tidelands, Texas took the treasure and reimbursed the company. In 1969 the State Antiquities Code established a special committee to control salvage and excavations on state land for the future. In 1972–1975 state archeologists located and excavated the wreckage of the *San Esteban*. Although the prospect of finding lost gold fires the imagination, the real fortune of Padre Island is found in mundane recreation and tourism.

The island had been officially explored in 1766 as a part of a coastal survey ordered by the viceroy of New Spain, but the Spanish king granted ownership to Nicolas Balli earlier in 1759. The Mexican government confirmed ownership to his grandson, Padre Jose Nicolas Balli, and his nephew, Juan Jose Balli, in 1829. The enterprising cleric established a church for the Karankawa Indians and a ranch on the southern tip and hence the name "Padre Island." John Singer, whose younger brother developed the sewing machine, bought land from the Ballis during the 1850s, but because of his Union sympathies, he was forced out during the Civil War. He left behind a legend of treasure buried in jars and lost in the shifting sands. In the 1870s Patrick Dunn gradually acquired most of the property for ranching purposes and fought an ongoing battle with trespassers who wanted to fish, hunt, and swim on the island. Dunn finally gave up and sold the rights to Samuel A. Robertson (1867–1938) in 1926.

Colonel Robertson, a railroad builder, World War I veteran, and sheriff of Cameron County, dreamed of developing Padre Island as a resort as he had done with the Del Mar Hotel on Brazos Island. In 1927 he built an open wooden bridge with troughs for automobile wheels from the mainland to North Padre Island. Drivers placed their tires in the troughs and drove three miles across the water. Robertson called it the Don Patricio Causeway in honor of Patrick Dunn. The promoter put up two hotels near the southern end and planned a road down the center of the island. The Great Depression and a hurricane in 1933, however, washed away the hotels, the causeway, and the dreams. Robertson sold out to Albert and Frank Jones of Kansas City. Albert Jones, along with M. E. Allison, formed the Padre Island Development Company to sell house lots on the north end, and the company struggled until the county built a causeway in 1950 that provided public access to the island. National Flood Insurance beginning in 1968 and home insurance from the Texas Windstorm Catastrophe Pool starting in 1971 stimulated construction in such coastal areas. Slowly, an expensive subdivision organized around marinas then grew on the bay side of north Padre Island.

There was only slight interest in tourism for the southern tip until Cameron County opened the Queen Isabella Causeway from the mainland at Port Isabel in 1954. This provided opportunity for John L. Tompkins, a thin, cigarette-smoking real estate salesman from Corpus Christi. "There was an absolutely untouched strip of land with a climate just as good as Miami's and a great deal better than anything the West Coast could offer," he said.[97] Tompkins lobbied for the causeway, bought land, sold lots, and built the first house for himself. Resort construction began in 1955 with restaurants and beach hotels. Condominiums appeared in the mid-1960s, South Padre Island incorporated as a city in 1973, and the first spring break students began to arrive in the early 1980s. Although the town lacked seawall protection, it was easy to foresee the same sort of coastal building that has strangled the Florida shorelines—hotels and high-rise apartments shoulder to shoulder to the edge of the sand. That was Tompkins' dream.

PADRE ISLAND NATIONAL SEASHORE

There were, however, some crosscurrents. David E. Colp, the former self-sacrificing chair of the State Parks Board had suggested a park on the island in 1936, but it was dropped because of the opposition of Governor James Allred. In 1955, however, the National Park Service published *Our Vanishing Shoreline* that pointed out the loss of the national coastline to private interests. That in turn prompted Texas to pass an Open Beaches Act in 1959. This gave the public the right to use the beaches from the low tide line to the vegetation line of the dunes. Therefore, hotel or homeowners could not fence off a beach for private use, and if a shoreline shifted, as it might in a storm, the public retained its right wherever the new beach might form.

There was also a growing concern about wildlife and endangered species. Connie Hagar at Rockport, near Corpus Christi, became noted for her bird studies along the coastal flyway, and at South Padre, Ila Loetscher became famous as the "Turtle Lady" who aided the survival of endangered Ridley turtles that nested on the sand barrier islands. In 1958, consequently, Texas maverick Democrat Senator Ralph W. Yarborough (1903–1996) introduced a bill in Congress to establish a national park on Padre Island, and later President John F. Kennedy, recommending public seashore recreation areas, supported the general idea in a speech to Congress. Yarborough testified at the hearing, "We in Texas do not want a Miami type of development here with stone fences run out from hotels and motels across the beaches and down into the ocean fencing away from the beaches and the water all the people except those in a few high-priced motels."[98] Hector P. Garcia, a Corpus Christi physician and spokesman for the poor, also commented, "For many hundreds of thousands of poor citizens in this area Padre Island is the only recreational area available to them . . . to some of these Mexican children the only gems and jewels in their life will be the beautiful shells they will find in this, our natural land."[99]

Conservative Republican Senator John Tower and land developers opposed the idea. John Tompkins, who would allow a small park, argued, "With it we must have private development, motels, hotels, homes, towns, and cities."[100] Padre Island National Seashore, nevertheless, became law in 1962 and after years of property negotiations and a cost of $23 million, the park was brought together on 67.5 miles in the middle of Padre Island. Lady Bird Johnson, who dedicated the National Seashore in 1968, said, "It has been said that wilderness is the miracle that man can tear apart, but cannot reassemble. So, I hope very much that these white sands, this dazzling dome of sky will be here, in all their freshness to be savored year after year."[101]

The National Park Service placed its visitors' center on the north end of Padre Island near Corpus Christi. The rangers respected nature and kept the island in a wild state except for a semiannual cleanup of the trash—two and one-half tons per mile per year—that floated in with the tides. A long sand barrier island with urban development on each end thus became one of Texas' most unusual and renowned parks.

THE PURPOSE OF PUBLIC SPACES

A century of park building in Texas has resulted in 2 national parks, a national seashore, 13 National Park Service areas, 4 National Forest Recreation areas, 124 state parks, 4 state forest recreation sites, 19 natural landmarks, 13 zoos, and countless urban parks. It amounts to an estimated 2 million acres. For the most part, the era of public park construction is over in Texas with the exception of municipal parks that will continue to be added as the cities expand. But a great lesson has been learned.

Human beings need respite from the abrasions of steel and stone, from the traffic lights and stop signs of their everyday lives. The sight of green shrubs, flowering trees, perhaps a heron fishing in a small pond glimpsed from an interstate highway offer a restorative balm. The park builders sensed this need and made an effort to reserve space for urbanized humanity to step outside to camp, picnic, hike on an unpaved trail, look at the stars, breathe deeply, feel the wind and sunshine, hear the birds, explore the natural history, and wonder at the beauty of a sculpted canyon or an unbroken line of seascape. The parks, large and small, reveal the place of interface, a door to the natural world from which humanity emerged. It is a world that offers perspective on life and renewal for the human spirit.

CHAPTER 3

The Great Stadiums

Across the expanse of Texas in every town and city can be found stadiums for football and baseball. They parallel in size and design the wealth and size of their community, from spare wooden bleachers for a handful of parents and students to enormous concrete bowls for tens of thousands of people. The stadiums, large and small, occupy valuable unused space for much of the time, and the revered playing fields thus offer testimony to the power of sport in Texan and American culture. Kyle Field at Texas A&M University can seat 82,600 fans; Darrell K Royal-Memorial Stadium at the University of Texas at Austin can accommodate 80,000; Rice Stadium at Rice University has a capacity of 70,000; and Jones AT&T Stadium at Texas Tech University can hold 52,700. The capacity at Kyle Field equals one-half the combined populations of Bryan and College Station; that of Jones AT&T Stadium amounts to one-fourth the number of citizens in Lubbock.

The games played within are important for entertainment—there is nothing better than the rising anticipation and thunder of a crowd welcoming its team to the playing field on a sunny, October, Texas football day. What takes place during the game touches the emotions, inspires conversation, engenders pride, and provides a common experience. "Gig 'em Aggies!" (Texas A&M, 1930); "Hook 'em Horns!" (University of Texas, 1955); "Guns Up!" (Texas Tech University, 1972) are statewide rallying cries. Sports provide a "glue" for community cohesion. Memories and loyalties are thus formed that are inseparable from a place.

There is much more that can be said about the history of stadiums, the arenas of action, than has been written. The design affects the game, particularly in baseball. Location is an element of urban development. The concessions, restrooms, and seats reveal a concern, or unconcern, for human comfort. Cost is always a factor for a city or institution. Technology, such as television or AstroTurf, can force adjustments in play. And the teams that participate mirror larger social concerns, such as the integration of black athletes into sports. Change is the essence of history, and in Texas history two facilities are particularly significant: the Cotton Bowl in Dallas and the Astrodome in Houston. One evolved gradually at the fairgrounds of Dallas to accommodate the growing popularity of football. The other dazzled the baseball world with such an advanced technological burst that stadium design changed forever. And both places, interestingly, reflected the long heritage of Western civilization even in faraway Texas, with a linkage, of all places, to the ancient Colosseum of Rome.

THE COLOSSEUM

This stadium, the most famous of the ancient world, brought together the technological mastery of architecture and the sports of the Roman Empire at its peak of success. The ancient Greeks, however, deserve credit for defining the primary elements of sport—rules, competition, and physical prowess—and also for constructing the first stadiums for the public viewing of athletics at places such as Olympia and Delphi. Their enthusiasm for sports also proved infectious. Lucian (117–180 CE), a Greek satirist and writer, speaks clearly to us across two millennia:

> If the Olympic Games were being held now . . . you would be able to see for yourself why we attach such great importance to athletics. No one can describe in mere words the extraordinary . . . pleasure derived from them and which you yourself would enjoy if you were seated among the spectators feasting your eyes on the prowess and stamina of the athletes, the beauty and power of their bodies, their incredible dexterity and skill, their invincible strength, their courage, ambition, endurance and tenacity. You would never stop . . . applauding them.[1]

Rome conquered Greece during the middle of the second century BCE and mixed its own athletics with those of the Greeks. The Romans inherited a stadium and an interest in chariot racing from their former masters in the Italian peninsula, the Etruscans. They expanded the stadium, called the Circus Maximus, to three tiers surrounding an oblong sand track where two-horse, four-horse, six-horse, or ten-horse teams traversed the course seven times for the glory of the god Jupiter. The crowds, as many as 385,000 people, cheered, gambled, and anticipated the bloody wrecks of horses, drivers, and chariots as the competitors careened around tight 180-degree turns. So popular were these races that they outlasted the Roman Empire by one thousand years.

The Circus Maximus could hold about one-third to one-half the population of Rome and was the largest stadium in the history of the ancient world. A modern comparison is the Indianapolis 500 automobile race, which attracts an estimated five hundred thousand people in recreational vehicles and in the stands. This is more than one-half the population of Indianapolis. The Texas Motor Speedway north of Fort Worth holds about 215,000 fans. Here and in other automobile stadiums can be found the same spectator enthusiasm for technical skill, speed, equipment, danger, and possible collisions. The Etruscans also gave to their Roman successors a certain blood lust, the desire to see the splattering of human blood in a sports or captive situation. The result of this interest was the construction of the most famous of all stadiums, the Colosseum.

After a civil war that followed Nero's forced suicide, Vespasian (9–79 CE), the successful general, restored Roman finances and began rebuilding the capital. On the site of Nero's private artificial lake in 72 CE, Vespasian ordered the construction of an amphitheater that would benefit the people and symbolize the strength of the empire. Vespasian died before completion and his son Titus (39–81 CE), who continued the Flavian Dynasty, opened the nearly finished stadium in 80 CE with one hundred days of gladiator contests. Titus, who died abruptly, maybe poisoned, reigned for only twenty-six months. His successor and younger brother, Domitianus (51–96 CE), completed the work before the dynasty ended in murder, terror, and violence.

The Flavian amphitheater became known as the "Colosseum," probably because of its colossal size or perhaps from a large nearby statue of Nero that had been converted to a sun god with a solar crown. The statue was known as the "Crowned Colossus." The current word "coliseum" relates to any large amphitheater, but the spelling "Colosseum" is reserved for the venerated stadium of ancient Rome. The amphitheater was four stories high. The first three stories featured repeated open archways with interior stairways that led to the seating for forty-five thousand people. The top level, an enclosed gallery, featured small quadrangular windows that supported a series of closely spaced posts that could hold up an awning, or *valarium*, that would be stretched over the seating areas to protect spectators from sun and rain. It is unclear whether it extended all the way across the top, or if it left a large hole above the field of action like Texas Stadium of modern times.[2]

In the shape of a large oval, the stadium was made of travertine limestone, brick, marble, concrete, and volcanic stone held together with iron clamps. Eighty entrances led to two tiers of marble seats set fifteen feet above the arena floor—beyond the reach of unhappy lions or vengeful human combatants. The first row of seats was reserved for senators, who were required to wear togas. Above them in ascending order were places for military personnel, married men, plebs, youths and their tutors, and women. The emperor and the vestal virgins occupied special boxes. Scattered fountains sprayed the air to cool it. The oval arena floor, 287 × 180 feet, was made of wood covered with sand to absorb blood. There was an entry way for the participants and another for the removal of bodies. Below the floor were lightless cages and cells for animals and people as well as a system of water tunnels for flooding the combat area for naval displays.[3]

The purpose of the Colosseum was to entertain the populace and to serve as a reminder of Roman power. A typical day featured animal fights in the morning, executions of criminals by starved beasts at noon, and gladiator fights in the afternoon. The gladiators were trained and armed to fight, if necessary, to the death. Seneca (4 BCE–65 CE), a Roman philosopher and politician, commented about a visit to the Colosseum, "I came home more greedy, more cruel and inhuman. Man, a sacred thing to man, is killed for sport and merriment."[4] Seneca was one of the few critics. Most Romans did not object to the sport or to the cost.

A weakened empire and Christian censure, however, brought an end to the gladiatorial games in 404. Outsiders invaded and sacked Rome in 410 and again in 455.

After that, the empire fell apart and the capital gradually declined and decayed. The Circus Maximus disappeared as segments of Rome reverted to pasture land. By 600 the Colosseum was silent and covered with wild grasses. It was damaged by earthquakes in 847 and again in 1231, and looters stole the iron clamps that held it together.[5] Chariot racing, however, survived at the Hippodrome, a stadium for fifty thousand citizens of the Byzantine Empire at Constantinople, until the invasion and sacking of the city by the Ottoman Turks in 1453. The Hippodrome was the last stadium for mass public use in the world until the Spanish erected a permanent bullring in Madrid in 1743. There were no stadiums in Asia, Africa, North America, or South America. The famous ball courts of the Maya in Central America were for the amusement of royalty only; there were no grandstands for the public.

The reason that the Colosseum became important was that the ruins survived and Europeans, starting with the Renaissance in the fifteenth century, became curious about the ancient Romans. In the early nineteenth century, exotic vines, flowers, and shrubs covered the site and botanists studied the flora. There was speculation that the unusual plants had grown from seeds that had been part of the food fed to the wild beasts by the old Romans. The Colosseum became a tourist attraction that writers and poets wished to see by moonlight, and in 1871 archeologists cleaned up the site to reveal its history.[6] It became a part of the grand tour of historic places for the educated elite and so wealthy Europeans and Americans visited Rome. The Colosseum thus became the prototype for public stadiums—permanent, monumental, urban, open-air, intimate, and accessible.

The ruins spoke to those who would listen. In the mid-1950s, for instance, a self-made millionaire and former judge from Houston toured the grounds of the Colosseum. He listened to the stories, but he was most intrigued by the minor aspects of an awning to keep off the sun and fountains to cool the inside of the structure. And, he mused to himself, "Why not?"[7]

FOOTBALL AND TEXAS

The game of American football resulted from a melding of soccer and rugby, both imported into the eastern colleges from the boys' schools of Great Britain. McGill University of Montreal played two games with Harvard in 1874 in which they changed the rules for each game. Harvard played Yale the following year and used a combination of regulations. In order to compete with each other, Columbia, Harvard, Princeton, and Yale formed the Intercollegiate Football Association in 1876 to codify the rules. During the 1880s, American football diverged from both soccer and rugby, inspired largely by the suggestions of Walter C. Camp (1859–1925), the coach of Yale. Under his influence, the line of scrimmage, downs, gridiron markings, and an assignment of points were defined. The game became so popular that in 1905 sixty-two colleges formed the Intercollegiate Athletic Association to regulate the sport and prevent undue injury to the players. This organization became the enduring National

Collegiate Athletic Association in 1910. Football thus started as a collegiate game for men, spread through the colleges, and then filtered down into the high schools and secondary schools.[8]

The game of football appealed to the mythic Texas frontier personality—rough, gritty, masculine, combative, competitive. The game required teamwork, but allowed for individual stars. It was controlled by rules and limited by time, and thus football was a reflection of emergent American capitalism. The schoolboy game, furthermore, was fun to play and enjoyable to watch. Football came to be a social focal point for conversations and parties and school activities, and thus, it became ingrained in the Texas personality.

It is difficult to pinpoint precisely when football came to Texas, but some scattered facts are known. In 1886 a group of young men in Houston played a sandlot game without a rulebook. After casting off their coats, vests, cravats, and collars, they ran about kicking and yelling until they flopped on the grass without enough breath to pump up the ball again. There were additional sporadic games of this sort in the 1890s in Houston, and in 1901 the town high school began to play on a fairly consistent basis.[9]

The game appeared on Galveston Island in 1890 when the local YMCA, clubs, and high schools began to play one another. In 1892 the Santa Fe Rugbys challenged Ball High School. The Ball fans created a cheer set to music: "Brekekekex, coax, coax. Bredededex, coax, coax. Ball High School! Ball High School! Yellow and blue, rah! rah! Boom!!!" The Santa Fe team listened in amazement and then went on to beat Ball 14–0. Central High, the black school in Galveston, also formed a team and tried to find an opponent. Apparently no group would accept their offer.[10] Dallas High School fielded a team in 1900 following the organization of a Dallas Football Club in 1891.[11] There was enough high school activity by 1910 so that the Texas State Teachers Association had to take steps to regulate eligibility. Too many "ringers" were being recruited off the streets for important games. This effort resulted in the ultimate formation of the University Interscholastic League to manage high school athletics.[12]

In 1896 in Dallas an independent heavyweight team—they would be called an all-star team today—beat the University of Texas. The Dallasites used a cheer: "What's the matter with Dallas? Is she all right? Is she all right: well I should scream. There are no flies on the Dallas team."[13] The University of Texas began to play football in 1893 with a home-and-home schedule of four games with San Antonio and Dallas University. They played Texas A&M in 1894 and 1898, and then began the traditional end of the season game with the Aggies in 1900. By 1914 Baylor, Texas Christian, and Rice had teams and the Southwest Conference (1914–1995), including Oklahoma, began its supervision over regional athletics.

Edgar Odell Lovett, the first president of Rice, deliberately installed football on his campus in 1912 after attending a game between the University of Texas and Texas A&M. "I've never regretted it," he later said, "although I believe I have spent more time on football problems than anything else. The mischief is that you have to win. The week after you win a game everybody is happy and things go well. But when you lose, they are miserable around school and that is bad for studies."[14] As any college president would tell you today, nothing has changed.

At the end of the nineteenth century and beginning of the twentieth century, then, football took root in Texas. Teams played on vacant lots, high schools cleared ground for football games, and universities began to build stadiums—for example, Memorial Stadium at the University of Texas in 1924 and Kyle Field at Texas A&M in 1905. In Dallas the directors of the State Fair of Texas, an association of Dallas businessmen, included the sport into its annual October celebration. Teams competed inside the horse track oval in front of a grandstand. Texas played Sewanee and Oklahoma played a Dallas all-star squad in 1902. In 1912 Texas played Oklahoma next door to the fairgrounds in Gaston Park. In 1921 the association built a 15,000 seat wooden stadium without locker rooms at the south end of the racetrack for football, and the directors scheduled teams from Baylor, Southern Methodist, Texas A&M, and Texas. The players dressed for the games at home or in their hotels. Starting in 1929, the Texas-Oklahoma contest, the "Red River Shootout," became a regular feature.[15] The interstate rivalry was prime entertainment and good business for Dallas and its fair.

The Cotton Bowl

In 1930, Depression-era workmen at the fairgrounds pulled down the wooden stands and proceeded to build Fair Park Stadium, a 46,600-capacity amphitheater on the 60-acre racetrack grounds. The playing surface was placed 24 feet below the surface of the land and the dirt piled up to form 46-foot embankments around an oblong hole. Concrete beams placed atop the dirt mound supported a wooden deck with redwood benches for the spectators. The design provided only landscaping for the outside edge of the embankment to protect the underlying soil. This neglect resulted in a later problem. A large tunnel at the south end provided an entry for the players. The stadium was built mainly of wood, cost only $338,000, and was the largest in the South. The purpose of the amphitheater was to serve college and high school teams in the city and state, and it opened with a high school game, North Dallas versus Sunset on October 7, 1930, followed by Texas versus Oklahoma on October 18, and SMU versus Indiana on October 25.[16]

The stadium acquired its name, the "Cotton Bowl," through the personal effort of J. Curtis Sanford (1903–1972). "Jimmy" Sanford was a tall, rugged, free-wheeling, rich promoter who made his fortune in the rough East Texas oil fields in the early 1930s. In 1936 he rode the Rose Bowl Special, the 100-car train that carried fans from Dallas to Pasadena for a championship game between SMU and Stanford. Southern Methodist lost 7–0. On the return to Texas, Sanford began to figure that fans should not have to ride all the way to California for a bowl game and that since Dallas was midway in the continent, it should have a game of its own. The Rose Bowl, which started in 1902, was the earliest, but the Sugar Bowl of New Orleans, the Orange Bowl of Miami, and the Sun Bowl of El Paso all began in 1935. In 1936 TCU, a Southwest

Conference team, beat LSU in the Sugar Bowl 3–2. So, the idea of bowl games was in the air.

Sanford put together a committee to promote the "Cotton Bowl Classic" and offered $10,000 for the winner and $6,000 for the loser in a 1937 New Year's contest. As with the Sugar Bowl and Orange Bowl, the Cotton Bowl name related to the predominant agricultural product of the region. Sanford copyrighted the name and rented Fair Park Stadium, which, after this game, became known as the Cotton Bowl. Although Arkansas was the Southwest Conference champion, Sanford chose TCU to play against Marquette in the initial game. He thought that All-American quarterback "Slinging" Sammy Baugh of TCU, who had turned the college game into an exciting aerial circus with his sidearm passing, would attract more spectators. The Marquette players were out of condition—their regular season had ended at Thanksgiving—and they chose to run to cover receivers rather than to rush the passer. This gave Baugh the time he needed and he picked his end, Leo "Little Dutch" Meyer, the nephew of the head coach, for all their points. TCU won 16–6. "We came over from Fort Worth on the bus that morning," Meyer said laconically, "played the game and went back on the bus that night."[17]

The committee gave the players a banquet after the game, but felt disappointed about the 17,000 attendance in the 46,600-seat stadium. Meager numbers continued until the Cotton Bowl Athletic Association in 1940 made an agreement with the Southwest Conference to always host its champion as the home team. It was good publicity for the conference and it was good business for Dallas. In 1941, consequently, when Texas A&M beat Fordham 13–12, the stands filled almost to capacity at 46,000.[18] The turning point of the game came in the second half when Aggie fullback Earl Smith trotted to the sideline and pretended to leave the field. He didn't, Fordham players did not notice, Aggie quarterback Marion Pugh threw him a pass, and Smith streaked sixty-two yards for a tying touchdown.[19]

THE HOUSE THAT DOAK BUILT

The Cotton Bowl Classic games continued through the World War II era and were introduced into postwar prosperity with the 40–27 victory of the University of Texas over the University of Missouri. Bobby Layne, the Texas quarterback, ran for four touchdowns, threw for two touchdowns, kicked the extra points, and completed eleven of twelve pass attempts. He actually hit his receiver in the mouth on the single incomplete play. "It was one of those afternoons when both teams just ran up and down the field," said Layne. "They couldn't stop us and we couldn't stop them." A former teammate of Doak Walker (1927–1998), Layne was a sensational halfback and a five-sport athlete from Highland Park High School in Dallas. Just out of school, both joined the merchant marine at the war's end and were shortly released. Layne committed himself to the University of Texas, but Walker decided to stay home at SMU after he had traveled on a train to New Orleans to watch SMU play Tulane.[20] Walker was fated to become the catalyst for the transformation of the Cotton Bowl into a modern stadium.

At a time when football players often remained on the field to play both offense and defense, Walker became the best all-around performer in Southwest Conference history. Substitute players could only come onto the field during a time-out and it was not until 1948 that referees were required to call time-out when the control of the ball changed sides. After this, coaches began to use platoons of defensive and offensive specialists. Although physically unimposing—5 feet, 11 inches and 170 pounds—Walker could play both ways and his statistics were impressive. He possessed a natural talent for the game. In his college career, he gained 2,076 yards rushing, completed 138 passes for 14 touchdowns, caught 29 passes, made 11 interceptions as a defensive back, scored 303 points with touchdowns and extra points, and led his team to two championships. He was selected for All–Southwest Conference and All American honors in 1947, 1948, and 1949. In 1948 he became the second Texan (Davey O'Brien of TCU was the first in 1938) to receive the Heisman Trophy, given to the best football player in the nation. In that season SMU won the Southwest Conference and beat Oregon 21–13 in the Cotton Bowl Classic. During that season Walker rushed for 532 yards, passed for 304 yards, intercepted 3 passes, returned 10 punts for 169 yards, kicked an average of 42 yards per punt, and led the conference with 88 points. The Doak Walker Award for the best running back in the nation began in 1989.[21]

The Walker era at SMU predated television coverage and, therefore, overflow crowds pushed into the small 24,000-seat Ownby Stadium on the campus to witness the games. Dallas fans had noticed the exciting halfback when SMU won the Southwest Conference in 1947 and, consequently, to accommodate the spectators, SMU switched its home games to the Cotton Bowl in 1948. The managers of the bowl had been thinking about remodeling after the whiplash from a September hurricane had washed the exposed dirt embankment down onto the playing field. The simple landscaping had not held.

Walker came along at the right time. Dallas was prosperous, and the State Fair issued $1.28 million in bonds to reconstruct the stadium. Any holder of a $100 bond had an option to purchase a good seat for the season. The Cotton Bowl thus was remade with reinforced concrete with an upper deck on the west side in 1947–1948. At the end of 1948, Walker won the Heisman Trophy and a second deck added to the east side brought the capacity of the Cotton Bowl up to 75,500 seats. This gave the stadium its modern configuration: an open, oval bowl of lower seats with two separate flanking upper decks. In 1986 the Fair Park officials, in recognition of the stadium's history, placed a plaque at the main entrance that simply stated: "The Cotton Bowl, the House that Doak Built."[22]

Players trotting through the tunnel into the stadium and meeting the deafening roar of so many fans experienced a rush of excitement. Bob Folsom, who played for SMU in 1947–1949, the Walker era, recalled, "It was a pretty warm feeling when you came out and 60,000 fans were cheering—you knew that at least 80 percent were for you." Raleigh Blakely, who played for the Mustangs at the same time, said, "There was so much noise, you soon weren't aware of noise. All you could do was to pay attention to what you were doing, and you could barely hear the calls." SMU quarterback Chuck Hixson, 1968–1970, commented, "Coming down the tunnel you realized how many other players have done the same thing." At his first game, Hixson was overwhelmed by the mass of people, the sound, the colors, and the playing of the national anthem. Assistant coach Dudley Parker noticed as Hixon's eyes widened and glazed over. Grinning, Parker nudged Hixon and said, "This is a long way from the south side of San Antonio, isn't it?"[23]

John Eisenberg, who grew up as a fan in the 1960s and later became a sportswriter for the *Dallas Times-Herald* and the *Baltimore Sun*, commented about the view from the stands:

> The Cotton Bowl was a colorless, outdated concrete stadium, but it seemed as glamorous to me as a floodlit Broadway theater. It had no luxury suites, few bathrooms, little legroom, and no amenities other than small electric scoreboards in the end zones—but to me it was the ultimate setting for a game, a monolith that seemed to stretch from the earth to the sky. I had never seen a place so big, or so grand.
>
> .....
>
> The allure was the history, not the stadium itself. The Cotton Bowl was just a big concrete tureen, a Depression-era project incorporating none of the amenities that have become standard features in stadiums around the country in the '70s. The scoreboards provided only the score, time, down, and distance; no highlights, statistics, or advertisements. The concession stands sold hot dogs, peanuts and sodas; no nachos, ice cream, or sausages. There were no luxury suites, no escalators, no plush premium seats.[24]

MOMENTS TO REMEMBER

Both Eisenberg and Hixson, however, heard the echo of athletic history from this amphitheater speaking from its concrete bowl like the ocean's voice from a large conch shell. What happens in places of entertainment is important for memory, and fans at the Cotton Bowl had astonishing moments to recall. For example, at the Cotton Bowl Classic of 1954, Tommy Lewis, the senior fullback for the University of Alabama, stepped from the sideline to stop Dickie Maegle of Rice who was streaking down the field on his way to a touchdown a few yards in front of the reserve Alabama players. The event was shown repeatedly on television for the next twenty-five to thirty years.

Late in the second quarter, Maegle, an All-American running back with blazing speed, took the handoff from a T-formation, broke loose at the Rice five-yard line, and headed up the sideline. "I'm going to put on the afterburners," Maegle recalled, "when I see this guy out of the corner of my eye. It did dawn on me that this guy's coming off the bench, but I did say to myself, 'The guy's got no headgear on.' I said, 'Look back and see where Oliver [an Alabama pursuer] is,' when here comes this clown. I took one step to my left. I believe to this day if I hadn't taken that one step he would have broken my leg or my back." Maegle flipped into the air, the wind knocked out of him, but landed uninjured on the ground.[25]

Lewis, with no explanation for his action except that he was "so full of Alabama" and with no helmet, had thrown himself in front of Maegle. As a Rice cheerleader, one of the identical Reba twins, pointed her finger at him, Lewis rushed back to the Alabama bench, sat down, put his hands in his face, and murmured, "My God, my God, what have I done?" The stunned crowd of seventy-five thousand sat silent: there was no booing about this illegal, surprising, and unsporting act. The Rice coach Jess Neely accosted the Alabama coach Red Drew and exclaimed in his southern accent, "Red! Red! What prompted you to send that boy off to tackle ma boy?" Drew replied that Lewis had done it on his own. The referees briefly huddled and awarded Maegle a ninety-five-yard touchdown. With tears in his eyes, Lewis apologized to Maegle and the Rice team at halftime. Rice went on to win 28–6, and Maegle had his best game with 265 yards and 3 touchdowns on 11 carries.[26]

When Lewis apologized, Neely put a comforting arm around the crying Alabama player and said, "Son, get ready to live with it. You're going to live with it the rest of your life." And so it was. At the *Ed Sullivan Show* in New York several days later where the two players were interviewed, the network gave them a joint room at the Waldorf-Astoria Hotel. Maegle insisted on separate rooms and explained, "He just jumped off the bench to tackle me. I don't know how stable he is. He may have a nightmare and might want to throw me out the window." Maegle went on to a career as a professional football player until 1962 and then became a hotel owner and bond trader. Lewis, whose wife suffered a miscarriage on the night of the ill-fated game, played a year of professional football in Canada and coached high school football until one of his own players committed the same sort of off-the-bench tackle. He became an insurance agent and said forty years later, "If there were anything in the world in my life that I could take back, it would be that."[27] Neely was right: the disgrace lasted a lifetime.

Other moments stand out in Cotton Bowl history. In 1970 Coach Darrell Royal's Texas Longhorns, on their way to their second national championship, played Notre Dame down to the final minute. After deliberately avoiding postseason games for forty-five years, the Irish returned with Joe Theisman as quarterback to help celebrate one hundred years of college football. On a final drive, Texas stalled on fourth down at the Notre Dame ten-yard line. James Street, the Texas quarterback, convinced his coach that he could complete a pass play to his end, Cotton Speyrer. Street threw a wobbly pass and Speyrer made a diving catch at the two-yard line. "If I had drilled that ball it might have been a touchdown," the self-effacing Street later said, "but me being the great passer I am, the ball just barely got to him."[28] On the next play, Billy Dale, a blocker for the great Texas running back, Steve Worster, carried the ball into the end zone while the diverted Notre Dame defenders ganged up on Worster. Dale remembered, "I was so wide open I tripped myself in the end zone. I was an average football player, but I worked hard. That play, though, probably gave me a spot in college football history."[29] It has. Texas won the game 21–17 and the national championship title.

Theisman muttered afterward, "I hope they wear it [the number one rating] well for a year. We'll be back."[30] Sure enough, the following year Theisman and Notre Dame once again faced the University of Texas in the Cotton Bowl Classic. This time, however, Texas suffered six turnovers of the ball and lost 24–11 as Notre Dame broke a string of thirty Texas victories. In 1978 and 1979 Notre Dame, led by quarterback Joe Montana, returned to haunt the Cotton Bowl Classic. These games underscored a basic problem for the Cotton Bowl that portended a future difficulty—Dallas winter weather. In 1978 the Irish stuffed Longhorn Earl Campbell, a Heisman Trophy winner, and stopped the vaunted wishbone offense to beat Texas 38–10 in freezing temperatures.

The weather was worse the following year when Notre Dame nipped the University of Houston 35–34. The temperature was twenty degrees with a windchill of minus six degrees and the groundskeepers had to scrape ice off the artificial playing surface. After two quarters of play, Montana, who had had flu all week, was shivering uncontrollably with a body temperature of ninety-six degrees. During the halftime, the trainers wrapped him in blankets and fed him hot chicken soup. By the time his temperature was back to normal and he could return to the game, it was the fourth quarter and Houston led 34–12. With seven and a half minutes left in the contest, Notre Dame scored on a blocked punt, a Montana touchdown, and two two-point conversions. Houston failed on a fourth-down play at their twenty-nine-yard line and Notre Dame took over, six points behind and with fewer than two minutes to play. Montana drove the team to Houston's eight-yard line with six seconds left on the clock. A pass play to the right side of the end zone failed. Two seconds left, and Notre Dame repeated the play. End Kris Haines cut across the goal line; Montana rolled to his right and threw the ball low and away; Haines dove for the ball, caught it, and rolled through the end zone. The score was 34–34 with no time left on the clock. After a penalty for illegal motion, a substitute kicker booted the extra point for a second time and Notre Dame won.[31]

"I've never played such a weird game," said Montana. "By the time we scored that last touchdown nearly everyone in the stands had left to find someplace warm. All through that fourth quarter I kept telling everyone we would find some way to win it. But after we did, I was too sick and cold to even think about celebrating."[32] He was so bruised and beaten up that the trainers had to cut off his pants. When the doctors finished with him and he returned to the hotel, Montana found that his teammates had already departed to a party without him. "I had no idea where they were. So I sat in the hallway of the hotel, all alone with a case of beer, and celebrated the end of my college career."[33]

INTEGRATION

The Cotton Bowl was a witness not only to football heroism, but also to the profound social change of black integration in American society. Sports led the way with the introduction of Jackie Robinson to the infield of the Brooklyn Dodgers in 1947. Black athletes, however, began to show up at the Cotton Bowl at a time when segregated Dallas would not even let Negroes use the public library. During Emancipation Day, June 19, at the 1936 Texas Centennial Exposition, an integrated track meet of high school and college athletes took place on a sandy dirt track at the stadium.[34]

In 1940 the Cotton Bowl Classic hosted Clemson and Boston College. The Boston team included an African-American starting halfback, Lou Montgomery, who was excluded from play at the insistence of the Cotton Bowl officials and with the acquiescence of the college. In 1948, however, when SMU played Penn State to a 13–13 tie in the Classic, the northeastern team brought two black players to Dallas, and also an attitude. In 1946 Penn State cancelled a game with Miami because the Florida team refused to play against blacks. This incident prompted Penn State to issue the statement: "It is the policy of the college to compete only under circumstances which will permit the playing of any or all members of its athletic teams."[35]

Cotton Bowl officials carefully staged the event to avoid trouble and housed Penn State in the bachelor officer quarters of Dallas Naval Air Station in Grand Prairie fourteen miles distant. In violation of common segregation standards, the two black players, Wallace Triplett and Dennis Hoggard, attended the banquet in a downtown hotel. The newspapers withheld comment, and the *Dallas Morning News* in its bowl reports referred quietly to Triplett only as a "star Negro fullback." Meanwhile, the SMU team and its star Doak Walker attracted one hundred thousand mail order requests for tickets in four days. This helped sell the public on the need to buy the bonds necessary to expand the Cotton Bowl and the integration was hardly noticed.

The following year matched Doak Walker, the Heisman Trophy winner, and Norm Van Brocklin, the sterling quarterback of the University of Oregon. The Ducks included three black players and declined to stay at the Naval Air Station. The team instead stayed at a downtown hotel with the blacks housed in the private homes of prominent Negro citizens. This was a common tactic in the early days of integration. The blacks, however, ate with the team, and the Cotton Bowl reception committee included several Dallas citizens of color. This was a bold step for conservative Dallas, and it meant that the Cotton Bowl leaders had tentatively crossed the line of segregation. An overflow crowd at the game watched SMU win 21–13. The good feelings resulting from that hometown victory also eased the strain of social change.[36]

The biggest shift came in the mid-1960s, however, after Southern Methodist hired Hayden Fry as football coach in 1962. The school gave him permission to sign one Negro athlete and he found Jerry LeVias in 1965 in Beaumont. LeVias was intelligent and fast, and he wanted to go to a Southwest Conference school. Fry recruited him although he was only 5 feet 8 inches tall and weighed 160 pounds. LeVias recalled, "We never did talk about breaking barriers. It says something about fate and faith—that's how I went to SMU." However, it was not easy for the young black man, the only African-American player in the Southwest Conference. Students shunned him in class, no one would room with him, he had to wait for the shower stalls to empty before he could bathe, student trainers refused to tape his ankles, and in freshman football practice a player spat in his face. University of Texas fans held up nooses, Aggies released black cats onto the Cotton Bowl field, and, during the 1966 season, an anonymous caller to the SMU administration vowed to shoot "that dirty nigger LeVias."[37]

He was sustained by a kindly black janitor at the school, an aunt who lived in Dallas, and by the square-jawed Coach Fry, who had to deal with enraged boosters—"If you let that nigger play, I'll never give another dime." Both Fry and LeVias, who played as a wide receiver and punt return specialist, persevered with gritty determination. In his senior year during a tied ballgame at TCU, a Horned Frog linebacker tackled him, spat in his face, and growled, "Go home, nigger!" As LeVias left the field he announced, "I quit!" It was too much. He flung his helmet against a wall, sat down at the end of the bench, lowered his head, and wept. Meanwhile, the SMU defense held and TCU prepared to punt. As Fry searched for someone else to play the return, LeVias burst past him and blurted, "Coach, I'm going to run this one back all the way!" Fry handed him his helmet and casually said, "Jerry, you might be needing this." On the successful eighty-nine-yard return for the deciding score of the game, LeVias reversed his field twice before breaking into the open and eluded thirteen attempts to tackle him. "A lot of stuff had happened, and that was the first time I outwardly showed any real emotion. But sometimes you just get your fill," he explained.[38]

LeVias achieved All–Southwest Conference honors in 1966, 1967, and 1968. He became both an academic and athletic All-American and led SMU to a Southwest Conference title in 1966. By tapping an unused pool of talent integration improved the quality of college football. LeVias' abilities drew admiration and the barriers eroded. Fry recalled one of his players coming to him and apologizing. At first, the player admitted, he was repulsed about playing with a black, but he changed his mind. "I tell you what Coach, every time Jerry scores a touchdown he gets whiter and whiter."[39] Such an admission taken out of the context of the 1960s would be insulting, but it does demonstrate the power of athletics to blur racial prejudice. After the time of Jerry LeVias and Hayden Fry, the Southwest Conference and Cotton Bowl teams could no longer be exclusive to any color of human being.

THE PROFESSIONALS

Integration in Texas was also pushed by the coming to the Cotton Bowl of professional football teams with black players. There was an abortive attempt in 1952 with a National Football League team that included two African-Americans, but it posted a 1–11 record and left after one season to become the Baltimore Colts. Negro fans were segregated and forced to sit behind the goalposts in the worst seats. Lamar Hunt, when he started his professional team, the Dallas Texans, in 1960, did not repeat this error. The stands were open to all people.[40] Unable to obtain a National Football League franchise, Hunt of Dallas and K. S. "Bud" Adams of Houston founded the American Football League.

Fearing the competition, the NFL expanded to allow Clint Murchison Jr. to establish the Dallas Cowboys. Since Hunt got there first, the Texans played in the Cotton Bowl on Sunday afternoons. That left the Cowboys to play on Saturdays or Friday nights in conflict with the colleges and high schools. With twenty-four college and professional games in 1960 in the Cotton Bowl, the competition among the teams for a limited number of spectators was too much. It hurt everyone and in 1963 the Texans moved and became the Kansas City Chiefs.

Murchison, nonetheless, was dissatisfied and grumbled along with others about the flaws of the Cotton Bowl. There were not enough automobile spaces at Fair Park and people who parked on the streets of the unsafe slum neighborhood were subject to assault and theft. There were too many traffic jams and not enough drinking fountains. The wooden seats had no backs, were full of splinters, and demarked only by faded lines. People were so closely packed that a full bladder was a nuisance to everyone on the row, and the men's restroom where men and boys urinated into a trough was particularly foul. In September the stadium was too hot and in December it was too cold; the locker rooms had no air-conditioning and were too small; the press box was uncomfortable; and the playing field felt like concrete.[41] Murchison recognized, moreover, that "the amount of discomfort that people will put up with is decreasing as the quality of television is increasing."[42] He itched for change.

TEAM OWNERS AND STADIUMS

There was more to it. The Astrodome, which opened in 1965, had set a new standard for stadiums in regard to comfort and profits. Murchison hungered to participate in this shift. Like other owners, he wanted his own stadium and he did not want to have to pay for it. Stadiums had become too expensive for private investment, so the trick was to use public money. This involved the cooperation of three groups. The first were the voters. They had to be persuaded to tax themselves to back the bonds that provided the money to build the stadium. The voters, often fans as well, looked to a team for entertainment, inspiration, identity, and loyalty. They wanted to be proud of their Cowboys, or Astros, or Texans. Costs were not so bad when spread out per capita—a few dollars per year—and sometimes expenses could be shoveled off to outsiders in the form of hotel or rental car assessments. Fans tended to think emotionally and were readily persuaded to support the idea of a new stadium during a winning season.

The second group to be convinced were the local politicians. In most cases, this was also easy because the politicians were in a losing position. If the public wanted a new stadium and the leader did not, he or she might be voted out of office. Who would be blamed if an unhappy owner moved the team out of town? It was easier to go along with the emotional enthusiasm of the populace than to argue for better schools or hospitals. It was not difficult, furthermore, to be seduced by the often-used arguments that a new stadium would be cost effective, attract new business, or revitalize a decayed neighborhood.

Economists, incidentally, destroyed these justifications during the frenzy of stadium construction in the last part of the twentieth century. Most new venues, they pointed out, were unprofitable. The Superdome of New Orleans, for example, lost $3 million per year and the Silverdome of Pontiac, Michigan, lost $1 million per year. Tourists did not come to town to see games, and less than one percent of people at a convention went to a stadium. Analysis of the economic impact of the 1994 baseball strike revealed, moreover, little change in local income and in seventeen of twenty-four cities retail sales actually increased. Entertainment expenditures did not increase because of a stadium or sport, economists further observed. People just shifted from one type of entertainment to another, a simple reallocation of how they spent money. Revitalization, moreover, was likely to be beneficial only in a short run, especially if the team was a loser or moved to another city. Economist Robert Baade of Lake Forest College, one of the chief critics, concluded, "Constructing a stadium at public expense creates a reverse Robin Hood effect—taking from the poor and giving to the rich."[43] Economic arguments for the construction of a public stadium, therefore, did not add up.

The best argument for politicians was that the presence of a stadium and a major league team creates a "Big League" image that provides pride for the citizens and publicity for the city. A stadium had to be considered a part of the cultural infrastructure like a museum, library, park, or zoo—something that could not be measured in cold economic terms. An impressive amphitheater, furthermore, is similar to the ornate railroad stations that cities built in the nineteenth century in order to display civic accomplishment.[44] Every city needs a new stadium to testify to its worthiness. That was the safest argument. These arguments were all heard in the spectacular civic debate in 1989 that produced the $197 million Alamodome for San Antonio, a city still without an NFL team.[45]

For the third major group—the team owner and athletic league—the stadium issue is a question of profit. The league provides an exclusive franchise for the owner. Tolerated as a monopoly by Congress, the league makes certain that there is no other hometown competition and that there are never enough teams for the number of yearning cities that want them. In return, the league takes a share of the revenue from ticket, television, and merchandise sales. The rent from luxury seating and the money from seat licenses, a surcharge to season ticket holders, however, flows entirely to the team owner. This helps to pay for high-priced athletes and to generate enough revenue to satisfy bondholders.

To make certain of a favorable contract for the use of the stadium built by public money the team owner can threaten to move the team to another place that is willing to meet the owner's demands. In the stadium game, this is a card that is played openly and quickly to create anxiety among loyal fans. It is a tactic used by both baseball and football teams, and it is most effective when a team has a good season. For example, the Boston Braves moved to Milwaukee in 1953 and then to Atlanta in 1966; the Brooklyn Dodgers moved to Los Angeles in 1958; the New York Giants moved to San Francisco in 1958; the Baltimore Colts moved to Indianapolis in 1984; the Dallas Texans moved to Kansas City to become the Chiefs in 1963. The moves were often spectacularly successful for the owners and their ecstatic new supporters.

The abandoned fans in the old towns were simply left behind in bitter agony. When asked what owner Lamar Hunt should call his team in Kansas City, a disgruntled Dallas fan suggested, "The Kansas City Chicken Rat Finks." For the owners, it was a business, a question of profit, and Clint Murchison Jr. did not have a positive ledger sheet for the Cowboys until 1965.[46]

The Dallas Cowboys

The Cowboys, led by the free-spirited quarterback Don Meredith from SMU, became increasingly popular through the 1960s. Interest by fans in Dallas reflected that of the nation when football replaced baseball as "America's game." The Cowboys gave the city something to cheer about after the shocking assassination of John F. Kennedy on the Dallas streets in 1963. The team used high school cheerleaders, high school and college marching bands to entertain at halftime, the national anthem played on a solo trumpet, and the Greater Fort Worth Lions Club Band to make noise during the timeouts. The unofficial mascot was "Bubbles" Cash, a blond twenty-year-old stripper who would make her entrance to the stands in the middle of the first quarter during a lull in the action on the field. With piled-up hair, miniskirt, high heels, and carrying a large cone of pink cotton candy, she click-clicked down to her seat on the fifty-yard line. She became a tradition and the crowd would "Ahhhh" at her appearance, ask for autographs, and take her picture.[47]

The fans, mainly male, were an eclectic raucous mix, including a large number of blue-collar workers who could readily afford a $3 dollar unreserved ticket. Seating was without segregation, but blacks still tended to gather behind the goalposts to cheer the African-American players on all teams. Still, as fan and sportswriter John Eisenberg noted, "The simple act of a touchdown pass from Meredith to [Bob] Hayes, white to black, carried a great symbolic weight."[48]

Interest in Dallas and the Cowboys soared as the team began to win. In 1966 the Cowboys lost the National Football League playoffs to Green Bay in the Cotton Bowl 34–27 in the last seconds because of an offside penalty at the Green Bay two-yard line. Nonetheless, the team was a winner and the Cotton Bowl experienced sell-out games—eighty thousand for the 1966 Cowboy–Cleveland Browns game. The professional team provided about 58 percent of the stadium revenue and the Cotton Bowl managers made improvements to the venue. In 1967–1968 the stadium underwent a $2.6 million overhaul that provided aluminum chairback seats, a larger concourse, doubled restroom capacity, remodeled dressing rooms, more drinking fountains, and new turf on the field.[49] The thought of placing a dome over the Cotton Bowl was suppressed because the State Fair president, Robert B. Cullum, wanted a "pure football stadium."[50] In 1970, with a bow to better stadium technology, the managers installed AstroTurf on the field and put in new lights and a scoreboard. The artificial surface remained in use until replaced by grass for the World Cup games in 1994.[51]

None of this impressed Murchison, who saw the improvements as "pouring money into a hopeless situation." He wanted a new stadium at Fair Park or in downtown

Dallas. Mayor Erik Jonnson, State Fair President Robert Cullum, and the Dallas City Council, all of whom personally disliked the Cowboy owner, rejected his ideas, so Murchison paid $1 million for ninety acres one hundred yards west of the Dallas city limits in the suburban town of Irving. The Irving city fathers were much more cooperative, and Murchison proceeded with plans for Texas Stadium, most of which he designed himself.[52] Dallas thus missed an opportunity to add diversity to its downtown that would have offset the dangerous abandonment of that area on the weekends. Dallas also missed out on the publicity that the team could have brought to the heart of the city. The city leaders did not recognize the damage until it was too late.

Texas Stadium

Murchison might have changed the name of the team to the Irving Cowboys, but did not. The original name carried over into the new $25 million stadium that opened in 1971. The most striking feature was a large rectangular hole in the roof that allowed the rain, snow, sleet, and sun to smite the players on the artificial turf, but not the spectators in the stands. Murchison considered a sliding roof, but rejected the idea because he thought weather was an important element of the game. He purposely built the covering with light materials so that a dome could never be added. The current joke was that the roof needed to be open so that God could see his favorite team perform. The seats were placed on a steep incline in order to obtain good sight lines and intimacy for the fifty-eight thousand fans. There were 178 air-conditioned suites, actually bare concrete shells, encircling the top that people could rent for $50,000 per year and decorate themselves. Everyone was required to buy a $250 bond per seat, a surcharge, in order to purchase season tickets. "What could be fairer than having the stadium financed by the fans who use it?" said Murchison.[53]

The ticket requirements, however, cut out the lower classes. The cost was four to five times what it had been in the Cotton Bowl and only an estimated ten thousand fans followed the team to Irving. "If we discriminated against them, we discriminated against them," shrugged the Cowboy owner, "but no more than all America discriminates against people who don't have enough money to buy everything they want."[54] In a very real way, the change of stadiums left behind a group of agonized supporters just as if the Cowboys had moved across the country. Management showed no loyalty to their blue-collar friends.

A game at the new Texas Stadium became a social event for the upper class, for whom football was an afterthought. It was quiet and cheering was subdued, almost to the level of polite clapping. According to the players, it was weird and estranged. "We gave up the shoeshine guy for the lawyer when we moved," said player Jethro Pugh. "They have to beg for cheers at Texas Stadium," said fullback Walt Garrison. "No one ever had to beg for cheers at the Cotton Bowl." The field was sunk below ground level so that the elite spectators peered down at the players as in the old Roman Colosseum. "You know why they sunk the field?" offensive guard Blaine Nye asked offensive tackle Ralph Neely before a game. "So the gladiators can't get out."[55]

THE COTTON BOWL ENDURES

The Cotton Bowl thus lost professional football. It also lost SMU through no fault of its own. The school used the stadium as its home field for thirty years through 1978. The Ponies then played at Texas Stadium until 1987 when the NCAA halted its football program because of repeated violations about recruitment and alumni support of athletes. There is speculation that Southern Methodist never fully recovered from this "death sentence," but the school started playing again in 1989 at the dilapidated Ownby Stadium where Doak Walker had started, then at the Cotton Bowl from 1995–1999, and finally at its own new 32,000-seat Gerald J. Ford Stadium on the campus.[56] The Cotton Bowl thus lost an old friend.

In addition, the Southwest Conference broke up in 1994–1995. This severed the Conference's relationship with the Cotton Bowl Classic, and worse, the new and powerful Bowl Alliance of the Division I-A teams confined the national championship games to the Orange, Sugar, and Fiesta bowls. The Rose Bowl, initially, continued to match the Big 10 and Pacific 10 champions. The Cotton Bowl, with less money and a reputation for bad weather, was relegated to a second tier that meant that it could seek only second-rate teams for its New Year's game.

Recognizing the bowl's diminished status, the Mobil Corporation, which had sponsored the Classic for seven years, dropped its backing in 1995. On January 2, 1996, the forty-five thousand fans who came to watch Colorado beat Oregon 38–6 were pelted with rain and raked by wind. The upper decks and end zones were swept empty. It was the first game since the breakup of the Southwest Conference, and the *Dallas Morning News* commented, "It takes only four words to explain the low attendance at this year's Cotton Bowl Classic: cold, wet, no Texans."[57]

The Cotton Bowl, consequently, was left with a reduced New Year's Day game, an annual contest between Grambling State University and Prairie View A&M University, the yearly Texas-Oklahoma game, some high school games, and random miscellaneous events. Even the Longhorns and the Sooners began to talk about playing their games on a home-and-home basis after the end of their 2010 contract.[58] Worse, Jerry Jones, the owner of the Dallas Cowboys began building an 80,000-seat, 200-suite, retractable-roofed stadium between Dallas and Fort Worth in Arlington. Financed one-half with public monies from sales, hotel, and car rental taxes, with Jones left in control of the property, the stadium is scheduled to open in 2009. He was awarded the 2011 Super Bowl. The Cotton Bowl Association, with some lament, voted to move the Cotton Bowl game from the old stadium at Fair Park to the new stadium in Arlington in hopes of catching a prime position with the bowl alliance.[59]

Most of the time the venerable stadium remains unused if not unloved. Nonetheless, the old Cotton Bowl will probably endure as politicians and the public learn to object to the astounding cost of the new arenas that they are asked to finance for private profit. The Dallas area, moreover, has already expended its resources for such large projects: Texas Stadium in Irving for major league football, a new stadium being constructed in Arlington, and the Rangers Ballpark in Arlington (1994) for major league baseball. The Cotton Bowl remains attractive because it is solid, serviceable, and paid for. Thousands of high school athletes and their fans have yearned to play a championship game in this bowl for seventy-five years. The Cotton Bowl has been the prototype, the mecca, the mother of the stadiums in the Southwest. It has been the Colosseum of Texas and will likely live into the future.

BASEBALL AND TEXAS

Like football, the precise date of baseball's introduction into Texas is a bit uncertain. But here are some pieces of useful information. Alexander J. Cartwright (1820–1892) organized the Knickerbocker Base Ball Club, wrote down the first rules of modern baseball, and played a game in Hoboken in 1845. The "New York game" spread along the east coast of the United States and in 1857 twenty-two clubs formed the National Association of Base Ball Players. The Civil War helped to spread the game as bored Northern soldiers sought recreation in the lulls between battles. Geoffrey C. Ward and Ken Burns in their history of baseball quote a Union soldier who was participating in a game between the battle lines during the Red River campaign of 1864. Sudden rebel gunfire interrupted the sport and the center fielder was hit and captured. "The attack . . . was repelled without serious difficulty," wrote George Putnam, "but we had lost not only our center field, but . . . the only baseball in Alexandria."[60]

Southern prisoners of war soon learned the game and Northern soldiers taught baseball to local boys during the Reconstruction period. Easy to learn, the game required little equipment—only a bat and ball. It was played on empty green spaces in towns and it was slow paced. As the country evolved into an industrialized, urban nation, baseball reminded people of an idyllic rural past.

The soldiers in Texas played on a field north of the Ursuline Convent on Galveston Island and the men in Galveston formed a club in 1867. On San Jacinto Day, the R. E. Lees of Galveston lost 35–2 to the Stonewalls of Houston. Revenge came in 1871 when the Galveston Island Cities beat the Houston Pioneers 19–15. Local amateur teams formed, challenged others, fell apart, changed names, and reformed. Professional teams toured the state to increase interest in the sport in 1877 and 1887. Then in 1888, inspired by "Honest John" McCloskey (1862–1940), a touring professional, the Texas League formed with clubs in Austin, Dallas, Galveston, Fort Worth, Houston, and San Antonio. Although the league added and dropped teams over time, it has provided an ongoing diet of minor league baseball for Texans to the present time. A parallel Negro league formed in the 1920s that used the stadiums in off times.[61]

Both the quality of play and the configuration of the stadiums, as might be expected, were irregular. Galveston's Beach Park, for example, was made of wood and had a plank outfield wall on the beach. According to Nelson Leopold, an owner of the Galveston team, in the 1890s a Galveston player hit a home run over the fence and casually began to trot around the bases. A wave washed the ball back under the fence and the Houston outfielder picked up the sodden ball and hurled it to his catcher. The catcher then tagged out the surprised base runner. A huge brouhaha ensued that the umpire eventually settled by declaring that the home run would count. Galveston won the game, but the great Galveston hurricane of 1900 washed away the stadium and the storm of 1915 destroyed its successor.[62]

When it opened in 1928, Houston's 14,000-seat Buff Stadium—with its Spanish-style entry and convenient location near the Interurban tracks—was considered to be the best in the league. Major League Baseball commissioner Kenesaw Mountain Landis attended the opening ceremonies. With a deep outfield and a persistent breeze that blew toward home plate, the park discouraged sluggers and was considered to be a place that favored pitchers. It spawned "Dizzy" Dean's throwing career in the early 1930s. It was renamed Busch Stadium in 1953 in recognition of the team's long-standing, minor league connection with the St. Louis Cardinals, and the outfield fences were moved inward by twenty feet to help the hitters.[63] For the spectators, however, the stadium was noted for high humidity, rain, and mosquitoes. Cutter insect repellent was the perfume of choice. Still, there were stalwart fans who loved baseball and lusted for a major league team.

The Major Leagues

George Kirksey, a former sportswriter from Chicago and New York who ran a public relations business in Houston, began to talk about major league baseball to friends, politicians, and the city council in the late 1950s. He figured that Houston would need a 40,000-seat stadium, parking for 15,000 cars, and a population of one million people from which to draw spectators. Houston—then the eighth largest city in the nation—would qualify. In 1958 Kirksey put together a syndicate—the Houston Sports Association (HSA), led by banker William A. Kirkland—to promote the idea.[64] Twenty-seven men bought thirty shares of stock in the association at $500 per share. They shortly ran, however, into a "Catch 22" situation: the major league owners said that Houston needed a stadium before they would grant a franchise, and the local officials said that they would have to have a franchise before they would approve of a stadium.[65]

Some circumstances, however, offered a way through the impasse. Major League Baseball was in a mood to expand. Fan attendance had declined, Congress was reviewing baseball's monopoly position, owners were moving their franchises in search of profit, and Texas was an unexploited market. The Harris County Commissioner's Court, meanwhile, created a 17-member park board with William A. Kirkland as chair to investigate the feasibility of a sports stadium to serve the Houston area.

After investigating twenty cities, the board recommended the passage of a $20 million revenue bond issue to build a multipurpose facility that could be used for baseball, football, and other activities. With only a month to gain support, the bond issue was placed on the Democratic Party primary ticket in 1958 and endorsed by a 3–1 ratio. Since Texas at the time was a one-party state, approval on the final ballot was certain and preliminary planning began for the stadium. There were tangles to be unraveled regarding location, design, the Houston Buffs, and participation by the lucrative Houston Fat Stock Show. Time passed, and in 1960 Major League Baseball announced the expansion of the leagues by two teams each.[66]

Kirksey's sports association, which had received additional energy in 1959 when R. E. "Bob" Smith and his business partner Roy M. Hofheinz joined the syndicate, prepared to bid for a National League team. Bob Smith (1894–1973) had played semiprofessional baseball for ten years, made a fortune in the East Texas oil fields, and owned more land—some eleven thousand acres—in Harris County than anyone else. Roy Hofheinz (1912–1982) was a lawyer, Texas legislator, county judge, and two-term mayor of Houston. With his heavy, horn-rimmed glasses, the "Judge," as he was called, looked a bit like a cigar-smoking, portly owl. He made his fortune selling steel slag for road construction and through radio and television acquisition.

Hofheinz was fast moving, brilliant, determined, and flamboyant. Above all, he was a promoter and he called his vacation home on Galveston Bay "Huckster House." Kirksey, Hofheinz, and Craig Cullinan Jr., an oil heir and cofounder of the HSA, presented the Houston case to the National League at Cincinnati in October 1960 and returned home with the franchise. They were met at the airport by a crowd singing and a Dixieland band playing "Take Me Out to the Ballgame."[67]

Smith and Hofheinz bought controlling interest in the newly incorporated Houston Sports Association, and, under Hofheinz's leadership, the various tangles came undone. In short order, the sports association bought the Houston Buffs, named their team the Colt .45s, persuaded the Harris County voters to endorse $22 million in tax bonds rather than revenue bonds, bought a site on South Main from the Hilton Hotel Corporation, and obtained a 40-year lease from the county for use of the new amphitheater at $750,000 per year. This was enough to pay off the bonds. The livestock show agreed to use the facility and to build their pavilion next door.

Earlier, Kirkland and the park board had suggested constructing a multipurpose domed stadium for the county, and at the Major League Baseball presentations, the Judge promised a covered stadium. The plans were still somewhat uncertain, however, and they were considering a geodesic dome as conceived by Buckminster Fuller. For Hofheinz, who remembered the lesson of the ancient Roman Colosseum, some sort of covering was essential. "People in Houston aren't going to sit in big numbers in the hot sun and high humidity in the daytime or fight mosquitoes at night to see baseball. We've got have a covered, air conditioned playing field."[68]

The Astrodome

The general idea was to build a multipurpose facility that could be utilized for baseball, football, rodeo, and various special events. For a city, it made sense to have a single stadium, where the parking and seating could be used repeatedly for many purposes. It was cheaper and it conserved urban space. The best configuration for such a venue was a circle. It worked well for the shell-shaped playing field of baseball, but did not accommodate readily to the rectangular fields of football and soccer or the small courts of tennis and basketball.

The architectural answer was movable stands and flooring that could conform to the requirements of a sport. Some seating was lost when shifts were made, but it was a compromise that worked for most purposes. It was the best use of public money, and open, circular stadiums bloomed in Atlanta (1966), St. Louis (1966), Cincinnati (1970), Pittsburgh (1970), and Philadelphia (1971). The last of these round open stadiums, incidentally, came down with the demolition of Busch Stadium in St. Louis in 2005.[69] The Astrodome was also circular and designed for multiple use, but it was enclosed and air-conditioned. That was different, more daring, and much more difficult to accomplish. "If those Romans could put a lid on their stadium, so can we," said Hofheinz. "We'll build a stadium that will make Emperor Titus's playhouse look like an abandoned brickyard."[70]

At the time, there was little engineering doubt that a roof could be constructed to encompass an entire baseball field. The technology and materials, even for air-conditioning, were available. It was simply that it had not been done; it just had to be designed and put together. Hofheinz insisted not only upon an air-conditioned enclosure, but also upon a grass playing field. This meant that the roof had to emit sufficient natural light, an additional challenge. The Houston Sports Association hired two Houston firms to design the stadium—Wilson, Morris and Crane and Lott-Drake.

The architects studied other facilities and chose the circular shape because the main use would be for baseball. They considered a retractable roof like that of the Pittsburgh Public Auditorium (1961), but rejected that idea as impractical because of the demands of air-conditioning. They chose to use a diamond-shaped, lamella truss with steel beams to support an elongated arch to form a dome and lightweight plastic skylights to provide diffused light on the field. Agronomist George G. McBee of Texas A&M recommended Tifway Bermuda grass for the field because it grew well in low-light conditions. After three years of planning, it was time to start construction, and instead of the traditional turning of a spade, the principals gathered and fired Colt .45s into the ground.[71]

The site was seven miles southwest of downtown Houston, and Hofheinz leased a suite in the nearby Shamrock Hotel so that he could watch the construction through binoculars. He later moved into a personal Astrodome apartment beyond center field that eventually reached from ground floor to ceiling. The superstructure for the concrete and steel facility was up in four months for a dome attaining a clear span of 642 feet (710 feet in outer diameter) and a height of 218 feet—higher than any pop fly ball in baseball, higher than the 18-story Shamrock Hotel. Tested in a laboratory, the roof could flex over five inches in any direction and withstand hurricane-force winds. The air-conditioning system, tested for smoke removal from boxing arenas, was set at a steady seventy-five degrees all year. Otherwise, the humidity would form rain clouds inside the dome that would drip on the seats.

The playing field was placed thirty-six feet below ground so that fans would enter the stadium at midpoint. There were six levels of seats with each tier a different color like the rings of LifeSaver candy. The foam-padded, deep-cushioned, nylon-upholstered seats pointed toward second base. Fifty-three blue skyboxes ringed the top of the stadium, each one personally furnished by Hofheinz and supplied with closed-circuit television and food service. Spanning the centerfield wall was a 474-foot-long scoreboard that flashed animated messages as well as the essential information about the game and players. There was parking for twenty thousand automobiles. The stadium would accommodate forty-five thousand fans for baseball and fifty-two thousand for football through the use of ten thousand seats on tracks that rotated thirty-five degrees to form the football field. The architects had figured out how to square the circle.

The air-conditioning, the oversized scoreboard, the dome, the skyboxes, the cushioned seats—all of this was new, and Hofheinz was the innovative driving force. He said, "We are building something nobody else in the world has or will have for years to come, something that will set the pattern for the twenty-first century and we're doing it for less money."[72] He changed the name of the team to the Astros and nicknamed the stadium the "Astrodome" after Colt Firearms insisted on sharing the profits from the sale of team paraphernalia. The name officially remained the Harris County Domed Stadium, but the Judge took advantage of Houston's recent role in space exploration. Si Morris, one of the main architects, commented, "Without Roy's showmanship, there wouldn't have been an Astrodome. We can talk about it any way you want to, but Roy did it, and he created a completely new Houston identity by himself."[73]

The Astrodome was a stunning structure and it brought world attention to Houston as a place of high technology and daring. It was the first stadium since the Colosseum to draw people just to see the architecture, and the HSA began running tours even before its completion. About five hundred thousand people came in the first year. It was the most architecturally significant building ever constructed in Texas, and, at least for the moment, matched its hyperbolic description as the "Eighth Wonder of the World." The gentle arc of its white elongated dome provided contrast to the jagged, phallic thrust of the distant downtown office towers, and the cityscapes of North America would never be the same after this. The final cost was $45.35 million after Houston voters provided $9.6 million more in bonds. The total also included $4 million from property owners for rights-of-way, $3.75 million from the city and state, and $6 million from the HSA for restaurants, scoreboard, and skyboxes. There was no evidence of corruption, payoffs, or under-the-table deals in its history. The Astrodome began life as a stadium on April 9, 1965, when the Astros beat the New York Yankees 2–1 in an exhibition game. On that "giddy, spectacular night," wrote local sportswriter Mickey Herskowitz, "baseball moved this side of paradise."[74]

Problems in Paradise

There were two major difficulties, however. The roof leaked and the 4,596 Lucite skylights let in too much light. Throughout the stadium's history, despite layers of caulk, the skylights continued to leak rainwater and remained a nagging problem.

The ongoing joke was that fans did not get rain checks, just the right to move to a dry seat.[75] The sunlight that was necessary for the health of the grass, however, created an unforeseen and immediate obstacle for the players. It was a technical error that threatened the success of the entire enterprise.

A few days before the opening game, fielders discovered that they could not track high fly balls as they arced across the ceiling, lost in a glare of diffused sunlight amidst the dark crosshatched girders. The players tried sunglasses and different colored baseballs to no avail, and the outfielders began to wear batting helmets to protect themselves from the balls that fell a few feet away. It was all right at night, of course, and the Judge wryly announced to reporters, "Never fear. I will not be the first man to call a game on account of sunshine."[76]

The glare problem was eliminated by painting the outside of the dome with an off-white acrylic paint. This sufficiently darkened the interior for the players' eyes, but it slowly killed the grass. Hofheinz temporarily painted the dying grass green and looked for an artificial substitute. Fake undertaker's grass came to mind, but Hofheinz had heard of something better. Chemstrand, a division of Monsanto and American Viscose Corporation, had experimented with a nylon and acrylic carpet in the field house of Moses Brown School in Providence, Rhode Island, in 1964. The artificial grass was like a stiff nylon brush. Hofheinz tested a thirty-foot-long segment sent by Chemstrand by having University of Houston football players, baseball players, sheriff's horses, automobiles, and elephants run over it. He gave up his dream of natural grass under the dome and began to install what Chemstrand called AstroTurf in 1966, first for the infield and later in the outfield. It was a success and the use of artificial athletic turf eventually spread throughout the world.[77] Albeit by error, the Astrodome and Hofheinz provided another innovation for stadiums.

The Astrodome and Houston

The Astrodome met with a mixed reaction from players, critics, and fans. Baseball purists lamented the loss of open-air elements, players complained about injuries such as rug burn and turf toe, and critics made fun of the architecture. Larry McMurtry, Texas' foremost contemporary author, for example, failed to see humor in the brashness or beauty in the design and wrote that the Astrodome looked like "the working end of a gigantic roll-on deodorant." He continued, "Whatever it is will be bigger, better, sexier, more violent, and above all costlier, than anything we've had before. Houston is that kind of town." It was "echt-Texas," he sneered.[78] Roger Angell, who has spent his life writing about baseball, however, liked the architecture, the seating, and the conditions for the players. He abhorred, however, the intrusive scoreboard and the "vulgar venture" that treated baseball as sheer entertainment.[79] In contrast, news commentator David Brinkley said, "I've heard the jokes, but I like the idea of a town that is not afraid to be comfortable, that is not afraid to spend its money, that is not afraid of excessive luxury, and that has learned how to enjoy it. I don't see anything wrong with it."[80] Hofheinz's response to all the commentary was, "Nobody can ever see this and still think Houston is bush."[81] The Astrodome changed the image of the Gulf Coast capital.

In order to prove its worth and pay for itself, the stadium had to be used almost half the time. So, Hofheinz scheduled conventions, revivals, athletic contests, rodeos, and circuses. Billy Graham held a religious crusade there in November 1965 and left the Judge a small Bible inscribed, "The Astrodome is truly the Eighth Wonder of the World."[82] Ringling Bros. and Barnum & Bailey Circus set its single performance attendance record in June 1965, with rigging tied directly to the ceiling. Judy Garland and Andy Williams gave concerts in 1966; Elvis Presley performed in 1974. The Republican Party nominated George H. W. Bush for president in 1992. Over one million fans came during the first season to see the struggling, ninth-place Astros, and in 1973 a crowd of thirty thousand witnessed Billie Jean King beat Bobby Riggs in straight sets to prove that women could play worthy tennis. Muhammad Ali fought three times under the dome. The University of Houston used the Astrodome for its football games, and in 1968 fifty-three thousand fans turned out to watch Elvin Hayes stop Lew Alcindor (Kareem Abdul-Jabbar) of top-ranked UCLA 71–69 in the first basketball game played in the facility.

It would have seemed natural for Houston's professional football team, the Oilers, to move from the inadequate high school field they rented to the Astrodome, but Bud Adams, the owner, did not get along with Roy Hofheinz. The basic problem was that Hofheinz controlled the Astrodome and Adams did not. Adams stubbornly played at Rice Stadium from 1965–1967 and then moved to the Astrodome when rain dampened his profits. Hofheinz, meanwhile, bought control of the HSA from R. E. "Bob" Smith and began to build an entertainment empire. In 1967, along with Irwin Feld, the operating manager of Ringling Bros. and Barnum & Bailey Circus, he bought the circus, and in 1968 Hofheinz opened Astroworld, a theme park next door to the Astrodome. He later merged the circus with the toy manufacturer Mattel, the maker of Hot Wheels and Barbie dolls, but the toy maker had fraudulently misstated its 1969–1971 earnings and the Judge lost money in the deal. Hofheinz eventually won a lawsuit against Mattel, but for him it was too late.

In May 1970 Hofheinz, who smoked a box of cigars per day, suffered a crippling stroke. The Mattel stock that he had used as collateral declined after 1971, and in 1976 he had to sell his Astrodomain to the General Electric and Ford credit corporations. They allowed him to remove his furnishings from the Astrodome—some forty-eight vans—but they refused to let him rent a skybox. They did not want him around. Still a millionaire, the Judge retreated to his River Oaks home for the remainder of his life. At his death in 1982, the funeral cortege drove in a circle around the Astrodome on the way to the gravesite. In 1978 Ford bought out the General Electric interest and the next year sold the Houston Sports Association and the Astros to shipbuilder John J. McMullen (1918–2005) of New Jersey. The Astrodome remained the property of Harris County.[83]

Other Teams, Other Stadiums

McMullen was never popular in Houston in part because he fired long-term general manager Tal Smith and refused to renew the contract of outstanding pitcher Nolan Ryan. In 1992 he sold the Astros to Drayton McLane Jr. from Temple, Texas, who had made a fortune in the success of Wal-Mart. McLane wanted a new downtown ballpark that would make more money, threatened to sell the team, and narrowly won public approval for a new stadium in 1997 after the Astros reached the playoffs. The result was Enron Field (renamed Minute Maid Park following the 2001 debacle of the Enron Corporation), which boasted a retractable roof and natural grass. It could be air-conditioned, but only after the roof had been closed for three hours. The new baseball facility that opened in 2000 was one of the retrograde and nostalgic single-purpose stadiums that became popular at the end of the twentieth century.

The park let in the sunshine once more along with Houston heat, humidity, and mosquitoes. It seated three thousand fewer fans than the Astrodome and cost $265 million, with the bulk of the bonds supported by taxes on hotels, rental cars, parking, and liquor sales. In 1997 the state legislature authorized the formation of a local sports authority to collect such taxes. This was a new twist to the trick of spending public money for the profit of a private team owner. Travelers could now pay a share whether they used the facility or not. Yet, it seemed somehow emotionally worthwhile for Houston when the Astros reached the World Series in 2005.[84]

Bud Adams was not so fortunate. He still did not like the Astrodome and threatened to move the football team in 1987. He agreed to remain, however, with a ten-year contract in return for $67 million worth of improvements. This added ten thousand more seats and sixty-six luxury suites, removed the scoreboard and Hofheinz's old apartment, and attached four circular access ramps to the perimeter of the dome. Adams continued to complain that the Astrodome was not big enough for his losing team and agitated for a downtown stadium. His timing was bad and in this instance the threats of a monopolistic owner did not work. The City Council balked at his demands and so Adams yanked the Oilers out of Houston at the end of his lease and moved to a downtown stadium in Nashville to become the Tennessee Titans. Little love was lost with this divorce.[85]

When the NFL decided to expand once more, however, Robert McNair, a Houston billionaire and philanthropist, paid $700 million for a franchise to return professional football to Houston. When asked by his wife why he would spend so much money for a mere football team, he replied, "I think sports are an element within a community that can be a unifying force. I knew that we were missing something in Houston, and we needed to bring the NFL back."[86] He negotiated with Harris County to construct a retractable roof football stadium—the first in the NFL—next to the Astrodome for his team, the Houston Texans.

It cost $367 million and contained 69,500 seats along with 165 private suites. Public monies paid $250 million of this amount with the rest coming from the sale of seat licenses, proceeds from the rodeo, and Reliant Energy, Inc. for naming rights. The

Houston hotel surcharge tax soared to the highest in the nation as the Reliant brand was stamped everywhere upon the Astrodomain of Roy Hofheinz. Built wholly above ground, the new box-like Reliant Stadium, which opened in 2002, dwarfed the nearby Astrodome and raised questions about the future of the world's first domed stadium.[87] As newspaper critic Mike Tolson unsympathetically commented, "The Astrodome without the Astros is like Versailles without the kings. It imposes and impresses, but stripped of meaning it becomes just another place that used to be important."[88]

Houston is notorious for ruthlessly demolishing buildings and spaces that are not immediately useful. The Shamrock Hotel, for example, which was a symbol of Houston's oil boom heritage, was destroyed in 1987 to provide space for a parking lot. Houston is unzoned and spends only one-fifth the amount of money for planning than does Dallas. Houston is a city of action, exploitation, daring, and profit. There is, consequently, little respect for history or historic preservation. Yet, there is a curious hesitation about the Astrodome.

The old stadium sits humbled in Reliant Park, its graceful original symmetry obscured by Bud Adams' stuck-on spectator ramps and the stolid Reliant Stadium monolith next door. Although the Astrodome served as a refuge for the New Orleans victims of the Katrina hurricane disaster in 2005, it remains basically unused and unneeded. It costs $500,000 per year to maintain, and the space could make another dandy parking lot. Harris County, nonetheless, has paused in ordering an implosion like that of the Seattle Kingdome in March 2000. Suggestions about the Astrodome's future include building a city under the dome with schools, housing, shops, offices, and parks. But the sort of imagination that brought about its creation has faltered in preserving its future. No captivating plan has emerged.[89]

In spite of all the past criticism of the Astrodome, a certain reverence remains for what was first accomplished by the stadium—an enclosed air-conditioned baseball field, skyboxes, an entertaining scoreboard, comfortable viewing, multiple uses, Astroturf, and a reasonable cost for the public. It brought "big league" sports to Houston, became an emblem for the city, and inspired the building of some twenty-three other covered stadiums in North America. These stadiums in turn became defining landmarks for their cities. The Astrodome revolutionized thinking about amphitheaters, changed the jagged configurations of modern city skylines, and brought about an enduring excitement that could only have been matched by the ancient Colosseum. "The mere fact that it was the first of its kind makes it of transcendent importance," stated Stephen Fox, an architectural historian at Rice University.[90] Tal Smith, a baseball executive involved in both the Astrodome and the opening of the new Enron Field, commented:

> I want to be careful how I say this. We're all excited about Enron—the fact that it's downtown, the roof opens, it has natural grass. But for those who can recall it, the opening of the Astrodome was unique. It received worldwide attention. Domed stadiums are commonplace now. There were skeptics who didn't think baseball could be played indoors. Enron is more of a traditional ballpark. We had all kind

> of doubters. I remember the day they removed the support towers from the roof. You had people waiting to see if the dome collapsed . . . I believe Billy Graham was right when he called it the Eighth Wonder of the World.[91]

Perhaps the reason that the demolition of the Astrodome has been postponed is that no one wants to destroy one of the wonders of the world, and hope lingers that some alternative use can be found. It is still a sound building. Beyond that, there are community memories tied to the Astrodome, just as there are memories in Dallas linked to the Cotton Bowl, the "House that Doak Built." There is power in such history, the connection of people with place, but it may be insufficient to save what is considered to be an obsolete stadium in Houston, Texas. In terms of longevity, the Astrodome burst into the sports universe like a holiday skyrocket that illuminated the sky in brilliance and then burned out. It lasted but forty years, but oh what a light.

CHAPTER 4

The Pleasure of Libraries

When British scholar R. E. Wycherley listed the important facilities of the ancient Greek city-states in his book *How the Greeks Built Cities* (1969), he said that a city could not be complete for the Greeks without a wall for protection; an agora, or gathering place, for markets and public discourse; a field for exercise; fountains and springs for water; official buildings and shrines; homes; and an amphitheater for artistic presentations.[1] It was an evaluation based upon infrastructure, not upon simple numbers of inhabitants as with the U.S. Census Bureau's classification of urban places. The answer to the same question about modern cities—what makes a city a city?—would include such items as water and sewer systems, town halls, fire and police facilities, electrical systems, newspapers, post offices, radio and television broadcasting, business buildings, streets, stadiums, auditoriums, churches, and libraries.

A wall would be unnecessary, but modern citizens, like those of ancient Greece, still work together to make the city function. There are electrical workers to supply power for lights and machinery; politicians in town hall, firemen, and police officers to provide order and security; laborers, salesmen, engineers, and others in factories and offices to offer a way to make money; shopkeepers and merchants to make clothes and food available; rabbis, priests, and imams to open a door to spirituality; athletes, musicians, and actors to supply entertainment; pure water and waste disposal experts to ensure good health for citizens; street workers to develop efficient roads for transport; postal workers, reporters, and editors to furnish current information; teachers to produce an educated populace; and librarians to preserve the knowledge of the past. Without all these people working together in an integrated system, an urban place is something less than a city.

THE JOY OF READING

Libraries are so commonplace in the United States it would seem, at least for the moment, that they are integral to the definition of "city." Minor headlines at the end of 2004, for example, caused shivers across the nation when Salinas, California, the birthplace of novelist John Steinbeck, closed its public library due to a budgetary shortfall. Was this evidence of urban decline? Local retired schoolteacher Julianne Hansen said, "I think it's uncivilized. Everyone is so incensed. It's like closing down motherhood."[2] The library has since reopened for a few hours per week.

Was Salinas diminished as a city? Probably, but more to the point for this book, is the library a place of recreation, a source of pleasure? Well yes, sort of, in a sense, kind of, it can be in part. The answer involves several complex issues.

First of all, why do people read? People obviously read for pleasure, curiosity, education, and to find information that will help them. The motives are often mixed—there is no data for what goes on in a reader's head—but to exercise the sheer ability to read as an intellectual activity can be a form of recreation and pleasure. The quotation books are filled with comments about reading that hint at this.

"I seek in the reading of books, only to please myself, by honest diversion," wrote Montaigne, French essayist, in the 1580s. Benjamin Franklin, America's first philosopher, included in *Poor Richard's Almanac* (1732–1757), "Reading makes a full man, meditation a profound man, discourse a clear man." Irish dramatist, journalist, and politician Richard Steele said in number 147 of the *Tatler* (1709–1711), "Reading is to the mind what exercise is to the body." In 1854 Henry David Thoreau, essayist and poet, wrote in *Walden*, "How many a man has dated a new era in his life from the reading of a book?" Thoreau also noted, "Books are the treasured wealth of the world and the fit inheritance of generations and nations." In 1899, French jurist Montesquieu said, "I have never known any distress that an hour's reading did not relieve." Journalist and television commentator Harry Reasoner, who was born in San Marcos, Texas, observed, "Reading is about the only thing left in life that should be reserved for pure pleasure."

Scots novelist Robert Louis Stevenson's comment in 1881, "Books are good enough in their own way, but they are a mighty bloodless substitute for life," was countered in 1931 by Logan Pearsall Smith, British essayist, who said, "People say that life is the thing, but I prefer reading." A contemporary assessment not found in the common quotation books comes from Moby (Richard Melville Hall), a techno-musician. When asked why he started a book club for his fans, he replied, "Ozzy Osbourne used to snort ants. Led Zeppelin had sex with hookers on private planes. And I start a book club. Because one can only snort so many ants and have so much sex before one starts to long for the comfort and companionship of a book."[3]

Over time literacy, the ability to read and write, became the hallmark of an educated person and a worthy goal not only for the people of the United States, but also for the world. Educational ideas and institutions in America, like much else in the history of the United States, spread from east to west across the continent, following the path of Anglo settlement. Developments in Texas, with a touch of Hispanic influence, reflect this national history. The literacy rate improved in the United States from 80 percent in 1870 to 97 percent in 1950. In Texas during the same period, it changed from 27 percent to 97 percent. There was justifiable pride in this accomplishment, now almost forgotten, which was a triumph of teachers and libraries.[4]

It was also a tribute to the abiding desire, particularly by women, that children receive an education. In 1845, for instance, Captain Shapley P. Ross, a prominent Texas frontier ranger and Indian agent, decided to move his family from his raw land near Belton to Austin in order to find a school for his nine children. He had been haunted by the remark of a relative when he moved to the region six years earlier: "Ah well, let him go. In a few years he will come back from Texas in an old cart drawn by a crop-eared mule, and he will be followed by a gang of yellow dogs covered with mange. In that cart, and walking behind it, will sit a set of ignorant boobies, who would not know a schoolhouse from a hog pen or a schoolmaster from a Hottentot." Ross' wife, informed about his decision to move for the sake of the children, laconically commented, "You have been a long time coming to that conclusion."[5]

THE ART AND TECHNOLOGY OF PRINTING

The second major issue about the library as a place of recreation involves questions about what people read and where the reading material comes from. The era of laborious hand copies and carved wooden block printing ended with the perfection of metal moveable type by Johannes Gutenberg (1400–1468), who produced his famous 42-line Bible around 1455. It is right and proper that the University of Texas at Austin reverently displays one of the twenty surviving copies of this Bible at the Harry Ransom Humanities Research Center. The printed Gutenberg Bible is the work of a technological genius. The typography, which included ink mixed with linseed oil; paper made from rags; a press adapted from the ancient Roman wine press; and reusable type spread quickly from Gutenberg's home in Mainz throughout Europe, and within twenty-five years publishers produced more printed material than in all human history up to that point.

The books, pamphlets, and newspapers that poured from the presses used the vernacular of the people, not the dead Latin language of the church. Teaching and business negotiations no longer had to be conducted face to face. The new printing, consequently, stimulated reading and learning and thinking and more writing. The technology crossed national boundaries and no censor could follow it. Only the contemporary phenomenon of the Internet compares to this flood of unbridled information that challenged ideas and dug a new channel for the course of history.

The technique of printing remained virtually unchanged until the latter part of the nineteenth century, and it became a part of early Texas history. The revolutionist Francisco Xavier Mina (1789–1817) brought along a small English press and printer Samuel Bangs of Boston on his ill-fated attempt to wrest Texas from Spain in 1817. Bangs (1798–1854) produced the first imprints in Texas, escaped the execution that the Spanish dealt to Mina, printed materials for both sides of the conflict, and later published a succession of newspapers in Galveston, San Luis, and Corpus Christi.[6] Wherever the urban seeds were sown, printing presses, newspapers, and publishers popped up almost without fail to inform, serve, and sometimes irritate the local population.

When Ferdinand Flake (?–1872), the editor of *Die Union* in Galveston, for example, dared to criticize the secession of South Carolina in 1861, a mob broke into his office, destroyed his press, and scattered bits of type into an alley.[7] Editor William C. Brann (1855–1898) of Waco, another example, wrote with an acerbic pen about Baylor University and called it a "chronic breeder of bigotry and bile." He was kidnapped and beaten by Baylor students, about whom he wrote, "They take but two baths during their lifetime—one when they are born, the other when they are baptized." In 1898 a disgruntled assassin shot Brann in the back precisely where his suspenders crossed. Brann's gravestone, a symbol for an editor who had outraged just about everyone, became a target of drive-by shootings.[8] His life is an illustration of how a newspaper can amplify the ideas of an individual, for better or worse.

Although newspapers too suffered a high mortality rate, Texas could claim 38 daily papers in 1868; 34 in 1890; 89 in 1910; 110 in 1920; and 115 in 1950. Then the dailies declined to 83 in 1994 as chains, news services, urban population shifts, and new printing technology took hold. There had always been newspapers imported by ship or mail, and in 1948 the *Wall Street Journal* began to publish a southwestern edition in Dallas.[9] In Texas, as elsewhere, newspapers were the most popular form of reading material, but there were magazines, journals, and books as well. Most of these came from the eastern United States, but Texan publishers eventually emerged—such as Edwin B. Hill (1880–1949), Carl Hertzog (1902–1984), and William D. Wittliff (1940–)—as well as university presses at Southern Methodist University (1937), Trinity University (1961–1989, 2002), University of Texas (1950), Texas Tech (1971), and Texas A&M (1975). *Texas Monthly*, a sophisticated periodical of contemporary topics reminiscent of the *New Yorker*, began publication in Austin in 1973.

PRIVATE AND SPECIAL USE LIBRARIES

There are essentially four kinds of libraries: private, special use, academic, and public. Today almost every middle-class household and above has books, newspapers, and magazines. These people can afford the cost and welcome the printed materials. There is a proven and long-standing correlation among income, education, and reading.[10] For example, Frederick Law Olmsted, an educated, elite easterner, took a horseback tour through Texas in 1853–1854 and did not see anyone read a newspaper or book in the more settled region of East Texas. In a tavern he picked up a newspaper from a table and a man sitting nearby said, "Reckon you've read a good deal, hain't you?"

Olmsted replied, "Oh, yes; why?"

"Reckoned you had."

"Why?"

"You look as though you liked to read. Well, it's a good thing. S'pose you take a pleasure in reading, don't you?"

"That depends, of course, on what I have to read. I suppose everybody likes to read when they find anything interesting to them, don't they?"

"No; it's damn tiresome to some folks, I reckon, anyhow, 'less you've got the habit of it. Well, it's a good thing; you can pass away your time so."[11]

Although unobserved by Olmsted, there existed early Texans who collected books. From the Houston probate records of the 1840s, historian Kenneth Wheeler noted that the private library of John Scott held 221 volumes.[12] Dr. Ashbel Smith, whom Wheeler characterized as the "undisputed intellectual leader of the Republic," cherished a well-selected library of several hundred books that he kept in a separate building at his home on Galveston Bay. Of particular importance were the medical volumes that he carefully transported during the various moves of his life.[13] These books served as a personal special use library for his work as a physician. Merchants in the towns imported and sold books and magazines from Philadelphia and New York City. Book salesmen visited Texas and items could be ordered for delivery.[14]

Medical schools, law firms, architectural offices, government divisions, and businesses of various sorts accumulated the books that would help them. When Thomas A. Edison set up his famous laboratory for invention in Menlo Park, New Jersey, in 1876, he assembled in one place not only bright technicians and materials, but also a library of the latest books and journals about electricity. Edison and his assistants churned out a patent per week. When Bell Laboratories in Murray Hill, New Jersey, and Texas Instruments in Dallas established their facilities, they made room for a helpful library. Bell Labs maintained a collection of twenty thousand books and thirty-five thousand journals needed by its scientists and became a pioneer in the design of library information systems. It distributed two hundred and fifty thousand items per year and the laboratories averaged two patents per day in the 1970s.[15]

People, of course, continued to accumulate private libraries and at times such collections have played a role in the establishment of public and academic libraries. Prominent examples are: Robert de Sorbonne, who gave his personal library and money for upkeep to establish the famous library of the University of Paris in 1250; Reverend John Harvard, who bestowed three hundred books and a bequest in 1638 to a local college that now bears his name; Thomas Jefferson, who sold his six thousand volumes to the United States to restart the Library of Congress that the British had destroyed in the War of 1812; and Henry E. Huntington, a real estate and railroad millionaire of the nineteenth century, who used his money to purchase book and manuscript collections to create a research library in California. "The ownership of a fine library," he said, "is the surest and swiftest way to immortality."[16]

In Texas an unlikely bookworm dramatically advanced the library of the University of Texas. Swante Palm (1815–1899) immigrated from Sweden in 1844, lived first in LaGrange, moved to Austin, worked as a postmaster and accountant, served as Swedish vice consul, and collected volumes with "bookish energy" from England, France, Germany, Sweden, New York City, New Orleans, Louisville, Houston, and Galveston. He spoke English, French, German, Latin, and several Scandinavian dialects. Two years before his death, Palm gave his collection of ten thousand books to the University of Texas, which possessed only seventeen thousand volumes at the time. It was a 60 percent boost.

Palm served as an assistant librarian to care for the collection, and as he brought wagonload after wagonload of books to the campus, the sheer quantity forced an expansion of library space. The donation was the foundation of a collection of printed materials that in the next century expanded to become the best academic library between the two coasts of the United States. "What men have owed to books," wrote Palm, "is more or less what men have made of their civilization. Without records, human ideas would have vanished like uncaptive lightning."[17]

PUBLIC LIBRARIES

Since books, magazines, and even newspapers could be relatively expensive in a society of limited resources and literacy, there was an incentive in early Texas to share and borrow. Library formation generally takes place in an urban location where the concentration of population can afford the expense and where the demand for information and entertainment is greatest. The first organization, consequently, was the subscription library where literate people pooled their books, borrowed from the collection, and paid a small fee for maintenance and the purchase of additional volumes.

Taking the idea from Europe, Benjamin Franklin started the first North American subscription library in Philadelphia in 1732, and a little over one hundred years later the concept popped up in Galveston and Houston. Henry F. Byrne set up a 1,300-volume library in Houston in 1839, three years after the founding of the city. Subscription libraries, however, did not last long, except in the case of Franklin's "Library Company," which continues to the present. Most went out of business or converted into public libraries. Byrne's library failed in its first year when the State of Texas moved its seat of government to Austin.

The impulse for tax-supported, public libraries in the United States, like those that began in Britain in 1850, emerged from the reasoning that a democracy needs an informed, educated citizenry. Growing wealth made free libraries for the people possible and an expanding immigrant population made them necessary. Boston opened the first public library in the United States in 1854 after a board of trustees led by Brahmins Edward Everett and George Ticknor issued a famous report, which declared that a library should be free and open to all people and provide a variety of reference, rare, and popular books. Further, there should be a reading room with periodicals, where a taste for reading could progress from lighter materials, such as novels, to biography and history. The report said that the public library should be an institution of education, the "crowning glory" of the Boston system of schools.[18] Thus, the public library would be an open, accessible place of education and information. It became more than that. It became an oasis for desperate people seeking to escape the crush of urban life, where it was warm in the winter and cool in the summer. As writer Mary Antin (1881–1949), who immigrated from Russia, said of the Boston Public Library:

> I loved to lean against a pillar in the entrance hall, watching the people go in and out. . . . And I loved to stand in the midst of all this, and remind myself that I was there, that I had a right to be there, that I was at home there. All these eager children, all these fine-browed women, all these scholars going home to write learned books—I and they had this glorious thing in common, this noble treasure house of learning. It was wonderful to say, *This is mine;* it was thrilling to say, *This is ours.*[19]

A later immigrant from Russia, Bel Kaufman (1911?–) who wrote *Up the Down Staircase* (1964) about big city high schools, stated in 1976:

> I remember myself as a 12-year-old, newly arrived from Russia groping toward the mastery of the English language in my neighborhood library. . . . I worked each shelf alphabetically, burrowing my way from one end of the stacks to the other, relentless as a mole. I read by trial and error, through trash and treasure; like a true addict, I was interested not so much in quality as in getting the stuff.
>
> For many, the public library is the only quiet place in an unquiet world; a refuge from the violence and ugliness outside; the only space available for privacy of work or thought. For many it is the only exposure to books waiting on open shelves to be taken home, free of charge.[20]

Children and the Public Library

Children with imagination thrived in the atmosphere of children's programs and in the special rooms with reduced furniture sizes and in the open stacks of books that began to emerge in the public libraries at the end of the nineteenth century. The libraries took seriously their charge to promote lifelong learning, and receiving a library card was a rite of passage. Anne Carroll Moore, librarian of the New York Public Library at the time, coined an often quoted phrase, "The right book into the hands of the right child at the right time." The Cleveland Public Library formed a children's club of twelve thousand members and promoted, "Clean hands, clean hearts, and clean books."[21] The public libraries proved to be an incubator for literary talent. As a child, Amy Tan (1952–), who later wrote *The Joy Luck Club* (1989), submitted a comment to support the Santa Rosa Public Library in California:

> My name is Amy Tan, 8 years old, a third grader in Matanzas School. I love school because the many things I learn seem to turn on a light in the little room in my mind. I can read many interesting books by myself now. I love to read. My father takes me to the library every two weeks, and I check five or six books each time. These books seem to open many windows in my little room. I can see many wonderful things outside.[22]

Columnist and novelist Pete Hamill (1935–) said this about his neighborhood library located in a rough, dangerous section of New York:

> The library was on Sixth Avenue and Ninth Street on the south slopes of the Brooklyn hills and for a long time in my young life it was the true center of the world. . . . Inside, behind walls as thick as any true fortress, I always felt safe. . . . The attraction was not mere shelter. I was there on a more exciting mission: the discovery of the world. . . . On the streets I consumed the artifacts of what is now called popular culture. . . . The library took that instinct for the lurid and refined it. The books that were talked about in schoolyards and on rooftops gave me a need for narrative, for removal from the dailiness of my life. But they stood in relation to the books in the library as the raw does to the cooked.[23]

Far away in Houston, Texas, at nearly the same time, eight-year-old newsboy Dan Rather, who later became a television journalist and network anchor, met "Miss Rose," a social worker for the underprivileged at a park in the Heights subdivision of the city. "You know," she told him, "your only way out is to read," and pointed the way to a Houston branch library. Rather recalled that it was as if she had said, "Open sesame!" as he discovered the excitement of books. Miss Rose later escorted him on a bus trip to visit the central downtown Carnegie library. "When we got to McKinney Street I might as well have landed in Rome. The three-story library took up an entire city block and contained (so I later learned) 165,000 books. I gawked like the country bumpkin that I was." For Rather, that bus trip became "a defining adventure of my life."[24]

Lucia Rede Madrid, a retired schoolteacher with the same attitude as Miss Rose, set up a bilingual lending library especially for children in the corner of a grocery store in Redford, Texas, a half-mile from the Mexican border in 1979. She asked neighbors for book donations, used a simple checkout system with people registering on their own in a notebook, and offered a basket of free books to children. Families crossed the Rio Grande in a rowboat to go shopping and to check out books. "When a child picks up a book," said Madrid, "you are planting the seeds of knowledge."

She wanted youngsters to learn to communicate and for the best to leave Redford for greater opportunity. The store walls, subsequently, became a "Hall of Fame" with pictures of successful teachers, doctors, and engineers from the area. In explanation of their success, Madrid said, "It was the library." The news of her effort spread by word of mouth, book donations poured in from all over the United States—eventually twenty thousand volumes—and President George H. W. Bush honored her with a Volunteer Action Award in 1990.[25] She was one of the president's "Points of Light," an individual who makes life better for a neighborhood. Alas, Madrid went into a nursing home and died in the spring of 2006. When I visited Redford later in 2006, the library and grocery had closed, the school across the street was empty, people could not cross the river for fear of Marines and Border Control agents, and the town was dying. The light had gone out.

Librarians

Not many people have recorded their childhood feelings about their local library. It is not a common topic, but if asked about the memory, people find it stored like long ago treasured seashells kept in an old cigar box in the attic. Among the recollections of childhood are those about the librarian, the person who ruled the sanctuary, selected the books, and controlled the budget. For future novelist Eudora Welty (1909–2001), who grew up in Jackson, Mississippi, there was always an examination at the front door. "As you came in from the bright outside, if you were a girl, [the librarian] sent her strong eyes down the stairway to test you; if she could see through your skirt, she sent you straight back home; you could just put on another petticoat if you wanted a book that badly from the public library."[26] Writer Susan Allen Toth (1940–), who had early ambitions to become a librarian, commented about the leader of the Ames, Iowa, public library:

> Although librarians didn't make much money, my career guides warned me, they had something else that appealed to me as much as constant proximity to all those books. They had power. Not many women in Ames visibly wielded that, but Miss Jepson did. Even her deputy, Mrs. Erhard, had a derived air of stern authority. Miss Jepson, whose white hair and wrinkled pink skin made her seem agelessly preserved, was a definite-minded woman whose tongue had an almost audible snap. Whenever she submitted a budget request to the Ames City Council, she was able to get almost everything she wanted. No one dared to argue long with Miss Jepson. She personally selected each book the library ordered and gave the impression that she had read them all first. No detail of the library's operation escaped her inspection; she knew it so well I thought for a long time she must live there, in a secret suite connecting to her office.[27]

Although the chair of a library board was almost always a man, the head librarian was almost always a woman. There is a reason for this historic feminization of the public libraries. Women established about 75 percent of the public libraries in the nation as a project of middle- and upper-class women's literary clubs in the last part of the nineteenth and first part of the twentieth centuries. The clubs were apolitical and promoted the libraries as a form of "municipal housekeeping." These well-educated women had the time, money, and insight concerning the correlation of reading and success in American society. Furthermore, the public library was a virtuous alternative to the degrading dime novel and debilitating saloon. The women raised money, campaigned, and volunteered; they were also the greatest users of the collections.[28] This leadership of women can be seen repeatedly in the history of libraries.

When Melvil Dewey (1851–1931), famous for the Dewey decimal system of organizing books, established the first professional school to train librarians in 1887 in New York, seventeen of the initial twenty students were female. Ever since then, women have claimed the majority in the profession. Librarianship provided for women a needed career opportunity and for cities a competent and cheap employee. By 1910 almost 80 percent of the library workers were women. Dewey argued, "The natural qualities most important in library work are accuracy, order (or what we call the housekeeping instinct), executive ability, and above all earnestness and enthusiasm." He added in his support of female librarians, "There is hardly any occupation that is so free from annoying surroundings."[29] Women were paid less, however, and Dewey, reflecting the attitude of the time, said, "For many uses a stout corduroy is really worth more than the finest silk."[30] Equal pay for equal work was an issue that library administrators did not confront until the affirmative action protests of the later twentieth century.

Censorship

From the view of the library user, however, women did the work and ran the institution. By and large, the librarians bought the books and protected the collection. They usually purchased the bestseller list, the classics, and reference books, and they held fondly to the idea that the city library was a part of the educational system. There was an obligation to elevate the reading habits of the public. The librarians, therefore, played the role of censor, and their boards depended upon the instincts of their women librarians to do what was proper. Challenges to their hegemony were few and scattered at the grassroots level.

Historian Paul S. Boyer has recorded attacks on libraries by the religious right to remove J. D. Salinger's *The Catcher in the Rye* (1951), Maya Angelou's *I Know Why the Caged Bird Sings* (1969), John Steinbeck's *The Grapes of Wrath* (1939), and William Faulkner's *As I Lay Dying* (1957). One right-wing critic objected to *Making It with Mademoiselle* until he discovered that it was a collection of dress patterns. Blacks protested Mark Twain's use of the word "nigger" in *The Adventures of Huckleberry Finn* (1884), and feminists remonstrated about perceived pornography in the works of D. H. Lawrence and Henry Miller.[31]

Librarians removed German books from the shelves during World War I and Communist books during the Red Scare of the early 1920s. The book burnings by the Nazi regime in Germany, however, prompted sobering reconsideration about library collections. The American Library Association (1876)—the oldest library affiliation in the world—adopted a Library Bill of Rights that emphasized the goal of a balanced collection with diverse points of view. Thus, librarians resisted the anti-Communist pressure of the McCarthy era of the 1950s.[32] Besides, suspect books could be kept in locked cases or in restricted areas without the library incurring an accusation of censorship. Such action also protected the books from those who would defile them and satisfied librarians' primordial urge to preserve their collection.

The effort to elevate reading standards ultimately failed due to a persistent desire by the recreation-seeking public to read fiction and the need for public libraries to keep up their circulation figures. The war with "cheap" fiction, nonetheless, was of long standing. In 1871, for example, when Galveston first experimented with a public library, the leading demand was for current novels, followed by the more sophisticated works of literature.[33] It was human nature. In the November 1890 *Library Journal* appeared an anonymous poem that could be sung to the tune of a popular song from Gilbert and Sullivan's comic opera, *The Mikado*:

> At a library desk stood some readers one day
>   Crying novels, oh, novels, oh, novels.
> And I said to them People, oh, why do you say
>   "Give us novels, oh, novels, oh, novels."
> Is it weakness of intellect, people, I cried
> Or simply a space where the brains should abide
> They answered me not, or they only replied
>   Give us novels, oh, novels, oh novels
>
> Here are thousands of books that will do you more good
>   Than the novels, oh, novels, oh, novels
> You will weaken your brain with such poor mental food
>   As the novels, oh, novels, oh, novels
> Pray take history, music, or travels, or plays
> Biography, poetry, science, essays
> Or anything else that more wisdom displays
>   Than the novels, oh, novels, oh novels
>
> A librarian may talk till he's black in the face
>   About novels, oh, novels, oh, novels
> And he may think that with patience he may raise the taste
>   Above novels, oh, novels, oh novels
> He may talk till with age his round shoulders are bent
> And the white hairs of time mid the black ones are sent
> When he hands his report in, still seventy percent
>   Will be novels, oh novels, oh novels.[34]

Raising reading standards was a losing fight for librarians. The evangelical spirit gradually waned, and they gave up by the end of the twentieth century. There was, furthermore, a conflicting desire to provide books for everyone. As early as 1906, a Baltimore librarian admitted to her board, "When we consider that many of the readers lead a monotonous existence with little means to gratify their desire for amusement, we are glad of the opportunity to have them find books here which meet their needs."[35] In an important survey of reading habits, William S. Gray and Ruth Monroe discovered that over half the books borrowed from the Chicago Public Library in 1923 were fiction and read for recreation. The book sales at the local Marshall Fields department store, moreover, confirmed the interest: books sold were mainly fiction and bought by women. Texas, incidentally, in the Gray and Monroe report scored at the lower end for magazine reading and for the number of books in library circulation when compared to other states at this time.[36]

In a 2004 survey, the National Endowment for the Arts reported that 57 percent of American adults read an average of six books per year and that almost half were novels or short stories.[37] Nothing had changed. There was an abiding demand for fiction—"oh, novels"—and the advice of an examining committee for the Boston Public Library in 1867 retained its wisdom: "We may say that the best novels are seldom read in a way to do the most good; but that is a circumstance of course beyond any library's control, and there is a good deal to say in favor of supplying the masses with reading of even an inferior order rather than that they should not read at all."[38] Recreation, thus, was paramount.

Despite their control over book purchases, locked cabinets, and the demeanor of patrons, librarians' lives were not necessarily easy. Lillian Gunter (1870–1926) kept a diary about her administration of the Carnegie Library in Gainesville, Texas, in 1921–1924. The daughter of a plantation owner in the Red River Valley, she was educated at the Sacred Heart Convent in St. Louis and Wesleyan Institute in Staunton, Virginia. After the death of her father, she moved to Gainesville in 1901. She was a single, educated woman, thirty-one years of age. With the help of a local women's literary group, she took the lead in transforming the local subscription library into a public library and became its first librarian in 1914. She supplemented her education with a six-week summer training course at the New York State Library School in Albany and proceeded to run her small library with efficiency and accountability. She championed, without success, library access for blacks, but won support for county libraries and the Texas Library Association (TLA). A typical entry from her diary in 1923 recorded her actions and thoughts:

> The monthly report must be handed in to the new commissioner's court and it is not yet finished. The assistant librarian is at home, ill with the flu. I have a reference to look up, "Find a copy of a mock marriage." A high school history teacher who like Joshua, expects "the sun, moon and stars to stand still for her," is looking up books with my assistance, to put on reserve. Ten children want to use the same number of the "Reader's Guide." Ten more want to find a recitation or declamation. Six or seven are hovering around the loan desk to have their books charged or discharged. A branch librarian is selecting books to take back with her. Two teachers from the country want help with their work. . . . Ye Gods![39]

Andrew Carnegie and His Libraries

Gunter and Gainesville took advantage of the generosity of millionaire Andrew Carnegie (1835–1918), the richest man in the United States, to construct a public library building. Largely self-educated by borrowing from a private collection, Carnegie used his money for the establishment of free libraries for people who would help themselves. Between 1886 and 1917, Carnegie promised 1,679 libraries in 1,412 places at a total cost of $41 million. The town provided the site, books, and maintenance; he provided the building. Simple as it sounded, the proposal to construct a public library often fractured a community along class, gender, age, and racial lines. It was a progressive idea, and some groups just did not care for change. Children, women, and races should remain segregated, shouldn't they? Was it wise to educate the rabble? Why provide tax-paid shelter to verminous bums? And, what would the building look like? And, where would it be located? Wasn't Carnegie a robber baron who suppressed labor? Wouldn't a free library hurt the sales of bookstores?[40] So the questions went.

In the South of 1896 there were thirteen library books per capita. Texas was the lowest of the southern states with five books per capita. There was little understanding of the need and a library was considered a luxury. In Beaumont, a Texas community studied by library historians Donald G. Davis Jr. and Ronald C. Stone Jr., the Women's Reading Club and the women for temperance led a drive to obtain a Carnegie library in 1904. It was opposed by the *Beaumont Daily Journal*, which said that the money of the steel magnate was tainted "by the blood of toiling thousands." The Carnegie Foundation always negotiated with elected officials, and, at a time when women could not vote, it was at this juncture that the women lost control of their effort. The all-male city council voted 4–3 against the application. In 1917 a popular vote passed in favor of the application to Carnegie, but by then the foundation no longer funded libraries in Texas because of poor results in the state: two-thirds of the grantees failed to meet their obligations—the highest failure rate in the nation. Carnegie, who died in 1919, nevertheless, had given grants and construction money to thirty of the fifty-one public libraries existing in Texas in 1915.[41]

THE DALLAS PUBLIC LIBRARY AND CARNEGIE

According to city historian Darwin Payne, early Dallas was not noted for its devotion to books. The public collection housed in the city hall possessed only two thousand volumes in 1889.[42] Yet, Dallas provides a good historical illustration of a successful Carnegie library in the Southwest that was touched with the typical problems of growth, race, and censorship. The city became viable when two railroads marked Dallas with an "X" on the map after they crossed at that point in 1872–1873. This meant human and cotton traffic could move north and south and east and west; it meant the beginning of modern development in North Texas. When the town established public schools in 1884, the only books available for the students were an encyclopedia and a dictionary loaned by the principal. Pressure, consequently, grew for an adequate public library.

May Dickson Exall (1859–1936), educated at Vassar, president of the Dallas Shakespeare Club, and organizer of the Dallas Federation of Women's Clubs, initiated a library movement. Pauline Periwinkle, an intrepid local female newswoman, and the Commercial Club supported the idea. A new city charter of 1898 authorized $2,000 per year for a library. The *Dallas News* wrote, "The public institutions of a city are an index to the character of its citizenship, and a thoroughly appointed and well patronized public library is considered significant of the culture and intellectual standing of its people." A Dallas Public Library Association formed in 1899 with Exall as president, started a fund drive, and appealed to Andrew Carnegie. "Our citizenry are characterized by industry and sobriety," wrote Exall, "and there is nothing in Dallas of the wild frontier town." This was a slap at Fort Worth, the Dallas rival fifty miles to the west. Carnegie had already given $50,000 to their north Texas competitor.[43] So, in Dallas the city lined up to support a library.

Carnegie authorized $50,000, and the city increased its commitment of support to $4,000 per year and selected a site at Commerce and Harwood Streets, away from the commercial district and railroads. This was a bit unusual since city fathers often wanted to flaunt their culture to rail visitors. Somewhat embarrassing for Dallas, a Fort Worth architect, Marshall Sanguinet, won the architectural contest with a two story, neoclassical design with eight double-story Ionic columns and high arched windows. A large Aladdin's lamp perched on top as a symbol of learning. In the tradition of Carnegie libraries, the building included a children's room, reading room, and central checkout desk. The library also featured an auditorium along with an art gallery on the second floor. The gallery, suggested by local western artist Frank Reaugh, inspired the formation of the Dallas Art Association and eventually became the Dallas Museum of Fine Arts. The Carnegie Foundation grumpily refused to give more money for an expansion in 1907 and told the library it could move onto its second floor.[44]

A library board hired Rosa Leeper, who had six years experience in St. Louis as librarian; ordered thirteen hundred books; and adopted rules—no intoxication, no smoking, no eating, and no Negroes. The library opened in 1901 and cost $50,097, only a slight amount over budget. Exall, ignoring the black one-fifth of the population, exulted, "It is the aim and object of the modern library to have its books circulated as widely as possible so as to act as leaven on the whole community."[45] Across the Trinity River the central library opened an annex in Oak Cliff in 1903. The Boston Public Library and others had demonstrated that branch libraries circulated twice the books at half the cost. Carnegie provided $25,000 for a permanent Oak Cliff branch that opened in 1914, and, as might be expected, the major demand of the users was for novels.

Meanwhile, the black community grumbled about paying taxes for a library that they could not use. A black appeal to Carnegie failed because the Carnegie Foundation negotiated only with elected officials, and the white city council refused to endorse the request. The all-white library board, moreover, rejected black appeals for library aid. The only relief was the trickle of books the librarians quietly circulated to the black high school. Dallas, however, was not unlike other places in Texas. In the mid-1930s there were 147 counties with no public library service and only 16 libraries that loaned books to blacks. In the South two-thirds of the people lacked access to a public library, and as researcher Tommie Dora Barker stated at the time, "The library is one field in the South where it seems possible really to make a virtue of a present deficiency. There is very little to undo."[46]

Racial prejudice in Dallas, moreover, was palpable and represents a dark smudge in the history of the city. The community was segregated in housing, business, and politics. A crowd of one hundred and sixty thousand, the same size as the city population, gathered for Ku Klux Klan Day at Dallas' Texas State Fair in 1923. Hiram W. Evans, a Dallas dentist, reigned as the Imperial Wizard, the leader of the entire KKK for the nation. Yet, a city plan in 1925 included a black branch library along with three others for white areas. A subsequent bond issue passed in 1927, and in 1931 a branch library opened in a black neighborhood in north Dallas. It was heavily used until Dallas' first freeway, the Central Expressway, slashed through and divided the district in 1949. Afterward, the Dunbar Library slowly fell into disuse. By then, however, black patrons could be seated at the rear of the Carnegie Library and have materials delivered to them. Unrestricted, front-door access for blacks to the library system, however, did not occur until 1955 with the opening of a new central library building.[47]

The library was slow indeed to respond to what was then about 15 percent of the population, but it was ahead of integration in the Dallas Independent School District (1960–1961), ahead of the first black to play football at Southern Methodist University (1965), and ahead of the first blacks to go shopping at Neiman Marcus (1962). Moreover, it was ahead of the American Library Association, which added an addendum to its Library Bill of Rights in 1961: "The rights of an individual to the use of the library should not be denied or abridged because of his race, religion, national origins or legal views."[48]

The population growth of Dallas forced further expansion of the library system. The branch libraries thrived while the central library deteriorated with leaks in the roof, books piled on the floor, and no air-conditioning. Money was scarce during the Depression years and World War II, and the central library threatened to close. Bookmobiles delivering reading materials to neighborhoods became stopgaps while a campaign for a new main library gained momentum. Given voice by Lon Tinkle, the book editor of the *Dallas Morning News* and a respected intellectual, twenty-three book lovers formed the Friends of the Dallas Public Library led by Erin Bain Jones (1896–1974), an attorney and philanthropist. They organized a fiftieth library birthday celebration, an occasion forgotten by the city; bought another bookmobile; recruited members; and promoted a bond issue to build a new central facility. After initial recalcitrance, the public approved the bonds, and the city government took over complete responsibility for the public library system from the trustees of the private Dallas Public Library Association.[49]

Designed by George Dahl (1894–1987), the chief architect of Fair Park, the new library opened in 1955 on the same site as the old Carnegie library. After storing the one hundred and twenty thousand books of the collection at the Union Station for two years, it was a relief to move into the new structure, but the new head librarian James D. Meeks ran into some immediate problems of public censure. A privately donated piece of modern sculpture, depicting a naked man holding a book, hung over the new circulation desk. Following complaints by ultra-right conservatives, the artist put trousers on him. Then, the conservatives who also attacked the Dallas Museum of Fine Arts for showing the work of Communist artists, objected to a Picasso rug exhibit in the library because they thought the artist was a Communist sympathizer. Meeks took the rugs down and muttered that he wanted to save himself for battles over books, not art.[50]

The controversy with the super-patriots by and large brushed past the library and focused on the Dallas Museum of Fine Arts. It brought nationwide ridicule to Dallas and provided a forewarning about an endemic conservative virulency that set the stage for the later assassination of a president of the United States. Longtime columnist John Rosenfield (1900–1966) angrily wrote in the *Dallas Morning News* late in 1956: "This would be as good time as any for our fair city to arrive at a clear and simple code to govern the exhibition of paintings, the performance of music and drama, the circulation of books or any other expression of mankind's creative spirit or mental processes. This should be: If anyone objects yank it down, or ban it from the halls, or burn it up." The extremists then aimed their venom at Rosenfield, and his conservative newspaper declined to back his views. The following month he suffered a nonfatal heart attack, and biographer Ronald L. Davis claimed that the censorious event broke Rosenfield's spirit.[51] The cultural conscience of Dallas thus became silent.

Again, the population crush of Dallas forced the building of a new central library. The branch libraries continued to proliferate, but the central library was overcrowded despite its six levels of space and 800,000-volume capacity. There was little research space. Planning began in 1973 with Dallas architects J. Herschel Fisher and Pat Y. Spillman, and voters approved a bond issue in 1978. In addition, generous companies underwrote entire floors. The inside design was efficient and spacious with room for historical research on the top floor. The library later spent its $3.5 million endowment fund to rewire and go online in 1996.[52] The new eight-story library, meanwhile, opened in 1982 as part of a plan to enhance the area around the dramatic city hall, designed by I. M. Pei, built four years earlier. Situated on a broad, summer-hot concrete plaza, the city hall featured a series of cantilevered floors thrusting out thirty-five degrees over the entrance like an inverted pyramid. It was a grand gesture that architectural critic David Dillon said expressed the "bravura and panache of Dallas."[53]

Across the street, the outward design of the new library corresponded to the cantilevered floors of city hall with a series of progressively set-back floors with the same hard-edged straight lines and light-colored stone. The thrusting floors of the city hall seemingly pushed back the receding floors of the library tier by tier. It can readily be seen like the matching pieces of a giant jigsaw puzzle. David Dillon commented:

> The effect of all this nipping and tucking and color-coordinating has been to create an architecturally coherent public plaza that nevertheless has failed to attract the public. The extensive setbacks of the buildings only increase the feeling of emptiness of the plaza. What's needed, besides some shops and restaurants on the perimeter, is a building that marches right up to the curb, plants its feet, and talks back to City Hall instead of leaning back defensively.[54]

Dallas made a mistake, and, unfortunately, buildings tend to last a long time. The plaza is magnificent as a monument—it is overpowering and intimidating. After 5:00 p.m., it is also empty. There is no activity, no nightlife, no mixed uses, no vitality, and it is a dangerous place for people to linger. People using the library park in an underground garage and do not leave the premises. It is a problem for downtown Dallas in general: visitors become uneasy in the late afternoon as stores and restaurants close around them and leave them isolated and vulnerable in empty concrete canyons. The planners and politicians of Dallas failed to heed the lessons of venerable Jane Jacobs in *The Death and Life of Great American Cities* (1961). Jacobs taught that an urban space needs multiple uses for the enjoyment and safety of its citizens.

It should be noted that there has been a long-standing war between librarians and architects. Librarians want an efficient structure that will protect the collection and provide easy access for the public. Architects, understandably, often respond to the politicians, presidents, or donors who want monuments and who control the money. Thus, there is a history of ill-heated alcoves, spiral staircases, decorative Greek columns, grand entrances, picture galleries, awkward furniture, lack of workspace, and, of all things, lack of bookshelves. At the fourth annual convention of the American Library Association in 1879, librarian William Poole warned, "Avoid everything that pertains to the plan and arrangement of conventional library building." And the *Library Journal* commented in 1891, "It is far better that a library should be plain or even ugly than that it should be inconvenient."[55] Aside from its location, the Dallas Public Library seems to have satisfied both the architects and planners on the outside, and the librarians on the inside. That is an extraordinary accomplishment in an ongoing war.[56]

The Rosenberg Library and Patten's Dream

Carnegie's generosity inspired library philanthropy in others. A prime Texas example is Henry Rosenberg (1824–1893) of Galveston. Rosenberg migrated as a poor, serious-minded nineteen-year-old from Switzerland in 1843 to Galveston and became an apprentice to a dry goods merchant at $8 per month. He learned English, anglicized his name from Heinrich Rosenberger to Henry Rosenberg, worked hard, bought out his employer in three years, and made a fortune in dry goods, banking, real estate, and railroads. He married twice, had no children, no intimate friends, and died in 1893. He divided his $1.1 million estate among various community projects, including the construction and support of a public library "as a source of pleasure and profit to the people and their children and their children's children through many generations."[57]

Earlier there had been several subscription libraries, and the Chamber of Commerce opened the private Mercantile Library in 1871. The thought of making it available to all people came up almost immediately and in 1874 it became the Galveston Free Library with support from the city. The library closed in 1878 because of the nationwide depression and reopened in 1879 at the city hall with two thousand books. The

Galveston Lyceum, a private debate group, took responsibility for the library in 1881 and moved it to the top floor of the Masonic Temple. The Lyceum ran the library in sputtering fashion and the city took over again in 1890. The 1900 hurricane, however, ripped the roof off the hall and thoroughly soaked the collection, which had grown to seven thousand volumes. Only seventeen hundred of these books made the eventual transfer to the new library of 1904.[58]

After Rosenberg's bequest, the state granted a charter to the Rosenberg Library Association in 1900, which in turn created a board of twenty trustees. The board bought five city lots and held a library design contest. Winning architects William S. Eames and Thomas C. Young of St. Louis offered a two-story building in Italian Renaissance style with high windows and ceilings. It had a stately green tile roof; a lecture hall on the second floor; oak furniture; bronze trim; ornamental panels outside engraved with the names of great authors; shelf space for thirteen thousand books; reading rooms; an attic for storage; and a basement for toilets, a shop, and janitor's quarters.

No African-Americans were allowed to use the facility, but one year after the inauguration in 1904, a library opened in the black high school. The Rosenberg Library Association built a two-story addition to the school that provided a study hall for students and a reading room for the black community. It was administered as a branch, the first such branch library for African-Americans in the United States. Under rules of strict segregation, no whites were allowed to use the black facility. Much later, in 1949, bookmobiles served both races without discrimination.[59]

The trustees hired a librarian, Frank Chauncy Patten (1855–1934), who moved to Galveston from New York City in 1903 and remained until his death. He had been in the first class of library science established by Melvil Dewey at Columbia University. Tall, thin, shy, and kind, Patten was a bachelor who lived in rented rooms. He secretly gave a part of his salary to his employees, and when he died, his assistant was so upset that she refused to check out any books.

Patten opened the Rosenberg Library with 7,000 volumes and 125 periodicals. He doubled the collection in the first year, started a lecture series, bought reference and children's books, expanded to 55,000 volumes by 1915, and ran short of money. In the 1920s, Patten charged five cents for overdue books when other libraries fined only two cents. The annual circulation per capita was only one-fourth that of other public libraries, 2.1 versus 8.8, and the criticism was that he was building a reference and research center rather than a public library.

This was partly true. Patten had a passion for archives and a sense that materials about Galveston's past, a historic port city, were worth saving. In 1927 he appealed to his fellow citizens: "Let the letters, diaries, books of account and other manuscripts, the books, maps, all kinds of prints, photographs, pictures, paintings, historical relics—all of them—come to the Rosenberg Library to be recorded and put in proper condition and so preserved for the future historian." The materials poured into the library, and Patten was observed scrounging in the alleys to find discarded boxes that might be used as archival containers. He filled up the attic.[60]

An additional treasure trove of archival materials came his way. In 1871 a casual group of men formed the Galveston Historical Society in order to collect and preserve materials important for the history of Texas. The society operated sporadically, but accumulated various items, such as the papers of Lorenzo de Zavala, the vice president of the Texas Republic, and merchant James Morgan. Stored in the public library when it was in the Masonic Temple, the papers met the same storm-drenched fate as the books. The society, however, continued to collect materials, placed them in the new Rosenberg Library, refused to give them to the University of Texas, and transferred ownership of the collection to the Rosenberg Library in 1931.[61]

The result of this collecting activity was that the Rosenberg Library became a research repository for Texas history second only to the University of Texas at Austin. This was quite unusual for a public library, the main duty of which was to supply the reading public with current novels. The attic was piled high, and a survey by library consultants in 1967 said that the Rosenberg Library was "one of the great library collections of the country, and held together by baling wire."[62] I happened to see the attic at this time when taken on a tour by an assistant librarian, Bob Dalehite. As we followed an established path between the rafters, he gestured at the dusty unsorted letters, journals, and business records and said, "There is great history here." I had to agree.

A local fund drive, led by the chairman of the board of trustees, John W. Harris, raised enough money to build a somewhat jarring, box-like, light-colored, windowless, air-conditioned addition attached to the back of the older Italian Renaissance structure. Opened in 1971, it became the functioning public library while the old Rosenberg settled into museum somnolence. The addition worked beautifully, however, and on the third floor the librarians installed a state-of-the-art archival unit. A 1976 grant from the National Historical Publications and Records Commission allowed the archivists to process the materials of the dusty boxes and make them accessible for research by historians.[63] Patten's dream thus became a reality and the Rosenberg Library became a unique community facility.

The Texas State Library

The Rosenberg Library claims to be the oldest public library in the state. The state library is older, but its history is interrupted by gaps of inactivity, reorganization, poor management, shifting purpose, and abandonment. Established by the Texas Republic in 1839 for the use of politicians and the public, the library received irregular funding, interest, and materials. At the end of the Civil War, the state appointed Robert Josselyn, one-time secretary to Jefferson Davis, state librarian and appropriated no money to pay him. Before the removal of all state officials by General Philip H. Sheridan during Reconstruction, Josselyn completed a catalog that revealed a collection of five thousand volumes housed on the third floor of the capitol. Governor E. J. Davis appointed Joseph Lancaster state librarian in 1872. Lancaster found a room full of mutilated and stolen books, a "wreck of grandeur," without even a broom to clean up the mess.[64] The Constitution of 1876 created a commissioner to take charge of books and documents, but a fire in 1881 destroyed the capitol, the library, and the rudiments of the Texas State Archives. All was lost—documents, reports, maps, and books.

There was no library of any kind, except the special reference books of the Texas Supreme Court, until 1891 when Governor James S. Hogg and the legislature created the office of historical clerk, who functioned as a state librarian. This office collected mainly state documents and reports. In 1897, however, a conference of eighteen women's literary clubs met in Waco and founded the Texas Federation of Women's Clubs. In turn, the Federation started the Texas Library Association in Austin in 1902 for the promotion and expansion of libraries and the training of professional librarians. The TLA successfully lobbied for the establishment of a Texas State Library and Historical Commission in 1909; the County Library Law in 1917; and library schools in Austin (1919–1923) and at Texas State College for Women in Denton (1928) and the University of Texas (1948). Lillian Gunter from the Carnegie Library in Gainesville was one of the early agitators.[65] Interestingly, it was the women, again, who saw the need for libraries. Furthermore, it is interesting that these progressive Texas women flourished at the time when the distant Carnegie Foundation provided an opportunity.

The Texas State Library and Historical Commission supervised a state library that collected and made accessible to the public materials pertinent to state history, and it provided supportive services to help libraries throughout the state. A building to house the institution and its archives opened near the capitol in 1962. The County Library Law made possible that a bundle of at least fifty books could be sent to rural schools and communities with no library service. Even though an experiment of outreach in Jefferson County improved book circulation by three times in 1930–1934, distance and cost proved difficult to overcome. At the beginning of the twentieth-first century, only 94 of Texas' 254 counties indicated some sort of county library.[66] Generally, libraries are an urban phenomenon and the scattered rural population presents problems not easily overcome by the enthusiasm of public librarians.

ACADEMIC LIBRARIES

To serve their students and teachers, schools of all sorts acquired books and librarians. For the most part, the collections at colleges targeted the undergraduate community, but at the larger universities, archives and supportive collections became necessary for the faculty. Professors were expected not only to hold classes, but also to advance knowledge. This was the pathway of scholarship: to know what has been done before and then to reach beyond that point. It was no idle comment when Sir Isaac Newton of the seventeenth century praised his predecessors with his famous proclamation, "If I have seen further it is by standing on the shoulders of giants."

The library was essential because it provided the information about the current level of knowledge. It was a facility, a memory, a ratchet for humankind that removed the necessity of reinventing the wheel over and over and over again. An adequate library acquired, stored, and organized books, manuscripts, personal papers of important people, government documents, oral histories, photographs, music, and art. At times, certain acquisitions of no apparent value required a faith that someday the items would be important for research. The basic premise was that the bigger and more complete the library, the better. After being true for five hundred years, that assumption about the physical size of the library is now under attack.

In the United States, the largest repository is the Library of Congress with some 115 million items including 20 million books. In 1870 the government placed the copyright office with the Library of Congress and the copies of books donated for copyright confirmation became a part of the library. In 1901 the Library of Congress began to print and sell its catalog cards. These served as an index to the collection and contained the essential information about an entry, including some indication of the contents. Purchase of the individual cards that matched their own collection relieved librarians of a tiresome chore and spread the Library of Congress classification system (a letter followed by a number followed by a letter-number combination) that is now the norm.[67] The director of the Library of Congress, incidentally, has usually been a scholar rather than a librarian, and, ironically, the director has never been a woman. The largest university library is Harvard with 15 million volumes and the largest in Texas is the University of Texas at Austin with a little over half that amount. In sheer number of volumes, Texas also trails Yale, the University of Illinois, and the University of California at Berkeley, but competes readily with all the other major schools in the nation.

The University of Texas at Austin

The first chair of the Board of Regents of the University of Texas was Ashbel Smith, the physician of the Republic era who understood the importance of libraries. Book accumulation would not be overlooked and the Smith collection of four thousand volumes eventually found its way to the university in 1902. After receiving a boost from the eclectic book donation of Swante Palm in 1897 and a transfer of the Bexar Archives (Spanish and Mexican records from 1717–1836) from the commissioner's court of San Antonio in 1899, the University of Texas library experienced two major periods of expansion.

The first came under the direction of John E. Goodwin (1876–1948) from 1912 to 1923 and Ernest W. Winkler (1875–1960) from 1923 to 1934 when the library moved from a forty-third ranking in the nation to sixteenth for academic libraries. This happened in spite of warfare in 1917 with Governor James E. Ferguson, who vetoed the university appropriation, and in spite of the crippling Depression of the 1930s. Winkler, a bibliographer and historian, commented in 1933, "To my way of thinking [historical research] and the pleasure it brings is beyond comparison, superior to hunting, fishing, horse racing, or similar hobbies upon which men spend time."[68]

In 1918 the library purchased the John Henry Wrenn collection that contained fifty-three hundred first and rare editions of American and British authors. Purchasing primarily with private donations of money, the library added other rare book accumulations by George A. Aiken, Albert A. Bieber, and Miriam Lutcher Stark that gave it prominence for studies in English literature from the seventeenth century to the present. In 1921 Goodwin acquired the Genaro Garcia collection of three hundred thousand manuscripts and twenty-five thousand printed items that became the foundation for an unmatched Latin American research library. Garcia was a Mexico City bibliophile whose widow needed money to support their ten children. University representatives to the 1920 inauguration of Mexican President Álvaro Obregón learned about the availability of the collection. Goodwin and Winkler, moreover, possessed the good sense to give encouragement and freedom to pursue acquisitions to their special area librarians: Mattie Hatcher in Southwestern colonial history, Carlos Castañeda in Mexican and Latin American history, and Fannie Ratchford for rare books.[69]

Less sensational but equally important were the ongoing purchases of the Littlefield Fund, which amounted to twenty-six thousand items by 1938. Regent George W. Littlefield (1842–1920), who was from Mississippi and had fought in the Civil War, was disturbed about prejudiced interpretations of the Southern cause in the histories of the United States. He berated historian Eugene C. Barker and Barker told him that the problem was not with people who wrote the histories, but with the lack of resources upon which to base interpretation. Major Littlefield, who had made a fortune in cotton, cattle, and real estate, then provided an initial $25,000 in 1914 to buy appropriate items. He later added to the amount, and the fund continued after Littlefield's death in 1920 for the support of research related to Southern history. Littlefield also gave the money for the purchase of the Wrenn collection.[70]

A second great period of library acquisition came through the encouragement and energy of Harry H. Ransom (1908–1976), who was university chancellor and president in the 1960s. He was a career English professor and administrator with a passion for original manuscripts. He worked fourteen-hour days, wore horn-rimmed glasses and white shirts, exercised by walking, and danced only on demand. When Hazel Louise Harrod first came to UT from Waco a friend advised her to take Ransom's English class. She did, and told her friend at Christmas time, "I've got Harry Ransom." They married in 1951 and became an important couple among the campus elite.[71]

His pictures reflect a serious expression of amused tolerance. Texas writer Ronnie Dugger said of Ransom, "You sense around him a velvet-chambered continuum of silence wherein he wanders, reads, and muses, a little sadly."[72] Ransom once commented, "The University's main product is minds, its only real profits are ideas. The educational waste that is the unforgivable sin is the waste of intellect."[73] During his time, the number of endowed chairs rose from zero to forty-five, faculty salaries doubled, and the University of Texas became the leading producer of doctorates in the South and Southwest. This was a man who academics, particularly those in the liberal arts, would follow into hell. He gave them $45 million worth of archival materials, three-fourths purchased through donations.

The "Ransom Era" opened with the purchase of the Edward A. Parsons Collection in 1958 of forty thousand volumes and eight thousand manuscripts. Parsons was a scholar and bibliophile from New Orleans. Other purchases followed: T. Edward Hanley on contemporary literary manuscripts, Norman Bel Geddes on set design, Karl St. John Hoblitzelle on theater, Ben Weinreb on architecture, Helmut Gernsheim on photography, and others. Representatives of the University of Texas, checkbook in hand, aggressively appeared wherever collections surfaced on the market. With the idea that the oil endowment of the university could be spent for books as well as buildings, the voracious Longhorns became the terror of the book market as they swept it clean. John Silber, a former dean at the university, said, "[Ransom] could not tell the difference between the actual, the possible, and the totally inconceivable. He was, therefore, a man who could imagine new possibilities."[74]

T. Edward Hanley (1893–1969) and his books provide an illustration of the collecting frenzy. Hanley was a wealthy brick manufacturer from Bradford, Pennsylvania, who suffered an early, unhappy, brief marriage and remained a bachelor. In his loneliness, he became an addicted bibliophile in the 1930s and bought manuscripts from a former Brooklyn dentist, Jacob (Jake) Schwartz. An ingratiating dealer with a shop in London, Schwartz would buy rough drafts and manuscripts from writers and then resell them at a profit. Playwright Samuel Beckett, who needed the money, called Schwartz an "entertaining ruffian" who extracted Beckett's papers for a pittance. Schwartz would send the playwright small presents and request signed manuscripts. The generous Beckett complied, but commented at one point, "Schwartz is becoming rather a nuisance, soon he will be sending me his toilet paper to inscribe." Hanley bought somewhat blindly from Schwartz and the dealer was willing to let him pay with installments.

At Hanley's house in Bradford the disordered books and manuscripts piled up and spilled over—in the garage, in the basement, on the stairwell, in the attic, under the bed, everywhere. His insurance company refused coverage because the house was a firetrap. Then in 1945 at a Buffalo nightclub, Ed Hanley met an exotic dancer named Tullah who was half Egyptian, half Hungarian, and half his age. She wanted a wealthy man and so she and Ed married. Along with her dancing partner, a younger sister named Amy, they moved with Hanley to Bradford. The three of them got along remarkably well.

But Ed was an addicted bibliophile and he kept buying until he owed Schwartz $128,000. Tullah and Amy persuaded him to sell his 155,000-item collection. The Ivy League colleges gathered like flies to assess the collection—it would take weeks—but Ransom arrived, looked at the first editions under the bed and the other piled-up materials for two hours, and offered $1 million. Hanley sold to Texas and a guarded truck caravan brought the collection to Austin in 1958. The Texas librarians found treasures in each box they unpacked. That was how the papers of the famous Irish author Samuel Beckett ended up in Austin.[75]

In a final flourish, the Ransom Era concluded with the purchase of a Gutenberg Bible two years after Ransom's death. It was a part of a larger collection from New York City and, when asked by millionaire Ross Perot, who brokered the deal, if the Bible was worth it, librarian Decherd Turner replied that he would crawl to New York just to see it. The result of all this frenetic collection purchasing activity was that the University of Texas library became a world-class research institution.[76]

Meanwhile, the increasing numbers of students and faculty brought continuing pressure for better library facilities. In 1911 the library had moved into a two-story building, designed by nationally famous architect Cass Gilbert, that featured a handsome, high-ceiled reading room; large arched windows; and a red-tiled mansard roof. It was an architect's triumph and a librarian's frustration. The university librarian, Nathaniel L. Goodrich, was not consulted about the design and Gilbert ignored his entreaties. Its capacity was less than the old quarters, there was no elevator, and there were no book stacks. Some forty thousand books, along with bookcases, had to be moved onto the second story with a derrick. The building could not stand the weight of the books and the ceiling cracked. The move left a pile of materials in the basement that measured 31 × 17 × 7 feet, all waiting to be sorted by the staff.[77] As might be expected, the library soon filled up and individual departments began keeping their own books, thus, scattering the collection and causing confusion for students.

To halt the dispersion of the books, Main Library, with a 27-floor tower, opened in 1934 at the exact center of the original 40-acre campus. Complete with a clock and carillon, the tower provided an exclamation point for the campus. Carved across the broad front entrance of the library were the words from John 8:32, "Ye shall know the truth and the truth shall set you free." Imposing with a red-tiled roofline, expansive steps, and large, decorated, high-ceilinged reading rooms, the library was built with the aid of federal Depression funds. It was another architectural success and a librarian's nightmare.

Like the old library, the new facility used closed stacks, which meant that students had to look up the books they wanted from the vast card catalog, fill out a slip of paper with book information and their own identification, give it to a runner at the checkout desk, and wait for the runner to retrieve the book from the fourteen stack levels of the tower. Within the closely spaced book stacks, there was a small elevator and a narrow stairwell, and the runners moved like trained rats through a poorly lighted vertical maze. Faculty and graduate students could use stack passes to look for their own materials. The library was dedicated largely to advanced study, and, as library historian Carolyn Bucknall noted, "It is quite probable that tens of thousands of University of Texas students had gained initial academic degrees having made no use of the library except for its Reserve Collection."[78]

The tower became a sniper's perch for Charles Whitman on August 1, 1966, when the former Marine sharpshooter hauled a footlocker of food, water, ammunition, and guns to the open observation deck. The insane Whitman clubbed the receptionist, killed two, wounded two, and then began to shoot at the students crossing the quadrangle 231 feet below. With deadly accuracy, he shot victims walking bypaths, riding bicycles, peering through windows, and heading to class. In one of the nation's notorious cases of mass murder, Whitman killed seventeen and wounded thirty people. It could have been worse, but Whitman mistimed the attack and began firing just before the dismissal of classes at noontime. Once the situation was understood, professors held students in classes while others around the campus pulled rifles from their pickup trucks and pinned Whitman down with return fire. He was finally stopped and killed after ninety minutes by a courageous policeman and a volunteer who burst through onto the observation deck.[79]

I was in the bookstore across the street from the campus at the time and watched the drama unfold on the store's television sets. We were warned by the police to stay away from the windows and not to go outside. I could hear the "pop, pop" of shots being fired and see on television the dust puffs as bullets pocked the limestone of the observation deck. When it was over, I went home to assure my wife that I was all right, and, not knowing what had happened, she asked, "Why aren't you in the library?"

Much of the overflowing manuscript acquisition of the Ransom Era went to the Humanities Research Center, which opened in a separate seven-story library building in 1972. It was there that important personal papers could be found for writers like Christopher Morley, Samuel Beckett, Joseph Conrad, and Arthur Conan Doyle. The rate of acquisition, however, overwhelmed the curators, and in 1978 an audit revealed missing volumes, an improper relationship with a local book dealer, and an enormous backlog of unprocessed items. The director and his assistant abruptly resigned.[80]

Ransom, however, in his headlong buying of archival materials for research did not forget the need for lower-division student instruction. In 1963 the university opened a separate undergraduate library that featured 145,000 volumes with open-stack access, an audio library, and a reserve desk. It was not a new idea; Harvard had built a separate undergraduate library in 1949. Nonetheless, the students liked it and affectionately called it "Harry's Place." The Latin American Collection and the Barker Texas History Center that contained the Bexar Archives, the Austin Papers, and Ashbel Smith Papers moved across the campus from the Old Library Building into the new quarters of Sid Richardson Hall in 1971.

On the same sloping site the university placed the Lyndon B. Johnson Presidential Library and established a school of public affairs. Some fourteen moving van loads of political accumulation from his long career, 40 million pages of documents, moved from Washington, D.C., to Austin to be administered on the campus by the National Archives. It was the first presidential library in Texas and it functioned as a museum, a tourist attraction, and a research center concerning the life and times of Lyndon B. Johnson. A similar library came to the Texas A&M campus upon the retirement of President George H. W. Bush, and a third presidential library is anticipated following the tenure of President George W. Bush.

The main book collection of the university also moved to new quarters with the 1977 opening of the Perry-Castañeda Library. Serving both graduate and undergraduate students, the library was named for Ervin S. Perry (1935–1970), the first black engineering professor at Texas and in the South, and Carlos E. Castañeda (1896–1958), the specialist in Latin American history who immigrated from Mexico and learned English at the public library in Brownsville. The new library, the third largest academic library building in the nation, housed over 3 million volumes with ample room for reader tables and an electronic, online catalog. It was comfortable, efficient, open stack, and, at last, a triumph for the librarians over the architects.[81] It was not a monument to rich donors or presidents, the architecture was neither intimidating nor distracting, and it was named for two professors in the service of students.

THE PLEASURE OF LIBRARIES

It was at the Perry-Castañeda Library that I first felt the satisfaction to be found in a good library. I was pursuing information for my book on the history of Galveston and looking for an obscure article written by "T." It was an eyewitness account of a meeting with pirate Jean Laffite in Galveston in 1821. Information about Laffite was sketchy at best and this was a worthwhile lead. Supposedly, the article was in the *United States Magazine and Democratic Review* of July 1839. Whoever heard of that magazine, I thought, and if it existed, would there be the issue I needed? It might still exist at Harvard, or some other obscure and unreachable place. Oh well. I checked the electronic catalog, and there it was. Hmm. I went upstairs, walked through the stacks, found the magazine, sat down at a nearby table, and opened the old bound volume to the article by "T." "Wow!" I thought. "Here it is, right here at the University of Texas in Austin. On the bookshelf! At hand! What a joy, what a pleasure!"

Gene Lyons, a Graham Greene scholar, offered another example from the Humanities Research Center. He found a jotted note that Greene had written on the manuscript of *The Letters and Diaries of John Henry Newman* that "illuminated the man for me like a silent flash of summer lightning." Lyons went on to comment, "Fifty or a hundred years from now a person reading that scrap of dialogue who values Greene's work as I do will experience a chill as if the man himself . . . had come quietly into the room and touched his shoulder. Such experiences are what make scholarship exciting."[82]

THE INTERNET REVOLUTION

The long era of such research and quiet pleasure in libraries, probably, is coming to an end. Librarians everywhere are apprehensive about the rapid changes wrought by computers. The core purpose of a library, and of the book, as a tool to provide information is threatened. The library has been the honored citadel for knowledge since the Gutenberg book revolution five hundred years ago and pilgrims seeking information have humbly come to it. The Internet, search engines, and computers located anywhere, however, can provide information with an electronic click. What is the use, then, for a traditional library? That is the anxious question.

Librarians could see the changes coming for some time. The Library of Congress worked with photostatic equipment in 1912, and the Hoover Library at Stanford produced photocopies of materials in 1926. The University of Texas tried punched cards for circulation control in 1936. There were experiments with IBM computer equipment in the 1940s, and the National Library of Medicine developed an online database in 1964–1965. Microforms and microfilm came out at the same time, and in the next decade computer applications arrived apace.[83]

Libraries exchanged their card catalogs for electronic catalogs in the 1980s, and eventually went online so that their collections could be searched by an Internet service. Sharing was a time-honored library tradition and interlibrary loans were at least a century old. The card catalog became a dinosaur. The search capability of the Internet became increasingly efficient in the last part of the 1990s, and the administrators of Google, a major search engine, announced in late 2004 a project to digitize five major libraries—Michigan, Harvard, Stanford, Oxford, and New York Public. Why would anyone want to travel to a distant library when the desired information was instantly available at home, or in a dorm room, or on the back porch, or at a beach?

Observable examples of the computer revolution are abundant. Public terminal stations, keyboards, and mice are showing up on traditional library tables everywhere and people of all sorts occupy almost every terminal. A friend who works for Hewlett-Packard as an electronic engineer tells me that he almost never uses their special library resources. He uses the full-text copies of journals and magazines on the Internet for the information he needs in his work. Texas Instruments has discontinued its library and law libraries are falling into disuse as young lawyers are trained for Internet research. To answer why the 17,000-volume library on the Semester at Sea ship used by the University of Pittsburgh to take students and professors around the world was cut to 11,000 volumes, the director explained in 2004 that the students are using the Internet on shipboard for their class projects.

Scientists have been saying for some time that their use of the library is slight. It was the campus scientists who objected to Ransom's rampant purchase of expensive book collections at the University of Texas in the 1960s. In addition, Empire High School in Vail, Arizona, in 2005 issued laptop computers instead of textbooks to its 340 students. It was one of the first schools in the nation to become completely textbook free. Books and libraries, seemingly, are less needed now than they were even two decades ago. The computer ate the card catalog and now is eating books. Whither the library?

THE NEAR FUTURE OF LIBRARIES

At the moment, academic libraries and some public libraries remain attractive because they provide access to data banks that are too expensive for an individual to own. Furthermore, the libraries supply patrons with computers, writing programs, free Internet access, and technical instruction to help them become computer literate. In addition, there is still information in printed resources that has not yet been digitized, such as in older journals and newspapers. Digitizing, the translation from written to numerical computer format, is expensive and someone has to pay the costs. Even the Library of Congress plans to digitize only 10 percent of its collection because of the expense.

Archives, by and large, are not yet available for electronic perusal because it is technically too difficult to digitize handwriting. Researchers, consequently, still need to travel to library archives. It is not in the realm of science fiction, however, to imagine a time when everything in a library will be available through a lightweight laptop computer that can vary the font size to accommodate fading eyes. Our problem then will be to learn to swim in a sea of unfiltered, unsorted information. Professional librarians can be of service as Marylaine Block explained:

> Helping people to realize their potential is something librarians routinely do. Our collections reward self-motivated people, letting them learn whatever they desire to know, at their own pace. Whether they want to bake Irish soda bread, repair their cars, learn French, study opera, read Dostoyevsky, watch a Shakespeare play, or pass a civil service exam, we provide the necessary books, and video, and recordings. If we don't have what they need on hand, we get it for them from other libraries.[84]

Contemporary user studies indicate that about 40 percent of a total population does not use a public library at all. Dallas Public Library cardholders, for instance, amount to about 17 percent of the metropolitan population and 50 percent of the city population. About half of the people who do visit a library go for purposes of recreation. Worried library researcher Bernard F. Vavrek of the University of Pennsylvania, noting these facts, therefore has recommended that libraries become entertainment centers with an emphasis upon children's programs, best sellers, public access Internet terminals, music, genealogy, and local services to the community. Libraries, according to Vavrek, should coordinate with the local parks service, tourism bureau, and chamber of commerce. They should stock multiple copies of popular books. "Any library that neglects the fact that one of its core activities is service to women reading best sellers is flirting with disaster." Even the smallest library, he noted, could be a part of the global network and still fulfill a historic purpose as a public library.[85]

Transitions, however, are not clear, and they are messy with inconsistencies. In 2003 a record 165,000 new book titles were published, and Dan Frank, the editor-in-chief of Pantheon Books, commented, "Forty years ago you used to worry that a good book would not be published. Now *everything* is being published, and a lot of good books are being overlooked."[86] Newspaper readership, on the other hand, has declined every year since 1987, and the numbers of readers of literature have decreased since 1982.[87] What is going on? In 2004 the average number of hours spent on television, video recordings, recorded music, movies, and video games was five times greater than the time devoted to books, magazines, and newspapers.[88] A study in 2000 revealed the interesting dualism that 75 percent of people using the Internet also used the public library.[89] Perhaps the computer was simply a new tool and nothing to be afraid of.

Seattle, moreover, recently built a striking new public library to emphasize literacy on the home ground of Microsoft, while Columbia University, the birthplace of library studies, downsized its Teachers College Library collection to make room for collaborative learning facilities. In the Internet age, big is no longer better at Columbia. As Interim Director Gary Natriello commented, "We didn't have to fill the building to the brim with materials." Instead, there are cushioned chairs, coffee tables, and minimalist open stacks demurely positioned on the walls between the large windows.[90]

What it all means is not entirely clear. Libraries will not disappear before our eyes, but they will be different as computer terminals proliferate. They will be places of social contact and entertainment with librarians as facilitators. Dana Gioia, chair of the National Endowment for the Arts, however, fears a "vast cultural impoverishment" from this assault by the electronic medium: "Reading a book requires a degree of active attention and engagement. While oral culture has a rich immediacy that is not to be dismissed, and electronic media offer the considerable advantages of diversity and access, print culture affords irreplaceable forms of focused attention and contemplation that make complex communications and insights possible."[91] In 2007 the U.S Department of Education reported a decline in the reading proficiency—the ability to discern points of view from reading material—of high school seniors, from 40 percent in 1992 to 35 percent in 2005.[92] Therefore, although literacy may well improve in the cyberworld, being literate may decline as a cherished aspect of education.

School librarian Thomas Washington has experienced this phenomenon and complained to readers of the *Washington Post*:

> Typically, many people in my line of work no longer have the title of librarian. They are called media and information specialists, or sometimes librarian technologists. . . . We teach students how to maximize a database search, about successful retrieval rates. What usually gets lost in the scramble is a careful reading of the material. . . . I recently spoke with a junior who was stressed about her decreasing ability to focus on anything for longer then two minutes or so. I tried to inspire her by talking about the importance of reading as a way to train the brain. I told her that a good reader develops the same powers of concentration that an athlete or Buddhist would employ in sport or meditation. . . . She rolled her eyes, "That's your opinion about books. It doesn't make it true." To her, the idea that reading might benefit the mind was, well, lame.[93]

Libraries in Texas, as always, will float along in the mainstream of the national library evolution. The historical pattern in Texas has reflected the change from private to public libraries; from initial locations in large cities spreading to small cities and rural places; from an emphasis upon learned, serious books to popular literature; from racial segregation to integration. The history also reveals the constant influence of concerned women, sporadic attacks by groups who want to censor reading material, an abiding interest by readers in fiction, and the start of the computer revolution. Texas libraries also carry a historic burden.

A current study of literacy in cities based upon use of the library and newspapers ranked Texas, along with California, at the bottom. Among Texas cities, El Paso ranked lowest because of a high, non-English-speaking immigrant population. There were other Texas places on the bottom of the list—Garland, Arlington, San Antonio, Corpus Christi.[94] This would indicate that Texas libraries, particularly the public libraries, still have an educational mission for the poor migrants streaming northward across the Texas-Mexican border.

The general future outlook is foggy, but it would appear that serious books will become too long, too difficult, and too slow for most people. Words or sentences that require contemplation or the use of a dictionary will be dismissed as too hard, even by students. The pleasure of a library will be lost in the new helter-skelter, shallow, quick, cyberspace world. Perhaps, shallowness is the way it has always been for the majority of people, and, to echo the old wisdom of the Boston Public Library, it is better to have people reading the Internet than reading nothing at all. Still, it would seem that the joy found by readers in a good library will disappear within a generation and that the existence of such pleasure will become simply an arcane reference in the data banks of quotation.

CHAPTER 5

Theater and the Electric Revolution

"Live theater" is such an odd phrase—is there "dead theater"? Movies, perhaps, but we all know what the words mean. They refer to a presentation by in-the-flesh actors in front of a breathing audience. Live theater originated, apparently, at the dawn of humankind when people told stories and performed rituals of fertility, prediction, and myth. Even then the enactors used masks and costumes and performed before others. Theatrical history, thus, can be found in all cultures.

In Western civilization, the story winds across the marble amphitheaters of the classical Greeks, onto wagon beds of medieval morality plays, and hence to the raised wooden platforms of Renaissance London and William Shakespeare. The Greeks introduced comedy and tragedy to the stage, medieval Christians used farce to reveal imperfect humanity, Italians contributed opera, the French provided dance and ballet, and the English crafted comedies of manners, pantomime, and mocking parodies (burlesque).[1] The purpose, then and now, was to educate, inspire, and entertain an audience. Or, as historians Oscar Brockett and Franklin Hildy concluded, "The theatre, then, is one tool whereby people define and understand their world or escape from unpleasant realities."[2]

The activity on the stage focused attention upon the actors and the content of their speech and movement. In a modern theater with the stage at one end of a box-like room, the panorama is known sometimes as the "fourth wall." Commonly, the arena is separated from the audience by an arch and thus is known as a proscenium stage. In the eye of the patron, the wall is like a picture with motion framed by the perimeter of the stage—not unlike the rectangular frame of the modern television set. Technical particulars for theater changed over time, of course. When the actors moved indoors in the sixteenth century, for example, lighting became important and candles in chandeliers along with footlights of candles in canisters backed with tinsel or mica answered the need. At this point of theatrical evolution, migrants from France, England, and Spain took their notions of theater to the New World.

New England Puritans frowned upon acting as a sinful waste of time, but New York City merchants gave a license for a play presentation as early as 1699 and built a permanent theater in 1767. Williamsburg citizens possessed an amateur theater in

1716, and Charleston planters actually enjoyed a playgoers season in 1773–1774 of one hundred performances. French traders supported a professional theater in New Orleans in 1791, and Spanish magistrates welcomed three permanent companies of performers to Mexico City in 1601.

During its settlement, the people of Texas embraced this heritage. Spanish missionaries performed religious enactments; an officer of Don Juan de Oñate wrote and presented a play during the exploration of the El Paso area in 1598; and after securing the territory for colonization, San Miguel de Aguayo, during his return to Mexico in 1722, offered three dramas to astounded Texas Indians.[3] Along with native rituals, these were the earliest performances in Texas.

THEATER IN EARLY TEXAS

Theatrical groups appeared quickly along the trade routes and the Gulf Coast. John Salmon "Rip" Ford (1815–1897), a soldier, explorer, and politician, reported that W. W. Parker, the editor of a pioneer newspaper in San Augustine, organized a local thespian corps to present amateur melodramas and tragedies in 1838. Ford wrote two comedies for the group and his second effort was a success. He recorded, "It drew a large house, and increased the writer's vanity to an alarming extent. He imagined that lightning had striken [sic] him and developed in him a genius of sublime proportions."[4] Ford, however, moved on to other adventures, and San Augustine continued without him on its quest to become the "Athens of Texas."

In May 1842 William Bollaert had a theatrical experience in Matagorda when he passed through town. This small port city established a playhouse before it built a church, and he attended a presentation at the "pretty little theatre" of the Thespian Company of Matagorda. There he was recruited to sing two songs while dressed in costume. Bollaert, like Ford, also resisted the lure of the stage and left town the following day.[5] Beyond the saloon and drinking, amateur plays provided a major nightly recreation for early Texas.

Other examples are scattered in mid-nineteenth-century writings and document the entrance of professional actors. During their stay in Corpus Christi in 1846, officers organized an amateur army theater in an effort to offset the two hundred saloons distracting Zachary Taylor's soldiers on their way to fight a war with Mexico. The officers had to import a professional actress from New Orleans, however, after young Lt. Ulysses S. Grant proved inadequate for the role of Desdemona in *Othello*.[6] This mixed world of amateur and professional provided ample room for mishap.

An impecunious professional touring group in Houston at this time persuaded "Pudding" Stanley, a retired actor who was running a bar and gambling hall in San Antonio, to play the lead role in *Richard III*. "Pudding," who had received his nickname for his portly figure, thought that he was without peer in the part of Richard, and the people of Houston packed the theater to hear and jeer a barkeep spouting Shakespeare.

Puffed, padded, declaiming, and gesturing, "Pud" strutted around the stage and at one point almost fell into a box seat. As he straightened up, the ostrich plumes of his hat caught fire from the candles in the chandelier. Unaware that he was aflame, Pud glared indignantly at the laughing audience until the smell of burning feathers warned him of his danger. During the love scene with Lady Anne, a heckler warned her that Pud already had two Mexican wives in San Antonio, and in the final scene, as Richard III died, another yelled "keno" in reference to the conclusion of a gambling game. As the curtain descended, the king with his burnt feathers sat up and warned the harasser that Richard would "keno" him in the morning.[7]

More successful were the efforts of the resident stock companies that entertained in the young Texas capital of Houston. In 1838, with eight men and three women, Henri Corri launched a drama season with a comedy, *The Hunchback*, and a farce, *The Dumb Belle—or I'm Perfection,* to an overflowing crowd. He used a room in a building owned by businessman John Carlos and in the following season competed with Carlos, who set up his own stock company. Corri built a new theater on Market Street, but both failed after the legislature moved the capital to Austin and the Houston audience, as well as the economy, declined.[8]

Resident professional stock companies as attempted by Corri and Carlos, however, were rare in nineteenth-century Texas. Cities mainly depended upon traveling troupes and the ever-ready amateur productions to provide entertainment. German immigrants, for instance, became famous for their local singing and theater in Fredericksburg and New Braunfels. The staged presentations, at first, were given in large rooms provided by German social clubs, Masonic organizations, churches, city halls, or saloons.

Later, some of the drinking places offered dancing and low-level stage acts for the entertainment of customers. Most of the major towns sported such variety theaters, an institution that originated in the East and migrated to the West in the latter part of the nineteenth century. The variety theaters offered short acts of comedy, singing, and dance with scantily dressed women who performed on stage and then hustled drinks and sex between acts. It is for good reason that "actress" was a common synonym for prostitute in the census data of the time.

Among the best known of the variety theaters was Jack Harris' Vaudeville Saloon and Theatre in San Antonio. It faced south on Main Plaza with additional entrances on Soledad Street in a building constructed in the 1850s. The front half of the complex contained a mirrored bar, cigar store, and ticket office. Behind that was the entrance to a red-, gold-, and green-painted theater, which had seven rows of wooden chairs, a place for a small orchestra, and a small semicircular stage with a curtain and a backstage area. On the second floor above the bar were gambling rooms and an entryway to ten box seats that overlooked the stage. Electric lights replaced the gaslights in 1882.

Jack Harris began running the saloon-gambling-theater operation in the early 1870s and developed it in the next few years with a resident band and stock actors. He supplemented this house entertainment with new acts, such as banjo players or jugglers, as they offered themselves to the stage manager. The red stockings of the girls were famous in San Antonio, and it was said that once a man smiled at one of these stage fairies, his money was no longer his own. Harris' Saloon and Theatre lasted only until 1884, but it is easy to see the roots of modern Texas strip joints in the format popularized by Jack Harris.[9]

THE OPERA HOUSES AND HENRY GREENWALL

The variety theaters provided recreation mainly for a male audience. It was acting of sorts, although polite society considered it "illegitimate." A somewhat elevated type of variety theater, known as vaudeville, tried to offer cleaner acts that a decent woman might attend. (The use of the word "vaudeville" by Jack Harris thus was a misnomer.) At the same time, however, touring companies of actors traveling by railroad provided higher-level "legitimate" entertainment with presentations of Shakespeare and contemporary plays. As their cities grew, businessmen and promoters in Austin, Galveston, Houston, Waco, Dallas, San Antonio, and Fort Worth built "opera houses," so-called not because they specialized in opera, but because the title suggested an aura of sophistication. They were usually constructed in the downtown business sections in architectural harmony with the neighboring commercial buildings and often served multiple purposes with shops on the ground floor and a theater above them.[10]

The first opera house in Texas was the Tremont in Galveston, built in 1870–1871 by Willard Richardson, the owner of the *Galveston Daily News*. The exterior featured an iron and glass façade for the first floor, masonry on the upper two and a half floors, a stylish mansard roof, and tall arched windows. The first floor offered commercial rental space and a grand staircase through a lobby to the auditorium. The up-to-date stage had gas footlights with white, red, and blue filters. Impresario Henry Greenwall shortly leased the Tremont and used it until 1895 when he opened his own Grand Opera House.

This new brick "thespian temple" had a carved arched stone entry, marble tile in the lobby, fifteen hundred oak seats, boxes, yellow pine wainscoting, gas and electric lighting, heat and air ventilators, and a stage that measured seventy-five feet wide by sixty-eight feet high by sixty-eight feet deep. The drop curtain featured Sappho and her companions and it ascended for the first time in a gala performance of *Daughters of Eve* for a black-tie Galveston audience. Much later, in 1974, the Galveston County Cultural Arts Council took over the then-aged and time-abused Grand Opera House as a historic preservation project and restored it to its initial glory. It is the only Greenwall theater that still exists and is the finest example of its kind in the state.[11]

Henry Greenwall (1832–1913), who was born in Germany and reared in New Orleans, moved in 1867 to Galveston with his brother, Morris, to open a brokerage firm. That year they were inspired to help New Orleans actress Augusta Dargon, who was stranded on the island without funds. The brothers successfully set her up for performances in Turner Hall. The charming Augusta then went to Australia with Morris while the dour, rough-tongued Henry remained in Texas and became an impresario. He eventually put together a circuit of theaters including Houston, Galveston, Waco, Fort Worth, and Dallas before he moved back to New Orleans in 1888.

Greenwall hired actors and formed troupes in New York City, and then sent them on scheduled tours of his leased or owned theaters in Texas and the South. He was successful at competing with a larger New York organization called "The Syndicate," and at the end of the nineteenth century, Greenwall managed 566 employees, a $1.5 million investment, and $18,000 in weekly expenses. When he suffered a long illness in 1908–1909, however, it all fell apart. The competition with the monopolistic Syndicate proved overwhelming, and Greenwall died almost in poverty in 1913.[12]

During his time, however, Greenwall and other impresarios nurtured and elevated the theatrical taste of Texans—something not accomplished without effort. Actor Frederick Warde commented about performing in a room over a newly built store in Dallas in 1881:

> There were no dressing rooms in the Opera House. We dressed in our rooms in the Windsor Hotel, crossed on a diagonal covered bridge to the Exchange Hotel on the opposite side of the street in the rear, entered a back room, climbed out of a window, crossed a roof and entered the Opera House by another window that opened on the back of the stage. When a change of dress was necessary we had to make a return round trip by the same route, passing through a double line of colored chambermaids, Negro porters and bell-boys, whose characteristic laughter and comments on our appearance and costume were, to say the least, embarrassing.[13]

In Austin, on the same tour, Warde played the role of Iago in *Othello* and came close to being shot for his convincing portrayal. Toward the end of the play, a "countryman" became excited about the villainy of Iago, stood up in the audience, drew a six-gun, and declared that he would kill the "damn scoundrel." The editor of the local newspaper, who was sitting behind the agitated man, stopped the assault and explained that Warde was only impersonating a character. The man reportedly muttered, "He must be a damned villain, anyhow, or he couldn't act it so well, and if he doesn't stop abusing that woman (Emilia) he would shoot him, anyhow."[14]

Through the impresarios and their plays, Texans had the chance to increase their knowledge and appreciation of theater. There was even a circuit for Spanish-speaking troupes from Mexico City that toured El Paso, Laredo, and San Antonio and presented on crude stages such favorites as *La Cabana de Tom* (*Uncle Tom's Cabin*).[15] Literate Texans, therefore, learned to recognize good theater when they saw it; they were not hayseeds, rubes, cowboys, or unappreciative louts. Edwin Booth, an international Shakespearean actor, wrote to his friend Horace H. Furness in 1887: "My tour through Texas in the private car 'David Garrick,' was on the whole very pleasant. The towns are well worth a visit as embryo cities of wealth and beauty; the theatres excellent, hotels ditto, and the audiences very cultured and in full dress."[16] By the conclusion of the century, Texas audiences had seen great drama because of the work of people like Greenwall, but a major change was underway and his death in 1913 was symbolic.

THE ELECTRIC REVOLUTION

The manufacture of electric power and inventions for attendant uses transformed American cities beginning in the 1880s. Earlier demonstrations of usefulness came from telegraphs and telephones, but it was the electric streetlights, factory and office lighting, and trolley cars that marked the urban transfiguration. Built upon electrical knowledge, three inventions—movies, radio, and television—expanded the recreational choices of Texans and diminished the importance of live theater. The inventions, evolving with zigs and zags, false starts, and successes, came largely from outside the state and spread through the network of cities with the speed of, well, electricity. The technological diffusion was rapid, in a single lifetime, and the impact made Texas more urban, more American, and less regional in culture. Still, there were some Texan ideas and personalities mixed into the electric revolution that influenced its history.

Movies

The phenomenon of motion pictures depends upon a curious, long-noticed physical human factor called the "persistence of vision." What the eye sees remains briefly in the mind after the viewed object has shifted. A series of still pictures showing slightly changed positions, therefore, will appear to move when flicked, or quickly shuffled, in front of an observer. The sequential photographs taken by Eadweard Muybridge in 1877 to prove to Leland Stanford that a trotting horse indeed had all four feet off the ground at a certain time hinted at what could be done. With improvements in film and cameras, Thomas Edison turned out of his Menlo Park laboratory an electrically-driven "kinetoscope" that ran a continuous loop of Kodak film over a light and past a peephole with a magnifying glass. For 25 cents, people in New York City in 1893 could peep into the machines that provided, among other thrills, a fifty-second show of wrestling, boxing, a barbershop, a Highland dance, or roosters.[17]

Edison continued his experimentation, and in April 1896, he demonstrated his new Vitascope, a primitive projector, in New York City. Ten months later, there was one in operation at the Dallas Opera House, and variety theaters statewide scrambled to include a moving picture scene as a concluding act. In 1902 two Houston optometrists sold advertising to local merchants and set up a free outside theater on a vacant lot. It was a success in spite of neighborhood rapscallions who threw rocks through the screen and released a captive skunk into the audience.

In 1903 Edwin S. Porter, who worked with Edison, made *The Great Train Robbery*, a fifteen-minute, single-reel film that told a story. Such narratives prompted the establishment of storefront theaters called nickelodeons where a patron could see a series of short shows for five cents. These movie houses were easy to set up and provided cheap entertainment. The first one appeared in Pittsburgh in 1905. In 1908 there existed eight thousand nickelodeons in the United States and fourteen thousand in 1914. It was estimated that in 1910 about 26 million Americans, a fourth of the population, went to a movie every week.[18]

The nickelodeon wave that rolled over the nation left a residue of Vitascope houses in most mid-size and large Texas cities, wherever there was a place to gather an audience. A large sheet for a screen, plank benches or kitchen chairs for seating, a dark setting, a film, and a hand-cranked one-reel projector with an arc lamp was all that was necessary for thirty minutes or so of entertainment. A piano and a player added to the excitement.

Interest, innovation, and activity reached fevered levels as better equipment and movies poured forth. With its sunshine and studios, San Antonio might have become a movie production capital if Hollywood had not been so successful, but Dallas did become a distribution point. Theater operators traveled to Dallas once per week to purchase films to show to a ravenous and uncritical public.[19] The nickelodeon's time, however, was brief like that of a wondrous butterfly.

Multiple-reel stories, at first released one reel per week as serials, became feature films that the public gladly paid twice as much to view at a single two-hour sitting. This new economy meant that theater operators had to provide comfortable seats and restrooms. Competition among owners led to custom-built theaters with ornate lobbies, cushioned seats, nurseries, powder rooms, cut-glass mirrors, and decorative plasterwork. They were larger—as many as 750 seats—and were equipped with a stage and orchestra pit. After all, the movies were still silent and music added to the experience.[20] These new movie places were opera houses for film. And indeed, many of the original opera houses, such as the proud Grand in Galveston, became movie theaters.

KARL ST. JOHN HOBLITZELLE AND THE MAJESTIC

Improved, dedicated movie theaters popped up everywhere, such as the Texas in McGregor, Texas, in 1912; the Isis in Houston in 1913; the Queen in Houston in 1914; the Alhambra in El Paso in 1914; and the Isis in Fort Worth in 1914. Elaborate movie palaces evolved in the 1920s and Karl St. John Hoblitzelle (1879–1967) built the best. Born in St. Louis into a large family, he went to work at an early age and became acquainted with show business as secretary for the St. Louis World's Fair in 1904. With his brother and others, Hoblitzelle established a clean family vaudeville circuit in Dallas, Fort Worth, Waco, and San Antonio. He moved to Dallas and began to acquire theaters, the newest of which he always called the "Majestic."

To replace a Majestic that burned in 1917, he opened a new Dallas theater in 1921. This new Majestic announced itself with the largest marquee in the South—five stories of flashing lights topped with a bird on a whirling ball. With a stone French Renaissance–style exterior, the new theater boasted mirrored doors, chandeliers, a fountain in the lobby, ivory and gold paint, a Roman garden wall motif, a slanted floor for clear viewing in the auditorium, two balconies, a section for blacks with a separate entrance, ceiling fans, and a play area for kids in the basement. The theater employed a uniformed staff of seventy and opened with a black-tie gala that included seven vaudeville acts plus the dancer Olga Petrova who was engaged for $3,500 for the week.

After vaudeville died in the economic convulsions of the Great Depression, however, the theater's main purpose became to show feature films.[21] In 1973, as the locus of movie entertainment shifted to the suburbs, the Majestic went dark. Four years later, the Hoblitzelle Foundation gave the theater to the city for renovation into a performing arts center for the Dallas Ballet. The building thus survived as a sample of a grand era now lost, a time when it stood shoulder to shoulder with others on Dallas' Elm Street theater row.

As the head of Interstate Theaters, Hoblitzelle built another Majestic in Houston in 1923. It was the first air-conditioned theater in Texas and patrons leaving the cool building almost fell over from the oven-like blast of Houston's heat and humidity. (Houston can still have that effect.) Hoblitzelle also built a $3 million Majestic with 3,700 seats in San Antonio that opened in 1929. The second largest theater in the United States, it had a huge aquarium, plants of all kinds, and small live birds flitting about the lobby. Other elaborate movie theaters built at the time included the Palace (1921), a Hoblitzelle theater in Dallas with a $50,000 pipe organ that rose out of the floor; the Metropolitan (1926) in Houston, featuring an Egyptian temple motif; Loew's State (1927) in Houston, which displayed the furnishings from the Vanderbilt mansion in New York City; and the Aztec (1926) in San Antonio, a theater with a stage curtain depicting Cortez meeting Montezuma.[22]

Hoblitzelle—tall, courteous, and aristocratic—retired and sold his chain of 175 theaters, to RKO in 1929 just before the stock market crash of the Depression. After RKO and Paramount pictures fell into receivership in 1933, Hoblitzelle took over their bankrupt Texas assets in order to salvage the Texas movie industry. In effect, he sold high and bought low, and made a fortune. A good man, he returned this wealth to his home city and state through generous philanthropy.[23]

THE IMPACT OF MOVIES IN TEXAS

Motion picture technology, meanwhile, matured with cartoons (1913), sound (1927), color (1934), and safety film (1916–1950) that reduced the fire hazard of cellulose nitrate base film. Although it cost musicians their jobs, the elimination of live music offset the expense of installing sound systems. The earlier invention of the phonograph in 1878 pointed to the possibility of adding sound to film, and the change came swiftly. The popular *Jazz Singer*, with Al Jolson's voice, first sounded in October 1927 in New York City; it was shown in Waco five months later.[24] The mighty Wurlitzer organ, treasured for its ability to imitate all sorts of sounds—galloping horses, birds, steamboat whistles, rain, trains—thus became a relic.

Movies in the 1930s followed their audience to suburban shopping centers, such as the Village in Dallas, and catered to moviegoers in their automobiles with drive-in theaters, such as the Texas in Corpus Christi. Theaters often allowed black customers to sit in the balcony, but there were also exclusive black movie theaters in Corpus Christi, El Paso, Fort Worth, and Dallas that obtained black films from distribution companies in Dallas and San Antonio. Hispanic theater, supplied with films purchased in Mexico, started with tent shows for field hands and then evolved into a circuit of small theaters in South Texas.[25] Almost every town of any consequence in the state possessed a movie theater by 1960. The 23-page appendix of Richard Schroeder's book, *Lone Star Picture Shows* (2001) lists 1,914 movie theaters, but he estimates that 4,000 is closer to the true number.[26] Such a great number supports the thought that almost every Texan went to the movies at least once per week.

The movies offered cheap entertainment—from 25 cents to one dollar, or so—and a chance to cool off. Like live theater, the movies could be educational and inspirational, but they were also easier to see. The movies provided close-up, panoramic, and exotic pictures that live theater could not produce. The Hollywood movies, the gossip about the star performers, and the machinations of the movie moguls supplied weekly grist for local conversations and, for better or worse, a broader view of the world for common folk. And there was the communal experience. Critic, actor, and screenwriter Syd Field, reflecting upon a lifetime of movie attendance, wrote, "Once members of an audience are joined together in the darkness of a theater, they become one being, a single entity joined in a 'community of emotion,' an unspoken and deep-seated connection to the human spirit that exists beyond time, place, and circumstance."[27]

From the beginning, Texas furnished enduring movie themes of cowboys and Indians, pioneers, and gunfighters, but the movies tended to homogenize and liberalize the culture.[28] The cultural homogenization, however, was a rough mixture. On the streets of modern urban Texas, where 80 percent of the population eventually came to live, three-piece suits, Cadillacs, Rolex watches, and ermine coats can be seen, along with blue jeans, cowboy boots, and Stetson hats. The horses disappeared, but kids still reflected a Western and Southern heritage by saying, "Yes, sir" and "No, ma'am" and "Y'all." It can be argued contrarily that the movies actually strengthened some of the Texas myths and stereotypes, such as that of fighting for freedom at the Alamo, as well as the fashions in dress and language. Regionalism did not disappear, but the movies projected the same images in Texas and across the United States. The movies thus provided a common national experience. And not all of it was considered good.

CENSORSHIP

Sex and salty language in the movies periodically brought about national and local spasms of censorship. Flicked peep show pictures of "Dolorita's Passion Dance," for example, brought protests and cancellation of the "houchi kouchi" in Atlantic City. New York Mayor George B. McClellan briefly closed the nickelodeons of the city in 1908 because of protests that they were "recruiting stations of vice."[29] Then, the arrest and trial of comedian Fatty Arbuckle in 1920 on rape and murder charges splashed Hollywood scandal for the first time onto the front pages of newspapers.

Fearful local groups agitated for regulation, and in 1921 there were almost one hundred state bills in the United States introduced to ban any sort of sexual matter in the movies. In Houston a board of censors dedicated to the review of movie and stage productions in the 1920s censored parts of 2,600 programs and rejected 225 completely.[30] Dallas and Fort Worth carried out a similar program. The manager of the Palace Theatre in Dallas commented about Ethel Boyce, the city censor, "Mrs. Boyce was tough. You couldn't reason with her at all. She'd tell you, and that was it."[31] Karl Hoblitzelle reviewed the films shown by his movie chain to be certain that they were suitable for families.

To avoid constrictive legislation, the movie producers accepted the Motion Picture Production Code of 1930, along with later amendments to ban portrayals of brutal murder, drug traffic, adultery, animal abuse, excessive kissing, white slavery, miscegenation, childbirth, profanity, and nudity. This self-regulation sufficed for the 1930s and 1940s, but slippage after the brutality of World War II brought demands for new censorship from the Roman Catholic Legion of Decency (1934). *Stromboli*, *The Moon is Blue*, and *Baby Doll* had eased through, but the rough language in *Who's Afraid of Virginia Woolf?* (1966) precipitated the crisis.

Ultimately in 1968, the Motion Picture Association of America (MPAA) replaced the old Production Code with a classification system that differentiated movies for general, mature, or restricted audiences. The system was established under the leadership of former presidential assistant Jack Valenti.[32] With subsequent gradation refinements, the classification system has remained in place as a compromise between a movie industry that knows sex and hard language sell films and the groups that wanted restraint. Now, after being warned, viewers could decide for themselves.

Radio

The movie industry that provided delight and added variety of recreation for people was not without competitors in the electric revolution. The invention of radio is well known—experiments in the nineteenth century with electromagnetic waves, the transatlantic signal of Guglielmo Marconi in 1901, the voice and music broadcasts by Reginald Fessenden in 1906, and the three-element vacuum tube of Lee De Forest that improved amplification.

The basic elements of radio involve the transformation of sound into an electromagnetic wave, amplifying it, and broadcasting it from an antenna. Radio waves have a particular frequency, or wavelength, that can be modulated to create distinct broadcast signals or stations. The radio receiver, or set, reverses the process by catching the signal through an antenna and amplifying it again so that it can be heard through a loudspeaker. The receiving set has a dial that can tune in a particular signal and exclude others. Most radio signals travel only a short distance, a few hundred miles, but can be influenced by the amplification of the signal. Such power is measured in watts—the more watts at a station, the stronger the signal.

Lee De Forest erected the first broadcast station in the Bronx in 1916, but the radio boom began after World War I. Stations KDKA in Pittsburgh began in 1919 and WWJ in Detroit in 1920, and at night, when the signals bounced off the ozone layer of the atmosphere for long distances, the evening was suddenly filled with voices. With no more than earphones, a crystal detector, and a coil wrapped around an oatmeal box, a person could hear them. Instructions for improved sets with batteries, antennas, and tubes became available, and a nation that was still half rural put on the headphones. In 1923 when Sears Roebuck first included radios in its catalog, there were 556 stations and 400,000 households with some sort of receiving set.[33] And there were no rules.

WRR in Dallas became the first broadcasting station in Texas in 1921. It was owned by the city and used for fire dispatch. Since there were long periods of no activity, the operators filled in the time with weather reports, jokes, sports, and music. The city needed new equipment in 1925 and decided to quit the station, but in ten days five thousand people signed a petition to prevent it. The public had tuned in and liked it. WRR thus continued, but the police and fire departments acquired their own radio frequencies in 1931.

WBAP started in Fort Worth in 1922 because Amon Carter (1879–1955), the owner of the *Star-Telegram*, had heard that radio was going to compete with his newspaper. Carter said to his circulation manager, Harold V. Hough, "If this radio thing is going to be a menace to newspapers, maybe we had better own the menace." As Hough bought secondhand equipment from a friend in a supply store, the friend asked, "How far do you want to listen?" Hough replied, "Listen, I don't want to listen. Amon wants to talk!" Carter gave a speech from the little 10-watt station and the following day a woman sent a post card from Mineral Wells fifty miles away that read, "Your speech came in fine." After that, Carter believed in radio and increased the power to 500 watts.[34]

About five thousand enthusiasts, in Texas and elsewhere in the country, erected backyard broadcasting antennas and invited their neighbors to play the piano on the air. A gas station owner in Amarillo would shut down to sell gasoline and then continue after the sale. As early as 1911, the University of Texas and Texas A&M used transmission equipment for teaching purposes, and in 1919, a Morse code relay from the stadium in College Station to the broadcasting equipment in the electrical engineering building provided the information for a play-by-play report of the Texas–Texas A&M football game for radio stations over a 400-mile radius. This was probably the first radio broadcast of a sporting event in the United States.[35]

In 1927 there were thirty-two commercial radio stations in Texas when the national Radio Act created the Federal Radio Commission to establish order on the chaotic airways. Overlapping signals and interference throughout the United States forced the commission to allocate broadcast frequencies based upon home city populations. In Texas fifteen of the stations received clear channels while seventeen were forced to share their frequency and broadcast time. WBAP, Amon Carter's station, for example, had to share time with KTHS in Hot Springs, Arkansas.[36] The temporary

Federal Radio Commission proved so useful that it became the permanent Federal Communications Commission (FCC) in 1934.

As U.S. rules tightened, radio entrepreneurs fled to the border to the largely unregulated Mexican stations such as 100,000-watt XEPN at Piedras Negras across the Rio Grande from Eagle Pass. In the 1930s XEPN specialized in cowboy singers such as Slim Rinehart and Patsy Montana and helped to popularize the western genre of music. W. Lee O'Daniel rented time from the station in 1935 to feature his Hillbilly Boys and advertise his flour. Bob Wills and his band, which had started on radio in Fort Worth as the Light Crust Doughboys, had already broken with O'Daniel and started on their famed career as the Texas Playboys.[37] It was Wills, the son of a sharecropper, who inspired western swing dancing with such songs as "One Star Rag" and "Cotton-eyed Joe."[38]

Radio offered a unique recreation experience for its unseen mass audience. People could tune in as they wished and go about their business with a pleasant companion. Music, news, and sports were common fare. Radio was democratic—anyone could listen—and it crossed political, religious, and class boundaries with ease. It was also free for the price of listening to the commercials that businessmen found beneficial from the very beginning. The public response, measured by listener ratings and product orders, determined the life and death of programs. Unlike movies or theater, there was an exciting immediacy about radio; it operated in the present.

Radio did not require visual attention, only hearing and imagination for the programs that evolved for evening entertainment. At the Majestic in San Antonio the operators would stop the film for thirty minutes so that the audience could listen in the lobby to *Amos 'n' Andy*, the most popular radio show of the 1920s. What did Amos look like? He was actually a white man imitating a black man. What did Jack Armstrong, Superman, the Shadow, Mr. District Attorney, the Lone Ranger, Tonto, and others look like? They were imagined in the mind's eye of the listener, and it might well have been better that way. In the first days of Dallas station WFAA in 1922, a woman climbed to the open door of the rooftop studio of the *Dallas News and Journal* building and asked to see the announcer. The man turned from the microphone and asked if she wished to see him. The visitor replied, "I did, but perhaps I had better stick to my imagination."[39]

Most programs, like *Amos 'n' Andy* from Chicago, originated outside of Texas and were relayed into the state through the networks that developed in the 1920s. Advertising promoter Lee Segall, however, started *Doctor I.Q.* in 1939 at the Majestic Theatre in Dallas. Roving announcers in the audience would identify participants with "I have a lady in the balcony, Doctor," or such, and Doctor I.Q. would ask them a question from the stage. The participant would then receive a cash prize and a box of Mars Bars for a correct answer. The program became popular enough to be picked up by the ABC network and sent on tour throughout the country. Eventually, it crossed over from radio to television and found a home at the Ritz Theatre in New York City.[40]

Usually, there was no distinct place, such as a stadium or opera house, where an audience gathered to enjoy radio recreation. Radio was everywhere there was a turned-on receiver. Bill Meeks, who worked for radio entrepreneur Gordon McLendon, said that their stations "looked almost like a restroom in a bus station, but they sounded great over the air."[41] Lee De Forest, one of the radio inventors, commented, "I discovered an Invisible Empire of the Air, intangible, yet solid as granite."[42]

There were 12 million sets in 1930 across the United States and 40 million in 1940. Following World War II, there was pent-up demand and the majority of new automobiles came equipped with a radio. Almost every household came to own at least two receiving sets and they became part of the furniture. The instrument was ubiquitous and the leading agent of recreation at the moment, but radio's time of preeminence was short. Television took over as the most important entertainment medium in the 1950s.

GORDON MCLENDON, THE OLD SCOTCHMAN

During the transition period, the radio networks transferred their talent—programs, technicians, staff, and announcers—to television and left radio to find a new path. At this juncture, Texas provided a pioneer of radio format, Gordon McLendon (1921–1985). His father took his mother across the state line so that his son could be born in Paris, Texas, but Gordon grew up in Idabel, Oklahoma. He attended high school in Atlanta, Texas; learned oriental languages at Yale; and served the Navy in the Pacific during World War II. McLendon tried Harvard Law School, but dropped out because he had always wanted to be a radio announcer. With the help of his father, who became his business manager, McLendon bought one-half interest in a dinky 100-watt radio station in Palestine, Texas. After he learned the trade, he sold his half back to the original owner and opened 1,000-watt KLIF in Oak Cliff to compete in the Dallas market in 1947.

The idea of this lanky loner was to give his listeners what they wanted to hear. He used all sorts of gimmicks to draw attention, such as a parrot that would squawk, "K-L-I-F" during station breaks. Most importantly, McLendon simulated major league baseball games. He rented an office in New York City and hired a man to listen to the games and teletype the information to Oak Cliff. There, McLendon recreated the action complete with artificial sound effects of baseball hits, crowd noise, the singing of the national anthem, and people selling hot dogs. Once in a while there would be gaps in the teletype, so he would fill in with made-up fights in the stands or dogs roaming the field of play. He once had a player foul off 109 straight pitches. He announced before and after games that it was a simulation, but people did not care. The basic facts were correct, and listeners enjoyed his humor and tried to catch his mistakes. "This is the Old Scotchman," he would say at the beginning of the program to identify himself, "eighty-three years old this very day."[43]

Baseball, America's pastime, was popular, but because of team restrictions broadcasted games were available only in the upper northwest quadrant of the nation. Stations having airtime to fill paid McLendon a fee to relay his simulations. He formed the Liberty Broadcasting System, basically a hookup, that had 40 stations in 1948 and 365 in 1952 as he provided the other three quadrants of the country with baseball. There were 60 to 90 million listeners. Writer Willie Morris, reflecting about his youth in Yazoo, Mississippi, wrote:

> The one o'clock whistle at the sawmill would send out its loud bellow, reverberating up the streets to the bend in the Yazoo River, hardly making a ripple in the heavy somnolence. But by two o'clock almost every radio in town was tuned in to the Old Scotchman. His rhetoric dominated the place. It hovered in the branches of the trees, bounced off the hills, and came out of the darkened stores; the merchants and the old men cocked their ears to him, and even from the big cars that sped by, their tires making lapping sounds in the softened highway, you could hear his voice, being carried past you out into the delta.[44]

Morris recognized the subterfuge of simulation by noting a difference with the shortwave broadcasts and paying attention to McLendon's disclosures. He pointed this out to his neighbors and then said, "I believe we all went back to the Scotchman not merely out of loyalty but because, in our great isolation, he touched our need for a great and unmitigated eloquence."[45]

Liberty Broadcasting System collapsed into bankruptcy in May 1952 due to complaints of minor league baseball, major league restraints, loss of his Western Union wire service, and a failed attempt to raise his fees. McLendon was left with just three stations. Television was starting to take hold as an important entertainment medium—people were watching as much as five hours per day in 1960—and radio had to accommodate or die. At KLIF the Old Scotchman turned to "Top 40 format" music programming. The idea had begun in Omaha, but McLendon improved it. "Top 40 format" meant employing disc jockeys for the repeated playing of popular music as determined by local and national record sales. McLendon refined this by targeting specific age groups, blending the personality of the deejays with the music, and shifting programs to harmonize with daily patterns of life, such as for drivers in rush hour traffic. Within several weeks, KLIF jumped from 2 percent to 45 percent of the Dallas market and the audience learned to leave their radios tuned all the time to the same station.

He still did some sports broadcasting, such as with the Dallas Cowboys, and bought small radio stations that would benefit from his format programming. McLendon tried without success some special arrangements, such as an all-"beautiful music" channel in Oakland, California; an all-news channel from a 500,000-watt "border blaster" station in Rosarita, Mexico, and another in Chicago; and an all-want-ads station in Los Angeles. Meanwhile, he wrote some five thousand brief radio editorials on all sorts of subjects. About President Lyndon B. Johnson he intoned, for example, "Mr. Johnson seems, as always, to speak in terms of high idealism. It is just that, as usual, we cannot understand what he is talking about. We is a simple country boy."[46] He made money on three B-grade movies filmed in Dallas and responded to a critic, "I resent your allegation that *The Killer Shrews* was one of the worst movies of all time. I made two other movies that were worse than that!"[47]

McLendon made an unsuccessful run as a conservative candidate for the United States Senate in 1964 and for governor in 1968. His aging father, meanwhile, wanted to disinvest and McClendon began selling off his stations in the 1960s. He gave up KLIF in 1972. He suffered esophageal cancer—a sad irony for a man known by his voice—and it eventually killed him in 1986. This maverick, innovative broadcaster, however, discovered the pathway that successful radio stations have followed into the present time.

Television

In 1946 David Sarnoff, the managerial genius who put together RCA and the NBC network in the 1920s, spoke to a meeting of the NBC affiliates in Atlantic City, New Jersey. He told them that he thought television would become a stronger medium than radio or newspapers and that they should seriously consider moving in that direction. The thought of transmitting pictures had been around as long as radio and a primitive broadcast had been used at the 1936 Berlin Olympics. By using a sequence of thirty still images per second converted into an electric signal, broadcasters could send an image by radio or cable to a receiving set that scanned the picture into a picture tube for viewing. Harold Hough, who had attended the meeting in New Jersey, returned home to Fort Worth and helped to persuade his boss, Amon Carter, to apply for a license.

East of town they found a dairy field on which to build a station. While they were walking the location, a Jersey bull spotted them in his field and began pawing the earth. Carter told Hough to ignore the bull, but Hough replied, "I'm getting out of here. I've got a wooden leg and the bull doesn't know who you are!" They reached the fence by a ten-yard margin. They constructed the station with three studios and seven cameras costing $26,800 each. The largest studio measured 82 feet long, 48 feet wide, and 28 feet high. This was the new theater stage for the electric age. As an experiment, WBAP-TV broadcasted the September 27, 1948, visit and speech of President Harry S. Truman in Fort Worth to the four hundred sets of the metropolitan region and then officially began telecasting two days later. This was the first television station in Texas and in the Southwest.[48]

There were twenty-four applications for Texas stations by 1948 when the FCC froze the licensing process in order to parcel out the limited number of Very High Frequency channels available at the time. Only WBAP-TV and five others under construction—three in Dallas–Fort Worth, two in San Antonio, and one in Houston—were allowed to continue over the next four years. When the FCC lifted the freeze in 1952, it allowed applications for the Ultra High Frequency band and that action adequately met the demand for new channels. One year later, the Bell Telephone System completed a series of microwave relay points and cables that allowed network broadcasting to span the state. The FCC made room for education and public channels; color television arrived in 1954; and by the end of the twentieth century, Texas had over one hundred stations scattered among forty-three cities.[49]

Like radio, television possessed an immediacy that made it a source for instant news. With a picture to see in addition to sound, television captured the magic of motion pictures, radio, and theater. Television was mesmerizing. Even today in places of crowded conversation, such as at parties or at a sports bar, if a television set is on, people's eyes frequently flit to the screen. In addition, it was a reliable electric nanny that calmed rambunctious children. Television became the major source of entertainment and recreation for Texas and the United States, and almost every household included a television set. Like the radio, it too became a part of the household furniture.

As with movies, some television programs followed Texas themes of cowboys and the West and even initiated a modern version with the international hit *Dallas* (1978–1991). For the most part, however, with the exception of local news, the programs originated outside the state and contributed to the homogenization of culture. National and global news became a part of network broadcasting. It was informative and good for a nation dependent upon an informed public. Programs could also be entertaining and inspiring like good theater, and for the most part, they were free to the viewer for the price of enduring the commercial advertising that paid for the programs. Television provided a great deal of recreation and it was fun.

As a form of recreation, however, television was relentless, constant, and numbing. It never wanted to be turned off to allow a viewer to analyze the content. There was no opportunity to argue or talk back. There was no discussion. In general, television has left Americans, including Texans, dumber, fatter, and lonelier. The ability to comprehend complex arguments has declined with the downward trend in library and newspaper usage, according to the National Endowment for the Arts. Since watching television was a passive activity, by and large, there was less time for exercise, and obesity is now recognized as a health problem for the nation. The term "couch potato" became a descriptive term of the television age in the early 1980s. And with all of the busy progeny of the electric revolution—television, computer games, cell phones, e-mail—there was less face-to-face interaction. More money is now being spent by Americans on video games than for movie tickets. People are electronically removed from one another.

According to Norbert Wiener, one of the early computer pioneers, when information filters through any medium something is lost. A simple e-mail, for example, may well convey important information, but lost in the conveyance is body language, scent, the tremor in the hand, and the presence of another human being. No wonder there appears to be a decline in the number of intimate friends. No wonder that poet T. S. Eliot said about television in 1963, "It is a medium of entertainment which permits millions of people to listen to the same joke at the same time, and yet remain lonesome."[50]

THE IMMORTALITY OF LIVE THEATER

For better and worse, Texas became a part of the television world, a part of the electric revolution that now seems nearing an end. In spite of the enormous increase in and variety of entertainment offered to modern Texans, there remained a curious persistence by scattered impecunious groups interested in live theater. Although most of the groups came and went, formed and reformed, they were as perennial and widespread as dandelions. As Don Williams of the Channing Players of Houston's Unitarian Universalist Church explained, "People would show up for a while, get together, get married, and never come back."[51]

A few groups endured and established a permanent place in their home cities. But the lasting interest in community theater is remarkable and the efforts of these groups served to salve the electronic numbness. The participants were stagestruck amateurs for the most part who wanted to express creativity or to protest by producing and acting in plays before an audience. "Acting satisfied a deep urge in me," said Irma Mangold of the Dallas Little Theater. "I never felt the deep down peace, the soul peace, like I did when I was on that stage."[52] Actors and playwrights found excitement and fulfillment in the effort, no matter how ephemeral.

In 1969, for example, the amateur El Teatro Chicano formed in East Austin to parody the police, raise political issues, and challenge history. It was a part of an active underground theater movement of the 1970s. The group presented, among others, the play *Papa Mexico* that featured Father Mexico and his five daughters—California, Colorado, New Mexico, Arizona, and Texas. Father Mexico befriended the first wetback, Stephen F. Austin, who then joined San Houston and Kit Carson to stab Father Mexico in the back and rape the daughters. The group explored bilingualism and cultural conflict, spoke in the mixed language of the audience, and eventually was absorbed into the Chicano movement at the University of Texas.[53]

Movies, sports, radio, and television, however, all brought about a general decline in Texas theater. As Mary Porter Vandervoort Jr., a theater enthusiast who remembered when Houston was a part of an intercontinental theater circuit, explained:

> In the early days, when the town was known as good box office and the touring companies brought their best efforts, all the good old names: Joe Jefferson, Maude Adams, Sothern, and Marlowe were household words to the children. In addition whole families went to the theatres of Chicago and New York whenever the cotton crop was good and the price of steers high. Our taste was formed by being exposed to the best the theatre had to offer and when that best was not so good, when the new stars refused to endure the rigors of the road, when rare productions arrived with mediocre actors, shoddy sets, and soiled costumes, we turned our backs on the theatre and would have no part of it.[54]

Vandervoort, however, conceded that "the love of the theatre dies hard" and she helped to establish and lead the Houston Little Theatre that was organized in 1925.[55]

This was a part of a "little theatre" movement of local amateur groups that began in the United States in 1915 in response to the crisis of the legitimate stage and swept through Texas towns after World War I. Between 1915 and 1930, two-thirds of the live theaters outside of New York City died—the numbers decreasing from 1,500 to 500—and continued to perish with the onset of the Great Depression.[56]

The federal effort to give jobs to the unemployed might have been expected to help actors in Texas, but it did not. Hallie Flanagan, who led the Federal Theatre Project for the Works Progress Administration (WPA), ran into resistance in the state. The Texas administrator of the WPA feared controversy and ordered, "Do old plays. . . . We don't want to get into the papers. Do the old plays that people will take for granted and not notice." The program in Texas presented some old one-act plays and marionette shows in schools and parks, a traveling tent show of comedy, and received little notice. The following year Texas lost its WPA theater budget. Flanagan concluded, "Texas was a hard nut to crack and we failed to crack it."[57]

A large part of the problem was that the federal government and the state poured money into the 1936 Centennial Celebration in Dallas. Architects reconstructed Fair Park in Art Deco style and included a new music hall that served the city for the following sixty-four years. Fort Worth jealously responded to Dallas' good fortune by building a 4,000-seat, open-air cafe amphitheater with a 40-foot bar. Called Casa Manana, it was designed and operated by New York impresario Billy Rose. He presented what amounted to a spectacular vaudeville show with chorus lines, Jumbo the elephant, Paul Whiteman's Band, and stripper Sally Rand dancing nude behind large balloons. She demonstrated, as she put it, that "the Rand is quicker than the eye." Fort Worth advertised, "Fort Worth for Entertainment; Dallas for Education" and attracted a million tourists to the show over four years time.[58] Although Casa Manana ended with World War II, it foreshadowed the popular dinner theaters of the 1970s.

Margo Jones and Theater-in-the-Round

In one of those nice twists of historical fate, the failed federal theater program provided opportunity for the most important person in Texas theatrical history, Margo Jones (1911–1955). Born in Livingston, Texas, she yearned from a young age to travel and to work in live theater. During her schooling at Texas State College for Women in Denton, at the Southwestern School for Theatre in Dallas, and at the Pasadena Playhouse Summer School in California, she was one of the few students who wanted to direct, not act. She possessed enormous energy; smoked Camel cigarettes constantly; drank Scotch; preferred to sit on the floor; danced wildly; collected turtle figurines; never learned to drive a car; read a new script every day while running her fingers through her short, dark hair; desired to direct untried plays; called everyone "Baby," or "Honey," or "Darling"; and talked almost exclusively about the theater.[59]

After an around-the-world voyage to visit drama sites as a part of a ménage à trois with a rich woman and a shared man, Jones took a job in 1935 with the Houston Recreation Department to start an amateur theater group with federal funds. Nine people showed up for the first meeting of the Houston Community Players in 1936; there were six hundred members in 1941. The community theater group attracted not only the stagestruck, but also the misfits, the poor, and the lonely. There were no dues, no rules, no officers—just Margo Jones running on nerves, enthusiasm, and faith.[60] "I believe that as a result of theatre life can be better," she said. "Both the people in the theatre and their audiences can live more lives through the theatre; their experience can be fuller and their understanding, too. . . . With more great theatre, great art, great music throughout the world, life is bound to be better."[61]

The Houston troupe produced sixty plays in five years, mainly at a small park building that had a stage. Jones experienced an epiphany along the way that determined her future. While in Washington, D.C., she saw a play produced in a hotel ballroom with seating around the entire stage. So-called "arena" staging was nothing new: it reached back, at least, to the ancient Greeks. But this play was inside, in an unusual setting, and in the blessed air-conditioning that sweltering Texans had learned to appreciate. On the train back to Houston, Jones startled the woman sitting next to her by leaping to her feet and exclaiming, "Why not?"[62]

At home she approached the Houston City Council to obtain special funding to rent a hotel ballroom. "Honey," she said to the assembled men, "I don't care what it costs, you got the money. Houston's got the money. Give me the grand ballroom in the Lamar Hotel. What the hell's a ballroom when you haven't got a damn ball? When you can have *theatah*, when you can have plays. Wonderful, magical plays. Honey, we got to have some magic, some wonder. Give me that ballroom!" They did, and Jones produced summertime plays at the Lamar Hotel and later at the Texas State and Rice hotels.[63]

World War II intervened, and Jones taught at the University of Texas, where she told her students to smoke in class. "Kids," she said, "you have to smoke because if you don't smoke, then I can't smoke, and if I don't smoke, I'll go crazy."[64] She dreamed about establishing a permanent arena theater, or theater-in-the-round as she called it, where stock professional actors would offer a series of plays in a season. It would be a theater where the actors would be fully employed, not amateurs taking the night off, and where fresh plays from contemporary writers could be presented. A theater-in-the-round would induce new approaches for staging and lighting, and it would bring the audience closer, intimately, into the action. There might be a network of such theaters across the nation. At the end of the war, she told herself that it was time to "put up or shut up" and chose Dallas for her experiment.[65]

With the aid of the Rockefeller Foundation, arts critic John Rosenfield of the *Dallas Morning News*, and interested wealthy people of the city, Theatre '47 opened in the Gulf Oil pavilion at Fair Park in June 1947. The idea was that actors and audience together would celebrate each New Year by changing the name of the theater—'48, '49, '50, and so on. The air-conditioned building, appropriately designed with the straight, long lines of International Style architecture—the only one in the Art Deco-styled park—had a small auditorium, lobby, and landscaped terrace. Gulf Oil permitted its use at no cost except for utilities.

Jones remodeled the building to accommodate an arena stage, 20 feet by 24 feet, surrounded on its four sides by 198 seats on carpeted, stepped planes. The first row was on the same level as the stage thus giving an illusion of being on the platform with the actors. Lighting, arranged by national set designer Jo Mielziner, was critical because the lights replaced the curtain used to open and close scenes. The lights, moreover, served to set mood and atmosphere, much as scenery on a traditional stage. The actors entered and exited the blackened stage by three aisles. An amplified sound system provided sound cues, post-show music, and music between scenes.[66]

Jones offered a diet of old and new plays to the Dallas audience, which she greeted before and after shows. She highlighted the work of playwrights whom she thought needed encouragement and nurturing, and 70 percent of the plays she produced were new scripts. Tad Adoue, a reader for Jones, for example, sent her a play from Malibu, California, written by Jerome Lawrence and Robert E. Lee. The script had been rejected by at least eight Broadway producers and had moldered in their files for five years. Adoue warned her that it would take a lot of courage to produce this play in Dallas, but she did it anyway. The play was about the Scopes trial of 1925 in Dayton, Tennessee, and it possessed a timeless lesson about demagoguery in American life. It premiered at Theatre '55 and went on to a three-year run in New York City. Author Robert Lee commented, "Margo saw in *Inherit the Wind* the conflict and drama which not one other person in American theater saw . . . she dared. As a result of this experiment in Texas, Jerry and I realized that theater must be allowed to escape from the little bird cage in mid-town Manhattan."[67]

In six months Margo Jones was dead. She had been drinking heavily and was found semiconscious in her apartment, which had just been cleaned with carbon tetrachloride. Apparently, the fumes caused a toxic reaction with the alcohol in her system and she died of kidney failure after ten days in the hospital. Living on the edge had extracted its price.

Dallas Theater and Opera

The theater Jones had founded stumbled on until 1959, but Dallas theater efforts continued with the building of the Dallas Theater Center. In 1954–1955 old-time little theater participants, urged on by John Rosenfield, developed the idea of establishing a repertory school where drama majors could make a transition to professional theater work. When she heard about it, Margo Jones had said, "Glory be to Betsy! I second the motion. Let's get started." Paul Baker from the Baylor University drama department agreed to become the director; Sylvan T. Baer donated a wooded site on Turtle Creek; Dallas philanthropists provided the money; and Frank Lloyd Wright designed the facility. "I will build a building that Paul Baker can work in and grow in, and that those who follow him can work in and grow in," said Wright.[68]

Wright and Baker, however, squabbled over design, and with Baer, who tried to take his land back. But, in the end, Wright provided a work of art typical of his organic architecture—his only public building in Texas. The $1 million white stone theater jutted out from a cliff with strong, bare, straight lines and a turret. There was parking below the theater with the main entrance in the back so that people could view the building as they entered. It had a center stage with a small revolving circular stage on one side. Lights could be hung from anywhere in the auditorium, and scenery could be lowered from an overhead grid. The repertory company had a separate entrance and a terrace isolated from the public. It was named for Kalita Humphreys, a deceased actress, whose mother gave $40,000 for the 440 seats needed to complete the theater for its opening in 1959. The theater, however, did not function as well as it looked, and in 1984 other architects gutted the interior to provide a greater rake in the flooring, an expanded stage, and more storage for props and sets.[69] The Dallas Theater Center, nonetheless, endured as a place of theatrical recreation for the city.

In this same ferment of Theatre '47 and the Theater Center, opera became a regular feature in Dallas. In 1956 the Dallas Symphony (1945), following the lead of San Antonio, moved to extend the employment of its musicians by adding a short opera season. Because the New York Metropolitan Opera had visited the town regularly since 1939 there was a ready audience, and so the symphony hired impresario Lawrence V. Kelly (1927–1974) from Chicago to promote opera in Dallas. "There isn't an art institution in this country which was not taken on in its first generation by some nut, someone who just lived, breathed, and slept it," said Kelly. The young, boyish, enthusiastic Kelly was the nut for Dallas. And he also knew the rising and still unappreciated Italian diva, Maria Callas.[70]

She sang for the first time in America at the Dallas Opera opening in 1957. The symphony and the opera used the 1925 State Fair Music Hall—seedy and cavernous, with shabby dressing rooms, a shallow inadequate stage with no trap doors, and narrow wings. Later, when Joan Sutherland performed there, she said the Music Hall "resembled a made-over aeroplane hanger."[71] With a capacity for four thousand, twice that of European opera houses, the Music Hall was one-third empty for the opening Callas performance. It looked bad. Already, Fair Park had a rough reputation, and Kelly, who thought an opera house should have supportive amenities, complained, "Many people in the community feel that area is dangerous to go to at night, and when they arrive, there is absolutely no pleasure, nothing except the performance itself."[72] He sounded like Clint Murchison, who said much the same about the Cotton Bowl.

In 1971 the city remodeled the Music Hall to enlarge the lobby and orchestra pit, refurbish the dressing rooms, and add a restaurant. The stage still lacked improvement and, of course, nothing could be done about the location. The attitude of the city, however, reflected that of powerful Mayor Robert L. Thornton, who told a group of bankers in 1957, "I don't give a damn about singing or dancing, but Dallas needs this, so you get behind it." It was not art for the sake of art, but art for the sake of business. Expensive opera in Dallas with sets and costumes made in Italy thus persisted, somewhat to the amazement of outsiders. Elsa Maxwell, an international socialite from New York and California, attended the first four seasons of opera in Dallas and, with a typical outsider's ignorance of Texas, commented in 1960, "It's really incredible—incredible—the greatest opera in the world in a little town like Dallas."[73]

In 1989 the city finished the $100 million Meyerson Symphony Center, a joint public-private venture designed by I. M. Pei, for the sixty-acre downtown arts district. It had horseshoe-shaped seating for two thousand people, but it cost twice what was expected, burdened the orchestra with debt, and projected questionable acoustical quality. City Councilman Craig McDaniel, however, justified it all in 1994. "These cultural institutions, this Arts District, this mosaic of cultural events are not worth further investment for arts' sake," he said. "They were worth further investment because they are critical to the success of Dallas and particularly to the success of downtown Dallas. A healthy central business district, which includes the Arts District will mean . . . a better off city."[74]

This consistent bottom-line, business approach of Dallas leaders to art irritated long-term commentator and Dallas writer A. C. Greene who observed, "Dallas salutes the person who can buy a piece of art, not the person who can create one." He groused about a Dallas Theater Center brochure that praised the facility as a "Blue Chip investment in Dallas" without a word about the theater's role in the "spiritual release and catharsis for the playgoer."[75] Greene was probably too harsh about the business language, but he touched a nerve. The value of recreation can be lost in a hard-driving city like Dallas where worth is measured only in terms of money.

The Houston Renaissance

Houston, the state's largest city, was also a business-oriented city, but more open and less self-concerned than Dallas. With a booming post–World War II economy fueled by the Houston Ship Channel and the petrochemical industry, wealth and people flowed into the city as it sprawled over the flat coastal countryside. This was the basis for a renaissance that saw Houston expand in all sorts of experimental directions: the Manned Spacecraft Center (1962), Astrodome (1965), Philip Johnson's architecture (1970s), Texas Medical Center (1960s–1970s), Rothko Chapel (1971), de Menil art gallery (1987), and the arts in general. It was a twenty-year burst of urban energy in the 1960s and 1970s with a momentum that carried into the depressed 1980s. The city had experienced the little theatre movement after World War I and the success of Margo Jones' community theater during the Great Depression. These provided context for the success of the Alley Theatre and dozens of other organizations, such as Theatre Incorporated and the Playhouse, during the city's renaissance.

NINA VANCE AND THE ALLEY THEATRE

Nina Vance (1914–1980), born in Yoakum, Texas, and educated in theater at Texas Christian University, Columbia University, and the University of Southern California, moved to Houston as a high school drama and speech teacher in 1939. She joined the Houston Community Players and Margo Jones assigned her to sell tickets and raise money. Vance explained that she was new in town, knew but few people, and did not know how to do it. Jones replied, "Baby, you take the phone book and you start with A and you go to Z." Vance later said it was the best lesson she had ever received for the promotion of theater.[76]

After Jones left Houston, Vance followed her mentor's lead and directed plays in the round with the Players Guild (1945–1947) at the Rice and Lamar hotels. The Players Guild fell apart for financial reasons, but her friends Vivien and Bob Altfield offered Vivien's dance studio for arena staging. Vivien had met Nina while acting for Margo Jones. According to legend, Vance had $2.14 in her purse at the time and bought 214 penny postcards to send to people who might be interested in founding a new community theater. One hundred people responded and in 1947–1948, the Altfields opened their studio for night performances. It was one large room with bleacher seating for eighty-five people, a sycamore tree that grew through the building, a leaky toilet located over the stage that once flushed through the ceiling during a performance, and an entrance located down a long alley-like corridor. Enthusiasm abounded and within one year there were five hundred members paying dues of ten cents each. After one season, the fire marshal made them move their so-called Alley Theatre.[77]

An S.O.S. went out to the members to bring a "buck and a brick," and "like a flock of magpies bearing morsels of brick, board, and baling wire," the membership moved their theater to a converted fan factory that became home for twenty years.[78] Carle Benson, an actor, recalled the volunteers constructing a 200-seat arena theater: "Everyone was devoting their time to it. People who didn't have a job spent eighteen hours a day there and people who did have a job would come in after work and stay until twelve or one o'clock."[79] The director, Nina Vance—large, calm, attractive, blue-eyed, dynamic, and dominant—shared Margo Jones' dream of eventually establishing a professional repertory theater. Therefore, in 1954, despite the hurt feelings of the amateurs, including the Altfields, Vance decided to hire professional actors.

She went on to present new plays and premieres, and the Alley became a nationally acclaimed nonprofit residential theater. Vance received supportive Ford Foundation grants in 1959 and 1960, and in 1962 Ford offered a construction matching grant of $2.1 million. Houston Endowment, a local foundation, donated land in the downtown area for a site and, after a financial scramble, the new Alley Theatre opened in 1968. Designed by Ulrich Franzen of New York, the building presented the outward appearance of a fortress with turrets and open-air terraces. Inside it contained an 800-seat auditorium with a stage thrust into the fan-shaped seating arrangement and, in the basement, a 300-seat arena theater reminiscent of the former theater. It won an honor award from the American Institute of Architects. The Alley, along with the Dallas Theater Center, ruled as the leader of avant-garde theater in the state and was renamed the Nina Vance Alley Theatre after her death from cancer in 1980.

The Alley became a part of an arts complex that included Jones Hall (1966), which was the venue for the Houston Symphony (1913), and the Houston Grand Opera (1955). Competition for seat space in Jones Hall from the Houston Ballet (1955) and the Society for the Performing Arts (1975) that booked touring shows brought about the construction of the Wortham Center in 1987. It had a troubled birth due to unrealistic cost estimates and the local economic downturn, but emerged with two side-by-side theaters, one with 2,225 seats, the other with 1,102. The Wortham Center was financed completely with donated money and turned over to the city.

The Wortham Foundation—established by Gus S. Wortham (1891–1976), the founder of American General Corporation, who often made up the deficits of the symphony—provided a major part of the funding. Under the direction of Ben Stevenson, a former dancer with the English Royal Ballet, the Houston Ballet developed a crisp English deportment that garnered invitations to perform in Europe, Canada, China, and across the United States. Matching the success of the ballet, the Houston Grand Opera, led by its open-minded enthusiastic former business manager, David Gockley, became famous for its premier operas—particularly *Nixon in China* (1987), which won both an Emmy and a Grammy award.

The Houston renaissance, thus, produced performances of world-class quality in permanent award-winning venues. This was the high point of Texas' accomplishment in the arts. It was the result of talent, enthusiasm, dedication, recognition, and philanthropy combining at the right time in the same place to produce places of human entertainment and recreation at the most sophisticated level.

Images of Recreation

Considering the many photographs that people take of vacations, sporting events, and other recreational outings, pictures about recreational history should be abundant, but they are not. For the most part, such pictures lie moldering in shoeboxes, closets, basements, attics, and home digital archives. Most are for family pleasure and are rarely shared with the public. In the same manner, business photographs for company use remain in the business records and do not become a part of the public domain. Many are lost, destroyed by fire or natural disaster, and after a death or business failure, the pictures end up in a dump. Classical scholars estimate that less than 10 percent of the documents of ancient Greece survived into the present time. After searching Texas archives, I would estimate, likewise, that less than 10 percent of the recreational photographs have survived. At least, they have not been made available in a public repository, probably because people thought them too personal or unimportant.

In Texas, nonetheless, a variety of libraries maintain photographs. Some of them, such as the Dallas Public Library and the Amarillo Public Library, have placed images online. The Austin Public Library, Houston Public Library, Institute of Texan Cultures, Daughters of the American Revolution Library, San Antonio Public Library, Lyndon Baines Johnson Presidential Library, and University of Texas at Arlington offer guide books or copies of pictures arranged in categories. All of them will provide prints for publication, but most libraries use private shops for reproduction. Understandably, they charge fees for this service—an average of $22 per picture. This supports the Chinese proverb that one picture is worth more than a thousand words. Three pages, or a thousand words, in a recent hardback book costs a purchaser only thirty cents. But the price tag is not the point; the proverb refers to what can be learned from an image.

There are frustrating gaps of photographic information in Texas—such as about the Save Our Springs movement—that perhaps could be filled by pictures in someone's attic or in a file at a newspaper. Newspapers, however, are notorious for losing photographs. The University of Texas at Arlington, smartly, arranged to inherit the photographs of the *Fort Worth Star-Telegram*, and the Houston Public Library acquired the collection of the defunct *Houston Press* newspaper. These and the lifetime collections of professional photographers are invaluable. It seems, however, that for most places the libraries take in only the photographs left on their doorstep. It would be useful for the study of history if archivists would actively and consciously collect pictures of current events of significance just as they promote contemporary oral histories. Much can be learned from a photograph.

THE LICIT AND THE ILLICIT

Tascosa, located at an easy cattle crossing of the Canadian River in 1878, became a trading and recreation town for the large ranches of the Texas Panhandle. When the nearby cowboys received time off, they galloped to local saloons such as the Equity Bar (photo 1a), built of adobe by Jack Ryan and run by bartender Jack Cooper in the early twentieth century. The cowboys wore the typical broad-brimmed hats, vests, kerchiefs, chaps, and high-heeled boots (photo 1b). Inside the building, the small bar featured a high counter to lean upon and a foot rail to give the cowboys a chance to rest their commonly sore backs (photo 1c). They carried no guns in Tascosa, probably because Sheriff Cape Willingham banned firearms within the city limits in 1880. Shortly afterward, Fred Leigh, foreman of the nearby LS Ranch, rode into town, found the sheriff on the street, challenged the regulation, and began to fumble for his six-gun. Willingham calmly raised a sawed-off, double-barreled shotgun and blew Leigh out of the saddle. Leigh thus became the second man buried in Tascosa's boot hill, and the law remained.

PHOTO 1A

PHOTO IB

PHOTO IC

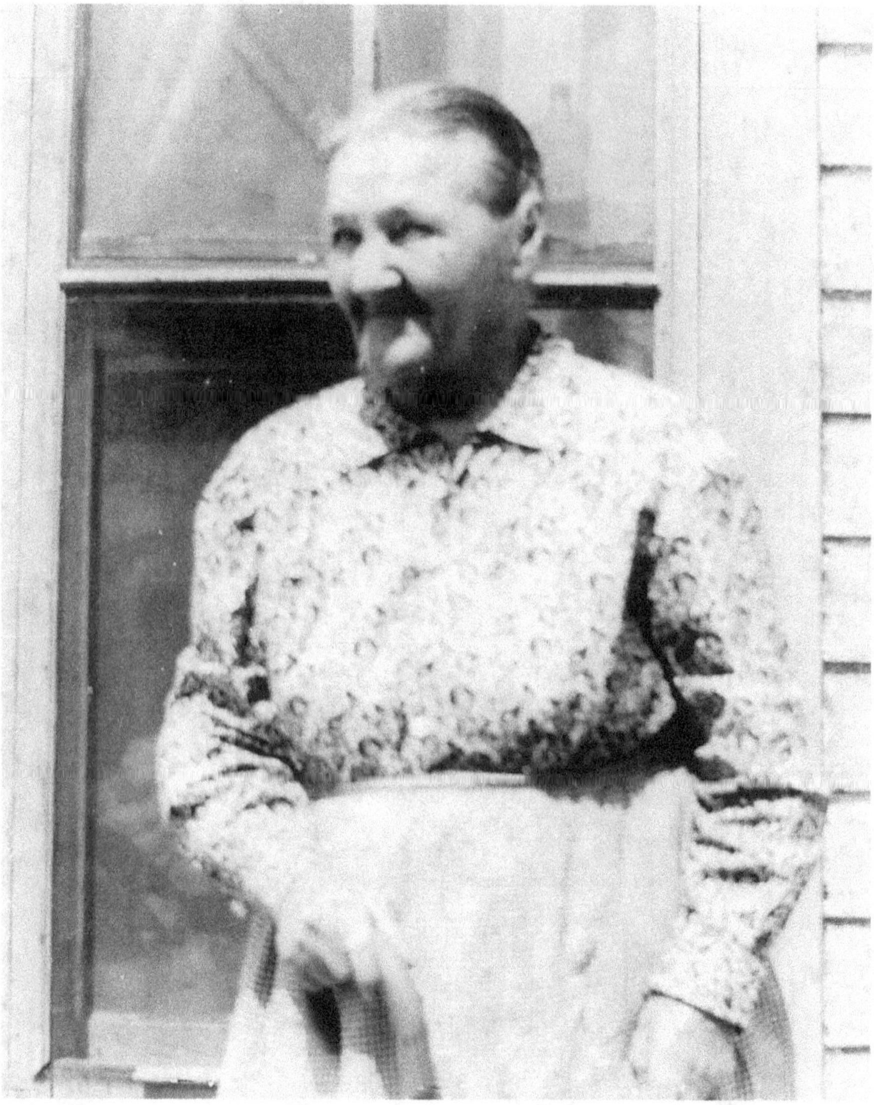

PHOTO 2

After a rambunctious decade, the railroad bypassed the town and people gradually moved elsewhere. Living on alone amidst the crumbling adobe buildings, Frenchy McCormick (1852–1941), a former dance hall girl, nevertheless remained loyal to Tascosa and to her husband who died there in 1912. Shown here in old age, (photo 2) she lived until 1941 and friends buried her next to her beloved "Mack" on a bluff overlooking Cal Farley's Boys Ranch, which is now located at the site (photo 3). Frenchy is a symbol of enduring love and loyalty in an unforgiving frontier.

(FRENCHY)
ELIZABETH McCORMICK
AUGUST 11, 1852
JANUARY 12, 1941
ERECTED BY EX-BOYS RANCHERS
AND INTERESTED FRIENDS.
1965
M. McCORMICK
FEB. 17, 1846
OCT. 7, 1912

PHOTO 3

Judge Roy Bean, proudly riding his black horse in front of his JERSEY 'LILLY' SALOON AND COURT HOUSE.

PHOTO 4

While serving a walk-in trade, saloons often provided the largest and most comfortable meeting places in town. They served multiple purposes—legal, business, and entertainment—as demonstrated by Judge Roy Bean (1825–1903). A notorious Texas character, he dispensed alcohol along with his own brand of eccentric justice at his famous Jersey Lilly Saloon and Court House in Langtry, Texas, near the Pecos River and the Rio Grande. The judge, shown here on horseback, sold refreshments to Southern Pacific train travelers and acted as the local justice of the peace in the 1880s (photo 4). There was no limit to guns and drinking at his saloon as can be seen with the man on the porch holding a rifle in one hand and a whiskey bottle in the other. The saloon possessed a billiard table for entertainment and since it was near the railroad, it could also sell the beer and ice that came by rail delivery.

Unlike whiskey, beer does not travel well, and Bean's beer probably was not very good. Heat, light, movement, and bacteria are problems; jostled beer loses carbonation and becomes flat. Even today, aficionados state that beer is at its best when fresh brewed. In the nineteenth century, therefore, beer was mainly made and consumed locally. In this photograph of the Degen Brewery (photo 5) in downtown San Antonio in the 1890s, the large wooden vat with a kettle inside was used to prepare the "wort," a heated combination of barley malt, water, and hops. The strange looking wooden overshoes were probably used to trample and crack the grain in order to facilitate the conversion of the cereal starch into sugars. At "blood warm temperature," the wort

PHOTO 5

then went into the large barrels, twice the size of modern kegs, in the foreground of the picture, and yeast was added. Fermentation and carbonation occurred as the yeast converted the sugars into alcohol. The man in the middle holds a hydrometer, "the brewer's compass," that can measure the ratio of sugar to alcohol and thus track the brewing process. The brewery appears to be located in a basement, which would help cool and age the product. The Degen Brewery was noted as the gathering place of the town "Bohemians" (Czechs), and it served the same function as microbreweries today where beer is created and consumed on the premises.

PHOTO 6

PHOTO 7

PHOTO 8

In contrast to the frontier saloons of Tascosa and Langtry, the White Elephant Bar of San Antonio in the 1880s was an elegant, urban drinking place (photo 6). It retained the traditional high counter and foot rail, but it also had a tobacco case, well-placed spittoons, a rack of wine bottles, electric lights, a belt-driven ceiling fan, a cooler for beer, tile floor, and a glittering back bar of mirrors and bottles. "White Elephant" was a common saloon name that could be found in Denison, San Antonio, Fort Worth, El Paso, Wichita Falls, and Fredericksburg. "Black Elephant" bars in San Antonio, Austin, and Fort Worth, according to historian Richard Selcer in *Legendary Watering Holes* (2004), catered to African-Americans. This one could be found at the corner of Flores and Nueva streets in San Antonio near the red-light district in the 1870s (photo 7). A white policeman seems to be standing in front, and a woman in a long skirt and broad-brimmed hat walks on the sidewalk.

For the most part, the bars were a male preserve for drinking, talking, pool playing, and gambling. This border saloon in Pecos, Texas, from the 1880s had a stove for warmth, coal oil lamps, several gambling tables, and a waiter to serve drinks (photo 8). According to information from the Western History Collection at the University of Oklahoma, the man seated at the table wearing a white hat was Jim Miller, who was later lynched in Ada, Oklahoma. He appears to be playing a gambling game like faro with chips placed on a mat. No guns are visible, and most of the men are spectators.

The gender of the customers had not changed in this picture of a saloon in La Grange, Texas, taken between 1910 and 1915 (photo 9). The bar, however, had acquired electric lighting for these men playing cards, drinking beer, and smoking cigars. The men, all Caucasian, wore coats, vests, high collars, and sported mustaches or beards. The person wearing the derby hat and boots, second from the right, was a traveling salesman according to the photograph data.

PHOTO 9

PHOTO 10

Women, generally, were unwelcome in the saloons of the nineteenth and early twentieth century. Jack Harris of San Antonio, however, broke this barrier and pointed to the future. If you checked into the Plaza Hotel on the north side of Main Plaza in the early 1880s, walked onto the balcony, and looked eastward up Commerce Street, you could see a sign for Harris' Vaudeville Theatre and Saloon (photo 10). Harris established a combination bar, gambling hall, and variety theater. He offered entertainment with a series of stage acts, and he hired women to hustle drinks and dance on the stage in red stockings. Such places across the nation developed both true vaudeville, which provided acts suitable for families, as well as blue vaudeville, which invented "strip" tease, or "illegitimate" theater. This particular establishment became notorious in 1882–1884 and closed after gunman Ben Thompson killed Harris and then later died in a shootout on the second floor overlooking the stage.

Prostitutes lingered in the shadows of saloons, but Billie Keilman, the owner of the Beauty tavern in the heart of San Antonio's red-light district, offered service as an advisor (photo 11). He published a guide to the area whorehouses complete with prices in 1912. As a result of two world wars and a purity crusade, however, the red-light districts closed and the bawdy houses disappeared. Only a few relics and curiosities remain in the state, such as Mother Harvey's in Galveston (photo 12) and Hattie's of San Angelo (photo 13). Hattie's, the two-story building on the left end of the historic block, has been restored as the only brothel museum in Texas. According to legend, a tunnel connected the bagnio to the old bank, on the far right with the date of 1884, so that ranchers could indulge in discreet hanky-panky.

PHOTO 11

PHOTO 12

PHOTO 13

PHOTO 14

Legal gaming stopped in 1905 and drinking halted in 1919. Law officers righteously destroyed gambling equipment, like these slot machines in San Antonio (photo 14),

PHOTO 15

and tried to find the hidden stills of the Trinity River bottoms, where everyone seemed to have a relative in the whiskey business (photo 15).

PHOTO 16

Prohibition then ended in 1933 while gambling remained illegal. Throughout this turbulent time, nightclubs, such as the famous Balinese Room of Galveston, subverted the laws. The Balinese Room offered gambling and drinking at the end of a long pier that extended into the Gulf of Mexico (photo 16). It was supposedly a private club and successfully frustrated the raids of the Texas Rangers until 1957. It took the Rangers three minutes to walk the length of the pier, but after a warning buzzer from the front desk at the seawall, the trained staff needed only thirty seconds to clear out the poker chips and dice tables.

The end of Prohibition in 1933 and the permission to sell liquor by the drink in 1970 slaked the public's desire to drink and some of the old-time places revived. Scholz Garten (or Garden) in Austin (photo 17) and Gruene Hall in Gruene (photo 18) carried on the tradition of German family drinking halls while the *Garten Verein* of Galveston, which had been damaged by storms and neglect, was restored as a public facility in 1923. The interior of Gruene Hall resembles an old-time western saloon with a high counter and foot rail (photo 19); Scholz Garten still has inviting tables and benches under the elm trees in back; the *Garten Verein* with its ornate wooden trim is a reminder of Galveston's Victorian age (photo 20).

PHOTO 17

PHOTO 18

PHOTO 19

PHOTO 20

PHOTO 21

Other entertainment halls emerged later such as the famous Armadillo World Headquarters, which, during its brief lifetime, provided a venue for blending contemporary and country music in Austin (photo 21). Older people sat on the folding chairs while younger fans sat on a floor of pieced-together carpet. The Armadillo, a phenomenon of the 1960s stimulated by youthful spirits, Lone Star Beer, marijuana, and innovative musicians, led to Austin's emergence as a music capital.

PHOTO 22

Gambling urges were eased a bit in Texas by lotteries and horse racing, but prostitution remained strictly prohibited. In spite of suppression, prostitutes nonetheless continued to proposition men in bars and on the street. In one surprising recent instance, three whores attracted an international clientele to a nondescript strip mall in Odessa. They worked in a massage parlor located in a small store to the right of the tattoo sign in the photograph (photo 22). It was much more discreet and quite unlike Hattie's of San Angelo. Nonetheless, bordellos of sorts still exist and the licit and illicit dance of drinking, gambling, and carousing, a historic aspect of human existence, continues into the present. Texans still like to gamble and gambol, but in a somewhat subdued manner.

PARKS AND OTHER PUBLIC PLACES

Following their instructions, Spanish town builders established the first Texas city parks. San Antonio, a leading city throughout Texas history, is a prime example with its central squares—Main, Military, and Alamo plazas. The large, open areas served as spaces for commerce, ceremony, relaxation, and battle. The founders built San Fernando Church on the west side of Main Plaza and it became a cathedral in 1873 (photo 23). Urbanization eventually reduced its plaza to a small park across the street from the front doors.

PHOTO 23

PHOTO 24

In the second half of the nineteenth century, nearby Military Plaza became noted as a farmer's market by daytime and for chili stands by night. In the background of the vegetable tables picture can be seen the Fashion Theatre, established by Billy Simms to carry on the tradition of Jack Harris after the demise of his partner's Vaudeville Theatre (photo 24). Women's skirts still reached the ground of this unpaved plaza.

PHOTO 25

When San Antonio placed a new city hall in the center of the plaza in 1891, the food stands moved briefly to Alamo Plaza before people began to worry about sanitation and this city tradition halted (photo 25). But for a half-century the markets and stands of the plazas measured the pulse beat of the city where all peoples ate together at the same long tables under the lamplight of tin lanterns.

PHOTO 26

Alamo Plaza may well have met the same fragmenting fate as the others. The Catholic Church sold part of their property to Honore Grenet, who built a wholesale grocery with wooden turrets and fake guns on top of the old compound walls where much of the fighting had taken place in the Battle of the Alamo. He leased the Alamo Church itself as a warehouse. Charles Hugo and Gustav Schmeltzer, whose names can be seen in this photograph of Alamo Plaza, purchased the business in 1880 (photo 26). Two decades later wealthy, educated rancher Clara Driscoll purchased the warehouse and held it for historic restoration after a hotel threatened demolition and conversion into a private park. This photo shows Driscoll in 1931 examining the new plans to expand the plaza in time for the 1936 Centennial celebration (photo 27). The Alamo and the surrounding grounds thus became a shrine for modern Texans (photo 28).

The 1880 picture of Alamo Plaza (photo 26) also contains another interesting point. In the lower left corner ladies are shown boarding a one-mule streetcar. The cars were not very fast, as balky as their motive power, but helpful in the summer heat when women wore skirts to the ground. Among other destinations, the mule

PHOTO 27

PHOTO 28

PHOTO 29

cars provided a cheap ride to San Pedro Park. The Spanish designated the park as public land in 1718 to protect San Pedro Springs, the source of San Antonio drinking water. This act makes San Pedro Park the second oldest municipal park in the nation, following Boston Commons. The spring eventually went dry as urban wells tapped

PHOTO 30

the underlying aquifer. The park languished, but the city restored it in 2000. These photos (photos 29, 30) show a party of youngsters at the park lake in the 1890s, and the restoration more than a century later that placed a shallow water swimming pool at about the same place near the headwaters of the spring.

PHOTO 31

Other municipal parks appeared as cities expanded, such as Old City Park in Dallas, Stewart Beach in Galveston, and Zilker Park in Austin. Old City Park, the first in the city, began as a land donation in 1876 and became a display area for local historic buildings in the late 1960s after freeways reconfigured the land use

PHOTO 32

of the area (photo 31). Stewart Beach developed when Galveston became a tourist destination in the first half of the twentieth century. As part of the price of tourism, it required the periodic cleaning of the sand, lifeguards, trashcans, and restrooms (photo 32).

PHOTO 33

Zilker Park began after World War I and its Barton Springs Pool became a vociferous point of environmental protection in the 1990s that affected the politics and growth pattern of the capital city. These photos show the changes and uses of the springs—a place for a turn-of-the-century outing (photo 33), a place of joyous holiday, and a place for the contemplative exercise of swimming. By 1939 the city had built a pool and it was crowded on this warm April day (photo 34). Men had shed the top part of their swimming costumes by this time, but still wore belts. The women wore bathing caps and tank suits with a small skirt. It was not nearly so crowded on this workday in 2007 with only two solitary lap swimmers and a lifeguard (photo 35). The trees were much larger. People remembered the park with affection and roused to protect it when urban developers threatened the springs with destruction.

PHOTO 34

PHOTO 35

PHOTO 36

The municipal parks initially became the location for the first Texas zoos, such as this early twentieth-century display of wild cats lined up in small cages at San Pedro Park in San Antonio (photo 36). This was typical of the early zoos. The Alamo City, however, constructed in 1928 the first Texas zoo to apply the ideas of Carl Hagenbeck of Germany in an old rock quarry at Brackenridge Park. Hagenbeck recommended exchanging cages and bars for moats and large open natural areas. Although the lions have retreated from the heat of the sun in this recent photograph from the San Antonio Zoo, the moat structure, protecting both animals and spectators, can be seen (photo 37). Hagenbeck tested the jumping ability of the large cats before prescribing the dimensions of moats. At the Houston Zoo, the moat was filled with water to give the Siberian tiger a place to swim (photo 38). It makes you wonder what would happen if a child fell into the water, but it does bring animal and viewer into close, unobstructed proximity. At the innovative Gladys Porter Zoo in Brownsville, built in the late 1960s, people and animals were separated not only by moats and water but also by elevated walkways (photo 39).

PHOTO 37

PHOTO 38

PHOTO 39

PHOTO 40

Fort Worth, which maintains the most visitor-friendly zoo in the state, also has the most experience—almost a century. The citizens had a long love affair with the elephant Queen Tut (1920–1964), who once saved a keeper from being trampled and who would curtsy to visitors (photo 40). Seemingly, a zoo is not considered a real zoological park until it possesses an elephant, even though pachyderms are expensive and responsible for the majority of zoo deaths per year. Fort Worth was also noted for the "hiss heard 'round the world" when Pete the Python escaped for a month in 1954. There was widespread panic in the city until Al the Chimp in the monkey section raised an alarm in the early morning that led to a recapture of the snake (photos 41, 42). Although zoos have been targets of animal rights activists, there has been no serious attempt to close them in Texas. Zoos offer too many educational opportunities and hold too many fond memories of family excursions.

PHOTO 41

PHOTO 42

PHOTO 43

While the cities and towns set aside public land, Texas developed a system of state parks, especially aided by federal grants of money and the labor of unemployed workers during the Great Depression. The Civilian Conservation Corps (CCC) constructed roads, paths, and buildings in the state parks, including the Pueblo-style Indian Lodge in the Davis Mountains (photo 43). Originally gold in color, it was put together with great difficulty regarding design and materials. At the time it was considered a "white elephant," and ironically, now it is painted white. It stands in stark contrast to the colors of the surrounding fields and mountains.

PHOTO 44

The CCC also worked at Palo Duro Canyon (photo 44), which became the brightest gem of the state park system. The Lighthouse, a rock formation symbolic of the park, can be reached only by a three-mile hike (photo 45). It can be seen with the aid of a telescope from the rim of the canyon.

PHOTO 45

PHOTO 46

PHOTO 47

PHOTO 48

For work on this small version of the Grand Canyon of Arizona, the CCC erected on the rim their largest encampment in the nation (photo 46). Paid $30 per month, equipped with World War I tents and clothing, and directed by U.S. Army reserve officers, the racially segregated young men built roads, trails, and campsites with pick-axes, shovels, wheelbarrows, and dynamite. This military direction can be seen in the uniforms and aligned tents of the men in the photograph. In a sense, it was good training for World War II. In most places, the CCC tried to put up structures that used local materials and blended in with the countryside such as the El Coronado Lodge, which now serves as an interpretive center (photo 47). Starting in 1966, the people of Canyon and Amarillo who had promoted Palo Duro development also began to present the summertime musical *Texas* from an amphitheater in the canyon. Using local talent, it is now the longest running, popular pageant in the state (photo 48).

PHOTO 49

PHOTO 50

PHOTO 51

The CCC also worked at Big Bend National Park, located in the remote curve of the Rio Grande of West Texas (photo 49). There was a long struggle to acquire the necessary free land for the park as required by the federal government, but Amon Carter of Fort Worth, who directed the fund-raising, was able to present a deed for over 700,000 acres to President Franklin D. Roosevelt in 1944 (photo 50). The park came to prominence in 1966 when the First Lady, Mrs. Lyndon B. Johnson, toured the area and floated in a raft down the river. In this picture, Lady Bird Johnson rides in front while Department of Interior Secretary Stewart Udall in the white shirt paddles behind her (photo 51).

PHOTO 52

Mrs. Johnson also presided over the dedication of the Padre Island National Seashore in 1968 from a platform made of driftwood. Praising the dazzling white sand and the brilliant dome of the sky, she formally acclaimed the permanent preservation of the island for the enjoyment of future generations (photos 52, 53). Then, while there, as might any visiting tourist, she responded to the invitation of the shore, took off her shoes, and waded into the soothing surf (photo 54).

PHOTO 53

PHOTO 54

THE GREAT STADIUMS

The prototype of all stadiums in human history is the Colosseum of ancient Rome. Although it was probably the Etruscans, perhaps the Greeks, who first built arenas for large numbers of people to view sports, it was the Romans who popularized mass entertainment. In order to provide for large numbers of people to witness an event, a stadium was necessary, and the Colosseum became the model for two millennia. Located in the heart of the capital, it seated forty-five thousand fans in tiers so they could easily see the recessed, oval field of action. It served multiple purposes, possessed a primitive air-conditioning system, and was easy to enter and exit. After the fall of Rome, the Colosseum endured through the ages as a ruin that was visited by countless travelers, particularly those of the nineteenth and twentieth century who toured Rome as a part of their education. In this picture of the Colosseum, the T-shaped walkway represents a part of the wooden floor that covered the cages and cells below (photo 55). The rows of foundation stone for the slanting tiers of seats, the oval shape, and the multiple exits can be readily observed.

Football spread from the eastern colleges to Texas in the late nineteenth century and became increasingly popular in the following decades. This photo from Mitchell County in central West Texas in the 1920s indicates the state of play at the time

PHOTO 55

PHOTO 56

(photo 56). The players had uniforms, cleats, helmets without face guards, shoulder pads, and thigh pads. Although some players at the time disdained helmets and shoulder pads, the tackler in the middle seems to have had his knocked off during the play. The playing field was simply a dirt field with chalk marks and the goalpost was made of poles lashed together. The fans, including a woman at the far right, lined the end zone with their cars and a few climbed to the top of a telephone pole for a better view.

In 1924 the University of Texas played Texas A&M for the first time in their new Memorial Stadium with temporary stands in the end zones and the capitol looming in the background (photo 57). Although an oval track surrounded the playing field, the stands did not curve to provide better visibility for those sitting at the corners. Texas won the game 7–0.

PHOTO 57

PHOTO 58

The "Red River Shootout" between Texas and Oklahoma began to be played regularly in Dallas in 1929 and the following year the city began construction of a large stadium on the racetrack at the State Fair grounds. Workmen piled dirt from a 24-feet-deep oblong hole along the sides, laid concrete beams on the mounds, attached a wooden deck, and affixed wooden benches to the deck. The workers left a large entry tunnel at one end for the teams. It was a huge oval stadium for 46,600 fans that was

PHOTO 59

the largest in the South at the time (photo 58). In 1936 Franklin D. Roosevelt gave a 26-minute speech in the stadium as part of an election campaign complete with guard units standing at attention before the speaker's platform in 89-degree heat (photo 59). Since Roosevelt could walk only a short distance, his automobile entourage drove directly into the stadium to the platform.

PHOTO 60

The stadium received its name, the "Cotton Bowl," after the first postseason game in 1937 (photo 60). To capitalize upon the sensational football talents of Doak Walker of Southern Methodist University, the city rebuilt the stadium in 1947–1949 with concrete and added two decks (photo 61). It became known as the "House that Doak Built." Walker, shown here sitting on a bench, was named to the All-American team three times although he was injured for much of his senior year (photo 62). The Cot-

PHOTO 61

ton Bowl was also the home stadium of Jerry LeVias of SMU, who broke the color barrier of the Southwest Conference in 1966. During his senior year, after a Texas Christian University player spat in his face and said, "Go home, nigger," LeVias took a punt, avoided thirteen tackles, and ran eighty-nine yards for the winning touchdown in a Fort Worth game (photo 63). Stadiums, thus, were places of witness not only for athletic prowess, but also for social change.

PHOTO 62

PHOTO 63

PHOTO 64

Over time there were alterations in the locker rooms, the seats, and the playing surface at the Cotton Bowl, but the basic shape with two upper decks remained the same (photo 64). It also remained a city-owned facility and a part of Fair Park. It was the Colosseum of Texas sports.

Complaints about control, amenities, and location finally led the owner of the Dallas Cowboys to construct Texas Stadium in Irving in 1971. This photograph shows owner Clint Murchison on the right with his general manager Tex Schramm at a luncheon in the new stadium while it was still under construction (photo 65). Jerry Jones, the owner of the Cowboys since 1989, in turn, is currently in the process of abandoning Texas Stadium for a new athletic field at Arlington that is scheduled to open in 2009.

PHOTO 65

PHOTO 66

In Texas this era of team owner–controlled, public stadiums began with the Astrodome. Jones, who toured the new facility in 1965, remembered more than forty years later, "When you saw that thing—glistening—I couldn't stand it. It sucked the air right out of you." (*Sports Illustrated*, July 16, 2007). Jones never forgot the experience, as was the case of most people. The Astrodome was a revolution in stadium design and was the most significant change in almost two thousand years—since the building of the Colosseum. It was a circular facility basically set up for baseball, but designed to be used for many purposes. Baseball, which emerged from the street games of New York City in the mid-nineteenth century, came to Texas with the Northern soldiers of Reconstruction following the Civil War. It was America's game before it lost that title to football during the 1960s. Until then Texans played bat-and-ball contests with enthusiasm, as shown in these two pictures of teenagers from Austin during the mid-1940s (photos 66, 67). They participated in summer league games with the boys play-

PHOTO 67

ing hardball, the girls playing softball. The contrast is interesting and demonstrates the gender difference in athletics at the time.

The boys played on an improved field with bleachers, protective fencing, and an embedded home plate. The catcher had a mitt, chest protector, baseball cap, and face mask. The girls, on the other hand, played on an open field with the home plate simply laid on the ground and with a softer ball. The catcher had no equipment and caught the ball bare-handed as did the fielders. The umpire stood behind the pitcher. In spite of his classic swing, baseball cap, and Keds shoes, the male batter popped the ball up. It can be seen in the upper right corner of the picture. The barefooted female batter did no better. The softball can be seen going through the legs of the catcher as the female fielders impatiently waited for something to happen. Although gender disparities in athletics gradually began to equalize after the passage of Title IX in 1972, the pictures illustrate the interest in baseball and in sports by both sexes during the middle of the twentieth century.

PHOTO 68

PHOTO 69

In Houston, baseball enthusiast Judge Roy Hofheinz led the construction of the Astrodome in 1962–1965. For the first time, an entire baseball field was enclosed under an air-conditioned dome; for the first time, there were private skyboxes and cushioned seats; and for the first time, there was a huge animated scoreboard and an artificial playing surface. Although it was circular in shape—ideal for the national game—the stadium accommodated other sports as well. Seats could be moved for the rectangular playing fields of football, soccer, basketball, and tennis. It was a rational, all-purpose arena where the same parking lot could be used for different events. The stadium changed the urbanscape, brought comfort to the fans, eliminated weather as a factor in sports, and, along with the Manned Spacecraft Center, gave Houston the reputation of a high-tech city where anything might be accomplished.

PHOTO 70

During construction on the outskirts of town, as can be seen in this set of pictures (photos 68–72), huge cranes lifted steel trusses supported by towers to piece together the dome. When workers removed the towers, people held their breath to see if the dome would collapse, but it did not. Skylights were attached to the outside curve and the inside seating was finished in rings of color. It was stunning and labeled the "Eighth Wonder of the World."

PHOTO 71A

PHOTO 71B

PHOTO 72

PHOTO 73

Long before this game between Houston and Pittsburgh in 1987 (photos 73, 74), the dome had to be painted outside to reduce glare, and artificial turf (AstroTurf) had to be installed because the grass died from lack of light. The photos show the extra-long dugouts ordered by Hofheinz—because he thought people like to sit

PHOTO 74

behind a dugout—and the intimidating scoreboard that led cheers and displayed artificial flying bullets and explosions whenever a player hit a home run. Opposing teams hated it; critics sneered at it; local fans loved it; and stadium architects copied it.

PHOTO 75

PHOTO 76

Hofheinz also pioneered in Texas the trick of gaining public funds to build a stadium that he could control in return for paying the mortgage—a public facility under private direction. This arrangement spelled doom for the Cotton Bowl and eventually for the Astrodome itself. In this image, Hofheinz is shown in the stands where every seat pointed toward second base (photo 75).

With the growth in the popularity of football, urban wealth, better technology, and hubris by team owners, Reliant Stadium for football and Minute Maid Park for baseball replaced the Astrodome in Houston—two stadiums for one (photo 76). "Form ever follows function," architect Louis Sullivan said in 1896, and the new Reliant Stadium reflected the inner rectangular playing field of football. Hulking and boxlike, it stands next to the Astrodome at the same site. The Eighth Wonder of the World represents now only relentless history, and its original elegant elongated curve is obscured by tacked-on pedestrian ramps and the behemoth next door. Texans, nevertheless, have passionately embraced sports as a part of their recreation and expressed this in the story of their twentieth-century stadiums.

THE PLEASURE OF LIBRARIES

In all but the smallest towns in the United States a public library for the education and recreation of citizens is commonplace. The idea started with the founding of the Boston Public Library in 1854 and reached Texas in the last part of the nineteenth and early twentieth centuries. In Galveston, the leading Texas port for the first sixty years, philanthropist Henry Rosenberg left a bequest to build a library as "a source of pleasure and profit" for all coming generations. It opened in 1904 and the first librarian,

PHOTO 77

PHOTO 78

Frank Chauncy Patten, embarked on an unusual quest for archival materials about the history of this important gateway. After thirty-one years of filling the library attic like a pack rat, Patten accumulated one of the best repositories of letters, diaries, and business records—the grist of scholars—about the history of Texas. This was most unusual for a mid-sized public library. The photograph shows the ornate original library building of Patten with the modern air-conditioned extension attached to the back for the benefit of his archives (photo 77). The architectural styles clash, but the library functions well for the people of Galveston and the scholars of Texas.

In the Lone Star State, as elsewhere in the nation, bright, educated, middle- and upper-class women inspired the drive to establish public libraries. Typical were the J.U.G.s (Just Us Girls) of Amarillo, Texas, an intellectual discussion group that needed books for their conversations and started a public library in 1902 (photo 78). Even though the J.U.G.s could not vote, no city council, no man, could withstand their determination.

PHOTO 79

During this same period, Andrew Carnegie, the richest man in America, expressed his faith in books and self-education by providing the money for over sixteen hundred libraries in the world, including some thirty places in Texas. In Gainesville, Lillian Gunter became the first librarian of a Carnegie Library in 1914 after she converted a local subscription library to public use in 1903 with the help of a women's literary society like the J.U.G.s (photo 79). The building eventually became a playhouse after the county established another library. In Dallas Carnegie provided an impressive two-story library with an Aladdin's lamp on the top at the behest of local women (photo 80). Children and their bicycles gathered on the steps for the photograph.

Most of the Carnegie Libraries, such as the units in Houston and Dallas, succumbed to old age and urban growth. Houston obtained a Carnegie Library in 1904, but replaced it in 1929. This Central Library lasted until 1975 when it became the Metropolitan Research Center after a new main library opened next door (photo 81).

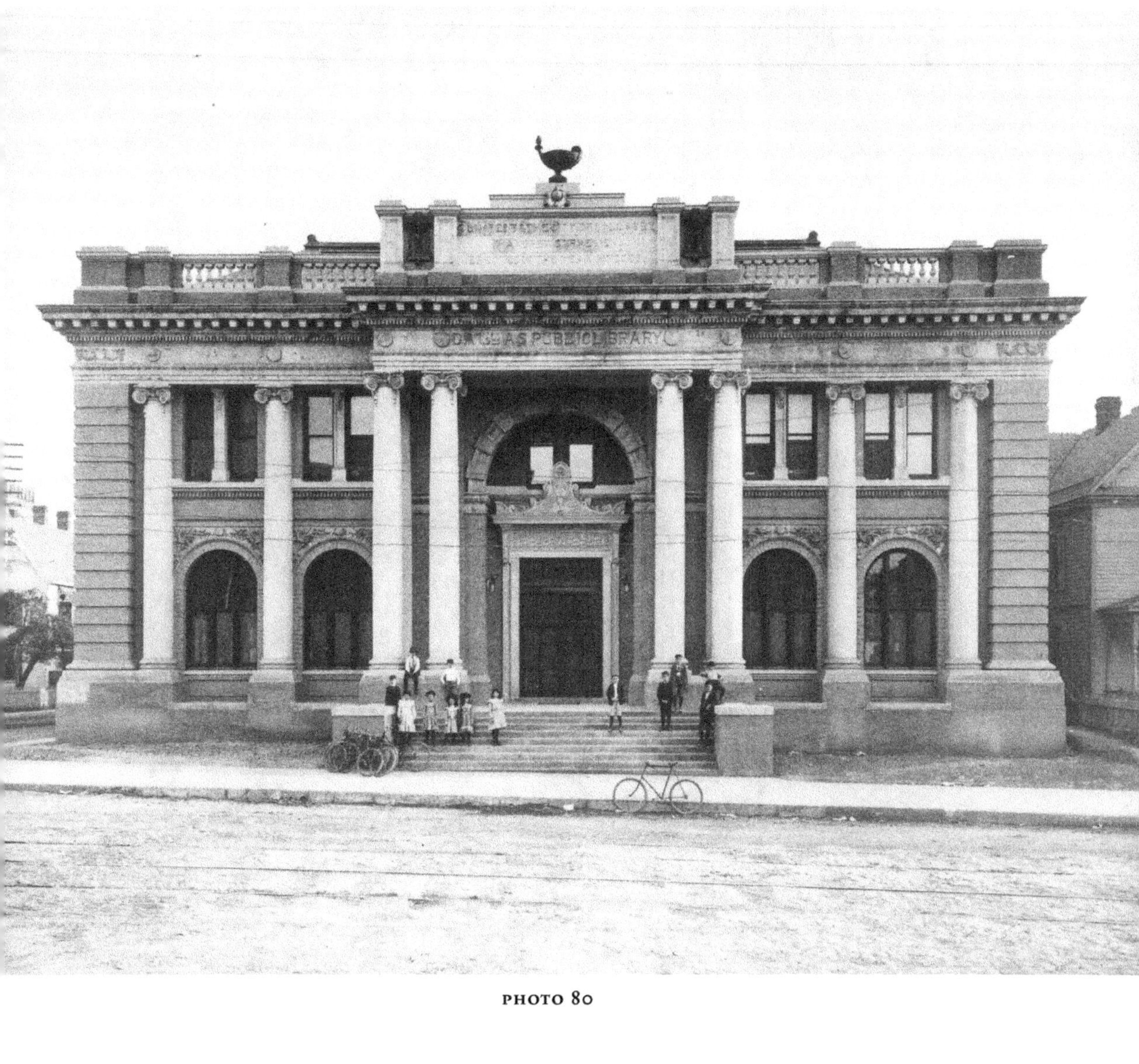

PHOTO 80

PHOTO 81

Dallas changed its main library facility in 1955 and again in 1982. Its present location in the City Hall plaza area brought some much-needed diversity of land use to that part of the city (photo 82). There is often disagreement between architects and librarians, but this is a building that seems to please both, a happy circumstance rarely accomplished. Its recessed floors counterbalance the cantilevered, aggressive, thrusting floors of the city hall across the concrete plaza—a building of civic action versus an edifice of contemplation (photo 83).

PHOTO 82

PHOTO 83

PHOTO 84

The foremost academic library in Texas and the Southwest is at the University of Texas at Austin. The holdings amount to about one-third those of the Library of Congress, the largest in the nation, and about one-half those of Harvard, the largest university library in the country. The University of Texas library expanded over the years through donations and by the aggressive purchasing of books and manuscripts. This resulted in a continuous search for space and the construction of new buildings.

PHOTO 85

In 1911 the university moved the collection into what is now Battle Hall designed by nationally acclaimed architect Cass Gilbert (photo 84). It was a handsome building with arched windows and red tiles that everyone praised, except the librarians. The ceiling cracked under the weight of the books and there was not enough space.

Main Library with a 27-floor tower opened in 1934 (photo 85), followed after mid-century with the Undergraduate Library, the Harry Ransom Humanities Research

PHOTO 86

Center, and the Perry-Castañeda Library (PCL). UT President Harry Ransom, shown in this picture at a formal reception in New York City in 1960 with philanthropist Karl St. John Hoblitzelle of Dallas (photo 86), directed and encouraged much of the growth after World War II. Ransom is on the right. The Undergraduate Library with the symbolic torch of learning passing between runners was known among students as "Harry's Place" (photo 87).

With its open-stack shelves holding 3 million books, the PCL replaced the Main Library in 1977 (photo 88). The open stacks meant that students and the public could search for information as they wished rather than waiting for librarians to serve them.

PHOTO 87

PHOTO 88

PHOTO 89

PHOTO 90

It was more efficient. Although bookshelves are so commonplace to libraries that their presence is easily ignored, it is in such places that rare intellectual pleasure can be found. Changes at the PCL also reflect the technological revolution that is overturning libraries. Computers have replaced the card catalog and taken over much of the space in the original reference room. (photo 89).

On the eastern edge of the campus, the National Archives placed the Lyndon B. Johnson Presidential Library in 1971. Alongside the library the university built Sid Richardson Hall, a long low building, to house its Latin American Collection and the Barker Texas History Center (photo 90). The Latin American Collection is preeminent in the world and the Eugene C. Barker Library of Texana, now a part of the Center for American History, is preeminent in the state. The LBJ Library was the first presidential library in Texas and functions as a research center about the life and times of Lyndon B. Johnson. Although its stacks are not open, the information about the politics of the time is readily available to the public by request. This is appropriate for the president who signed the Freedom of Information Act in 1966. The LBJ Library is also, incidentally, a prime tourist attraction.

The history of libraries is not without dips and bumps—seemingly, they are always short of cash—but in the twentieth century, Texans have built and endorsed libraries of public access. The abilities to read and to write and to think have been recognized generally as skills important for democracy, business, social exchange, and intellectual recreation. The Texas libraries stand as symbols of this recognition.

PHOTO 91

THEATER AND THE ELECTRIC REVOLUTION

Staged performances are integral in human society. They can be found in all places and at all times, and in early Texas the crude acting productions in bars and meeting halls were a welcome entertainment. During the last half of the nineteenth century, the small stages, such as that of Jack Harris' Vaudeville Saloon and Theatre, appeared and were followed by more serious opera houses in the large cities where there was enough population to allow a theater to be profitable. To present his high quality touring shows, Henry Greenwall (1832–1913) assembled a string of opera houses throughout the South that included Galveston, Houston, Fort Worth, Waco, and Dallas. He owned the Grand Opera House of Galveston, built in 1894. Greenwall's business eventually collapsed and his Galveston structure slowly decayed. It was restored in 1974 by the Galveston County Cultural Arts Council and is the only Greenwall opera house to survive (photo 91). Today it again serves its original purpose as a venue for touring stage shows. It was a typical opera house with an entrance on one side that opened to a grand staircase that led to the second floor theater. The design used common business architecture, blended into a downtown business setting, and left room for ground-level shops.

Live theater declined in the first decades of the twentieth century, and the administrator of the Works Progress Administration in Texas, seeking to avoid controversy, actually quashed efforts to introduce new plays. In spite of that, Margo Jones (1911–1955), a young, innovative director, persisted and later established a theater-in-the-round at Fair Park in Dallas in 1947. She read a new script each day, smoked incessantly, and collected turtle figurines as can be seen in this photograph (photo 92).

PHOTO 92

PHOTO 93

After her tragic death in 1955, her theater declined and is now used as a storage facility for the Texas lottery. Jones' legacy in Dallas, however, can be found at the Dallas Theater Center for young actors in the only theater building designed by renowned architect Frank Lloyd Wright (photo 93).

In Houston a Jones protégé, Nina Vance (1914–1980), shown in the photograph (photo 94), developed the theater-in-the-round Alley Theatre, which grew from an amateur group into a professional repertory organization with a permanent place in the downtown Houston Arts district. As a result of a performing arts renaissance that was going on at the same time, the Houston Symphony and Houston Grand Opera found permanent places in the district at Jones Hall and the Wortham Center (photo 95). With outstanding venues, money, performers, directors, and public support, the arts in Houston reached world-class stature.

PHOTO 94

PHOTO 95

PHOTO 96

The remarkable inventions in electronics, however, competed for the recreational attention of Texans. Motion pictures offered exotic scenery, close-ups of actors, cheap prices, and a great variety of stories. Silent movie houses, like the twenty-foot-wide Pastime in Houston (photo 96) and the Texas Theatre in Austin showing a Charlie Chaplin film, popped up almost everywhere. The 1916 Chaplin two-reel film of about twenty-two minutes featured his Little Tramp character in a tale of lost love (photo 97). Pianos and later organs provided musical intensity for the action on the screen. Stage theaters, such as the Galveston Grand Opera, converted to movie theaters, and dedicated movie palaces opened, like the $1 million, air-conditioned Loew's State of Houston in 1927 (photo 98). Not only was Loew's elaborately decorated with blue and white Wedgwood style plaques, it also had a proscenium-type stage with an orchestra pit for vaudeville acts. It could do everything.

PHOTO 97

PHOTO 98

PHOTO 99

The typical big city movie theater row that emerged on Elm Street in Dallas and flourished for a half-century included the Majestic owned by Karl Hoblitzelle (1879–1967). In this street scene of the theater row in 1923 the Queen, Jefferson, Old Mill, Palace, Rex, and Garrick theaters can be seen; the new Majestic is out of sight beyond the Palace Theatre on the left-hand side (photo 99). Hoblitzelle was tall, aristocratic, and courteous (see photo 86), and he made a fortune with his Interstate Theaters that featured family entertainment. He allowed segregated black patrons access to the balcony of the Majestic through a separate entrance. Interestingly, in "Deep Ellum," the black section of Dallas on Elm Street east of downtown, one of the earliest African-American theaters in Texas presented movies to the segregated community. In this picture from 1940, patrons in front of the Harlem look at the advertisement for a Ralph Cooper film (photo 100). Cooper was known as "the black Clark Gable."

PHOTO 100

PHOTO 101

The downtown Elm Street theater district, however, gradually declined as the movie houses followed people to the suburban shopping centers starting in the 1930s. The Highland Park Village Theatre of Dallas is an example (photo 101). With Spanish architecture, this planned, upscale, open shopping mall began in 1931. It was the second oldest development of its kind in the nation, following Country Club Plaza in Kansas City. The developers added the theater to the Highland Park center in 1935.

All the movie houses of Elm Street disappeared with the exception of the Majestic (photo 102), which was transformed into a venue for the Dallas Ballet in 1977. Other cities initiated such nostalgic and practical conversions to ensure the survival of a their downtown theaters. The Paramount of Austin is the finest example (photo 103). From

PHOTO 102

PHOTO 103

PHOTO 104

the 1930s, it was a premier downtown movie theater, equipped with the usual, complex projection machinery as seen in photo 104. A threat of destruction in the 1970s brought about a community reaction—Austin citizens are known for their attention

PHOTO 105

to such matters—and the theater was saved as a live performance venue (photo 105). The *Tuna, Texas* series by Joe Sears and Jaston Williams was effectively produced there in the 1990s.

PHOTO 106

Radio and television entertainment also came to Texas as a part of the electric revolution. A cheap radio set could pull voices out of the air, as it did for newsboy Frank Allison, who listened to the 1925 World Series with the help of an antenna tied to an iron window grill in a San Antonio alley (photo 106). Later, shortly after World War II, Gordon McLendon (1921–1985), the owner of station KLIF in Dallas, made radio history by providing simulations of major league baseball games, music disc jockeys, and radio interviews as shown in this photograph from the studio (photo 107). McLendon is on the left. Relying upon his celebrity, he ran as a conservative for the U.S. Senate in 1964 and for governor in 1968 (photo 108). He lost both times.

PHOTO 107

PHOTO 108

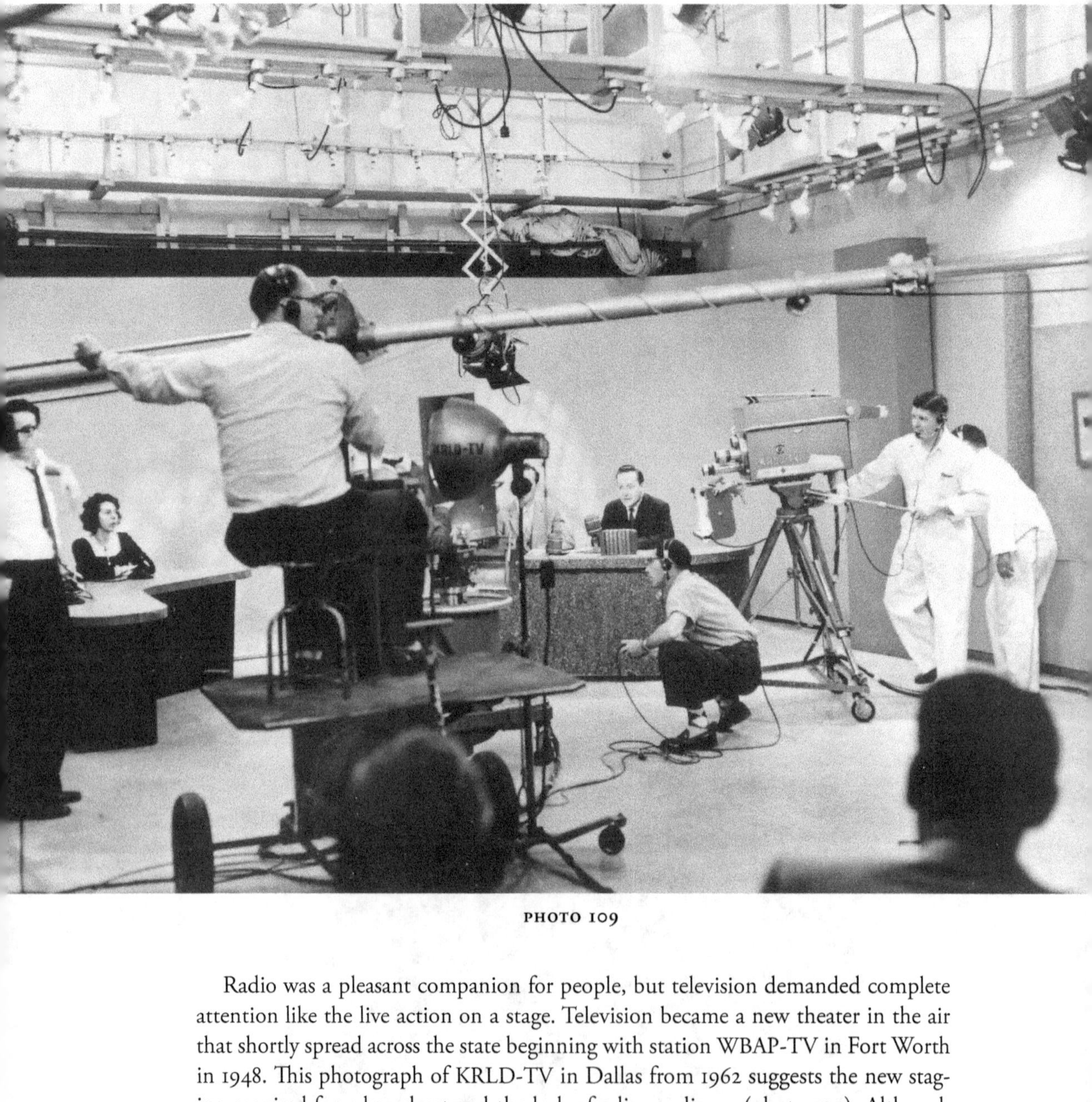

PHOTO 109

Radio was a pleasant companion for people, but television demanded complete attention like the live action on a stage. Television became a new theater in the air that shortly spread across the state beginning with station WBAP-TV in Fort Worth in 1948. This photograph of KRLD-TV in Dallas from 1962 suggests the new staging required for a broadcast and the lack of a live audience (photo 109). Although television became a mesmerizing form of theater that abided in the home, it never dislodged the performance of an actor on a stage.

Live theater survived, and along with the movies, radio, and television, the entertainment opportunities of the public greatly increased in the twentieth century. Texans had more choice than ever before to express their character and interests during their free time.

Conclusions and Afterthoughts

What can be learned about Texas by looking at recreation? That is, how do Texans answer that question mentioned in the Introduction, "What do you do in your spare time?" To transpose the question into historical terms, it would be, "What did you do in your spare time?" And does the answer indicate anything significant about the character of the people? Does history, an academic discipline that describes changes, have something to say? Here are some thoughts to consider.

Since many of the recreational ideas—football and baseball, parks, libraries, stadiums, theater, drinking and carousing, and the technologies of television, radio, and movies—came from outside the state, much of what occurred in Texas came from the larger culture of the country. In their recreation Texans, thus, were like other peoples from the United States and Mexico and reflected the same character and history. There was little originality.

Was there nothing unique or different in the Lone Star State? There were, of course, Texan themes—such as those involving cowboys, Indians, and oil booms—that turned up in plays, literature, and television. They enriched the culture. How could the novel *Giant* (1952), written by Edna Ferber (1887–1968) from Michigan, and the movie made three years later starring Rock Hudson, Elizabeth Taylor, and James Dean use anyplace but Marfa, Texas, as a setting? It is hard to imagine. Moreover, there have been Texas participants in various aspects of recreation from sports to theater—Virginia Mayo, Ray Walston, King Vidor, Doak Walker, Sammy Baugh, Mary Martin, for example. A complete quantification is not possible and other states can produce their own lists of notables, but there were obviously Texas flavors in the mix of national entertainment.

In addition to literary themes and the various participants in recreation, the land provided an unusual configuration and climate that distinguished the state. The parks were used to express this and have a distinct beauty that can be found only in the Lone Star State. Where else is there a Padre Island National Seashore or a Big Bend National Park that can dwarf the senses with their expressions of vastness and isolation? And, as elsewhere in the nation, Texas possessed its own sacred battleground parks, such as San Jacinto and the Alamo, that echo for those who listen the epic human struggles of the past. The land and what happened there, thus, make the parks unique. People who choose to recreate in such sites are able to feel the significance of a Texan place.

Also, there can be seen in the recreational history a demonstrated technological mastery—the most important of human attributes—in stadiums and theaters. The Astrodome was a thoroughgoing rationalization of the game of baseball for the comfort of fans. Nothing like this had been done before and it changed not only sport, but also the skyline of cities. Theater-in-the-round brought back an ancient technique of play presentation that reflected the determination of the producer and the faith of theatergoers in Dallas and Houston.

Recreational history delimits, moreover, the different roles of men and women in Texas. To be sure, it was Mother Neff who gave some of the first land to the state park system and it was Clara Driscoll who recognized the need to save the Alamo. But it was Governor Pat Neff who energized the state parks movement, Senator Ralph Yarborough who saved Padre Island, and Roy Hofheinz who built the Astrodome. Generally, it was the men who were interested in licit and illicit activities, sports, and the out-of-doors. Women, in contrast, played a greater role in the founding of libraries and establishing theaters. Certainly, there was strong male financial backing for places like the Rosenberg Library, Theatre '47, and the Wortham Center, but the spirit of women like Lillian Gunter, May Dickson Exall, Nina Vance, and Margo Jones drove the development.

In the history of the American West there is a cliché that it was women who imposed the civilizing standards of churches, schools, legitimate theater, and libraries. These institutions calmed the rambunctious male society and made possible the peaceful education of children. This cliché seems to be accurate. In the story of Texas recreation, it was women who worked for the institutions that would elevate the mind.

What does all of this say about Texas character in general? The history of theater and sports demonstrated an openness, willingness, and generosity to accomplish something new. The society accepted and supported innovators and entrepreneurs such as Margo Jones and Roy Hofheinz. Businessmen like Karl Hoblitzelle and Gus Wortham generated wealth and embraced an ethic to spend it for societal benefit. In their conservation movement, Texans demonstrated a love of the land by the establishment of parks. In addition, in the story of parks, theaters, and sports can be tracked a declining racial tension. Overt segregation no longer exists. Although ambivalent at times, Texans have suppressed prostitution and gambling and encouraged libraries. In general, then, recreational history reveals an emergent state citizen who respects the land, is open-minded and generous, opposes prostitution, accepts some gambling and drinking, tolerates racial and gender rights, loves zoos, supports libraries, takes pride in theatrical productions, and likes sports. The current Texan, thus, is more humane and civilized than the Texan of a century ago.

This image contrasts to narrower characterizations that possibly might be derived from the history of politics, war, or economics. The task of recreational history, however, has just begun. There is much more to be learned that might expand the image.

In the discussion about parks, for example, I focused upon public, not commercial, parks. What about profit-making operations such as Astroworld, Six Flags, and Sea World? Here is a history that deserves to be pursued that would take in the business aspects of recreation and provide an opportunity to explore the motivations of a mass market. Another example is a broad, long-term history of fishing that would take in the locations, technology, and the relationship of humanity to nature. The same sort of attention could be given to hunting. What about the history of golf, tennis, or sailing in Texas? Furthermore, beyond what I have hinted at in the discussion of electronics, the impact of video games deserves further study. What was it about the new Sony PlayStation that inspired the fifty fans I observed in November 2006 to camp out with sleeping bags and lawn chairs for two days in front of a store waiting for them to go on sale? So, there is much more for students and scholars to do.

What if there had been no Alley Theatre, Dallas Opera, University of Texas Library, Fort Worth Zoo, or Big Bend National Park? There can be only speculation, but as a people Texans would have been greatly diminished and they would have had less understanding of who they are. There would have been less inspiration, little reflection on life, less playfulness, and a dissatisfaction of the spirit. There would have been less connection with America and the world. There would have been less wonder and a great boredom in life. It would seem, then, that the history of recreation can contribute much to the definition of what it means to be Texan, and human.

Notes

INTRODUCTION

1. Benjamin G. Rader, *American Sports*, 2nd ed. (Englewood Cliffs, N.J.: Prentice Hall, 1990), p. 6.

2. Rhoda Thomas Tripp, *International Thesaurus of Quotations* (New York: Crowell, 1970), p. 708.

3. John R. Kelly, *Leisure*, 2nd ed. (Englewood Cliffs, N.J.: Prentice Hall, 1990), p. 23.

4. Steven Lagerfeld, a deputy editor of the *Wilson Quarterly* (vol. 22, Summer 1998, pp. 58–70), critiques scholars who have studied leisure and concludes that Americans are not very good at managing their free time. Stephen L. J. Smith in *Dictionary of Concepts in Recreation and Leisure* (New York: Greenwood, 1990), p. 253, defines recreation as "A pleasurable activity, which may be relatively sedentary, largely pursued for intrinsic motivation during leisure." His discussion of the meaning by various scholars illustrates how academics can tie themselves into knots over a seemingly simple word.

5. Vera Olivova, *Sports and Games in the Ancient World* (New York: St. Martin's Press, 1984), p. 43.

6. Kelly, *Leisure*, pp. 104–105.

7. *The World Almanac, 2001* (Mahwah, N.J.: WRC Media Company, 2001), pp. 134, 626.

8. Thorstein Veblen, *The Theory of the Leisure Class* (New York: Macmillan, 1899, 1912), p. 71.

9. Tripp, *International Thesaurus of Quotations*, p. 533.

10. See Gary Cross, *A Social History of Leisure Since 1600* (State College, Pa.: Venture, 1990), pp. 117–135.

11. Cross, *Social History of Leisure*, p. 2.

CHAPTER ONE

1. Shine Philips, *Big Spring: The Casual Biography of a Prairie Town* (New York: Prentice-Hall, 1943), p. 89.

2. Quoted in Vern Bullough and Bonnie Bullough, *Women and Prostitution: A Social History* (Buffalo, N.Y.: Prometheus, 1987), p. 16.

3. *The Holy Bible*, revised standard version (New York: Nelson, 1953), Luke 7:37–39.

4. Bullough and Bullough, *Women and Prostitution*, p. 245.

5. Margaret Swett Henson, "Susanna Wilkerson Dickinson" in Ron Tyler, ed., *The New Handbook of Texas,* vol. 2 (Austin: Texas State Historical Association, 1996), p. 637. Katherine Massey, "Angelina Elizabeth Dickinson" in Tyler, ed., New *Handbook of Texas*, vol. 2, p. 636. *Flakes Daily Bulletin*, July 20, 1869.

6. Alfred C. Kinsey, Wardell B. Pomeroy, and Clyde E. Martin, *Sexual Behavior in the Human Male* (Philadelphia: Saunders, 1948), pp. 193–194. Kinsey, a zoologist from Indiana University, placed emphasis upon biological factors, but later researchers who put emphasis upon social factors found basically the same thing, that sexual activity is greatest among young adults. See Robert T. Michael, John H. Gagnon, Edward O. Laumann, and Gina Kolata, *Sex in America: A Definitive Survey* (Boston: Little, Brown, 1994), pp. 116, 120.

7. Alfred C. Kinsey, Wardell B. Pomeroy, Clyde E. Martin, and Paul Gebhard, *Sexual Behavior in the Human Female* (Philadelphia: W. B. Saunders Co., 1953), p. 651. Leonard Shlain, *Sex, Time, and Power: How Women's Sexuality Shaped Human Evolution* (New York: Viking, 2003), pp. 76–77. Michael et al., *Sex in America*, pp. 145, 150, 156.

8. Kinsey, Pomeroy, and Martin, *Sexual Behavior in the Human Male*, p. 607.

9. Shlain, *Sex, Time, and Power*, p. 238.

10. Kinsey, Pomeroy, and Martin, *Sexual Behavior in the Human Male*, p. 607. Alexa Albert, *Brothel: Mustang Ranch and Its Women* (New York: Random House, 2001), pp. 103, 125.

11. Kinsey et al., *Sexual Behavior in the Human Female*, pp. 651, 682, 714–715. Michael et al., *Sex in America*, p. 156.

12. William H. Masters and Virginia E. Johnson, *Human Sexual Response* (Boston: Little Brown, 1966), p. 7. Shlain, *Sex, Time, and Power*, pp. 49, 51.

13. Desmond Morris, *The Naked Ape* (New York: Dell, 1967), p. 65. Modern social researchers divide sexual activities into procreational, relational, and recreational. See Edward O. Laumann, John H. Gagnon, Robert T. Michael, and Stuart Michaels, *The Social Organization of Sexuality: Sexual Practices in the United States* (Chicago: University of Chicago Press, 1994), p. 511.

14. Bonnie S. Anderson and Judith P. Zinsser, *A History of Their Own: Women in Europe from Prehistory to the Present* (New York: Harper & Row, 1988), p. 263.

15. Quoted in David G. McComb, *Galveston: A History* (Austin: University of Texas Press, 1986), p. 157.

16. Albert, *Brothel*, p. 31.

17. Albert, *Brothel*, p. 66. Jody Raphael, *Listening to Olivia* (Boston: Northeastern University Press, 2004), p. 7.

18. Anne M. Butler, *Daughters of Joy, Sisters of Misery: Prostitutes in the American West, 1865–90* (Urbana: University of Illinois Press, 1985), pp. xvii–xviii, 15, 48, note 40. See also Amy S. Balderach, "A Different Kind of Reservation: Waco's Red-Light District Revisited, 1880–1920," MA thesis (Waco, Texas: Baylor University, 2005), pp. 25, 50, 81. The college boy's answer to the trite question is for the prostitute to respond, "Oh, luck, I guess."

19. Roger M. Olien and Diana Davids Olien, *Oil Booms* (Lincoln: University of Nebraska Press, 1982), p. 131.

20. David G. McComb, *Texas, A Modern History* (Austin: University of Texas Press, 1989), p. 114.

21. Butler, *Daughters of Joy*, pp. 2, 4, 15, 27–28, 35–39, 51, 55, 58–60, 63, 67–68, 75, 78, 81–83, p. 10 (quote).

22. Butler, *Daughters of Joy*, pp. 74–75. J. Evetts Haley and William Curry Holden, eds., *The Flamboyant Judge: James D. Hamlin* (Canyon, Texas: Palo Duro Press, 1972), pp. 105–108.

23. David C. Humphrey, "Prostitution in Texas: From the 1830's to the 1960's," *East Texas Historical Association*, vol. 33 (1995), p. 29. Julia Kirk Blackwelder, *Women of the Depression: Caste and Culture in San Antonio, 1929–1939* (College Station: Texas A&M Press, 1984), p. 154.

24. Butler, *Daughters of Joy*, p. 62.

25. Pauline Durrett Robertson and R. L. Robertson, *Mystery Woman of Old Tascosa* (Amarillo: Paramount, 1995), pp. 5–12, 14–16, 20–24. John L. McCarty, *Maverick Town: The Story of Old Tascosa* (Norman: University of Oklahoma Press, 1988), pp. 186–187.

26. Quoted in McComb, *Galveston*, p. 157.

27. Butler, *Daughters of Joy*, p. 57.

28. Balderach, "A Different Kind of Reservation," p. 3, 7–8.

29. Butler, *Daughters of Joy*, pp. 102–103.

30. Bob Darden, "Best Legal Whorehouses in Texas," *Westward* in *Dallas Times Herald*, May 27, 1984. Aimee Harris Johnson, "Prostitution in Waco, 1889–1917," MA thesis (Waco: Baylor University, 1990), pp. 52–54.

31. Nancy Hamilton, "Ben Dowell's Saloon and the 'Monte Carlo of the West' (El Paso)," in Richard Selcer, David Bowser, Nancy Hamilton, and Chuck Parsons, *Legendary Watering Holes: The Saloons That Made Texas Famous* (College Station: Texas A&M University Press, 2004), pp. 140–141.

32. *The Blue Book: for Visitors, Tourists, and Those Seeking a Good Time While in San Antonio, Texas* (San Antonio, 1911–1912), pp. 21–27, p. 26 (quote).

33. Greg Davenport, "The District: Where Vice was a Virtue," *Magazine of San Antonio* (March 1978), p. 50 (first quote), p. 55 (second quote).

34. James T. Upchurch, *The Unchained Demon, and the Tribute Dallas, Texas Pays to Vice* (Arlington, Texas: Berachah Rescue Society, 1912), p. 25.

35. Elizabeth York Enstam, "Virginia K. Johnson: A Second Chance for the Wayward," in Michael V. Hazel, ed., *Dallas Reconsidered: Essays in Local History* (Dallas: Three Forks Press, 1995), pp. 217–218.

36. H. Gordon Frost, *The Gentlemen's Club* (El Paso: Mangan Press, 1983), p. 205. This book includes a rare interview with a prostitute, pp. 203–207.

37. Humphrey, "Prostitution in Texas," p. 31.

38. Granville Price, "A Sociological Study of a Segregated District," MA thesis (Austin: University of Texas at Austin, 1930), pp. 8, 18–21.

39. Price, "Sociological Study," pp. 11–13, p. 3 (quote).

40. Price, "Sociological Study," pp. 8–9, 14, 16, 31, 33, 34, 37–42, 70–71, 102.

41. Price, "Sociological Study," pp. 9, 12, 26, 34, 52–53, p. 82 (quote).

42. McComb, *Galveston*, pp. 158, 187.

43. McComb, *Texas, a Modern History*, p. 149.

44. *Dallas Morning News*, July 8, 1979. A busload of citizens from LaGrange gave a standing ovation to the play *The Best Little Whorehouse in Texas*, but a disgruntled Texas Aggie from the 1943 class said that the play made it appear that a lot of Aggies went to the Chicken Ranch. "I think the truth should be known," he said, "a lot of Aggies went to Mexico." *Dallas Morning News*, March 5, 1979.

45. *Austin American-Statesman*, June 1, 1980.

46. *Dallas Morning News*, July 8, 1979.

47. *Houston Post*, January 29, 1974. *Austin American-Statesman*, June 25, 1978.

48. *San Angelo Standard Times*, October 2, 1977.

49. Raphael, *Listening to Olivia*, p. 107.

50. Kinsey et al., *Sexual Behavior in the Human Female*, p. 300.

51. Bullough and Bullough, *Women and Prostitution*, pp. 297–298. Virginity at marriage for women was 93 percent for a group born in 1933–1942. For the cohort born in 1963–1974, female virginity at marriage was 36 percent. See Laumann et al., *Social Organization of Sexuality*, p. 602.

52. Humphrey, "Prostitution in Texas," pp. 36–38.

53. *San Antonio Express-News*, October 19, 1980 (quote); March 2, 1986; April 1, 1987; January 20, 1991; December 7, 1993.

54. *Fort Worth Star-Telegram*, February 27, 1981.

55. *Dallas Morning News*, July 11, 1985 (quote); September 27, 1985; July 17, 1989. *Dallas Times Herald*, June 10, 1991.

56. *Dallas Times Herald*, August 16, 1978 (lawyer). *Dallas Express News*, April 9, 1987.

57. *Dallas Morning News*, August 16, 1991.

58. *Dallas Morning News*, June 14, 2001.

59. *Dallas Morning News*, November 4, 1995.

60. *Austin American-Statesman*, February 16, 17, 19, 1994.

61. Katy Vine, "She Had Brains, a Body and the Ability to Make Men Love Her," *Texas Monthly* (January 2005), pp. 116–119, 193–198. *Odessa American*, July 28, 29, 2004; January 9, 2005; February 5, 9, 20, 2005; March 9, 2005.

62. Vine, "She Had Brains," p. 195.

63. Albert, *Brothel*, p. 234.

64. *DSM-IV* (Washington, D.C.: American Psychiatric Association, 1994), p. 194. *Barnes and Noble New American Encyclopedia*, vol. 1 (Chicago: Grolier, 1991), pp. 264–265.

65. Philips, *Big Spring*, p. 88.

66. W. J. Rorabaugh, *The Alcoholic Republic: An American Tradition* (New York: Oxford University Press, 1979), pp. 7, 9, 11, 21, 25, p. 18 (quote).

67. Frank M. Cockrell, "History of Early Dallas," *Dallas Morning News*, May 15–August 28, 1932, typescript in Barker Texas History Center, Austin, p. 60.

68. Gerald Carson, *The Social History of Bourbon: An Unhurried Account of our Star-Spangled American Drink* (New York: Dodd, Mead, 1963), pp. 11, 27–28.

69. Carson, *Social History of Bourbon*, p. 28.

70. Jack Gregory and Rennard Strickland, *Sam Houston with the Cherokees, 1829–1833* (Austin: University of Texas Press, 1967), pp. 78–79. James L. Haley, *Sam Houston* (Norman: University of Oklahoma Press, 2002), p. 74. Houston's use of the word "refreshments" is from William S. Red, ed., "Allen's Reminiscences of Texas, 1838–1842," *Southwestern Historical Quarterly*, vol. 18 (January 1915), p. 290.

71. Francis R. Lubbock, *Six Decades in Texas*, ed. C. W. Rains (Austin: Jones, 1900), p. 46.

72. Donald F. Schofield, *Indians, Cattle, Ships, and Oil: The Story of W. M. D. Lee* (Austin: University of Texas Press, 1985), p. 33.

73. Carson, *Social History of Bourbon*, pp. 88, 139, 152.

74. Richard Erdoes, *Saloons of the Old West* (New York: Knopf, 1979), p. 94.

75. W. Eugene Hollon and Ruth Lapham Butler, eds., *William Bollaert's Texas* (Norman: University of Oklahoma Press, 1956), pp. 19, 55–56, note 2.

76. McCarty, *Maverick Town*, pp. 173–174.

77. Madelon Powers, *Faces Along the Bar: Lore and Order in the Workingman's Saloon, 1870–1920* (Chicago: University of Chicago Press, 1990), p. 35.

78. Selcer et al., *Legendary Watering Holes*, p. 14.

79. Powers, *Faces Along the Bar*, pp. 16–18, 208–225. Selcer et al., *Legendary Watering Holes*, p. 36, note 9.

80. Stanley Baron, *Brewed in America: A History of Beer and Ale in the United States* (Boston: Little, Brown, 1962), pp. 14–18, 175–181, 239–240.

81. Michael C. Hennech and Trace Etienne-Gray, "Brewing Industry," in Tyler, ed., *New Handbook of Texas*, vol. 1, pp. 725–727.

82. Glen E. Lich, *The German Texans* (San Antonio: Institute of Texan Cultures, 1996), pp. 155–156.

83. McComb, *Galveston*, pp. 105–106, p. 106 (quote).

84. *Galveston Daily News*, March 28, 29, 1923. Vertical file for *Garten Verein* at Rosenberg Library, Galveston, Texas.

85. Geronimo Treviño III, *Dance Halls and Last Calls: The History of Texas Country Music* (Plano: Republic of Texas Press, 2002), pp. 128–132. The influence of the Germans can be seen throughout this listing of dance halls. See also Daniel P. Green, "Gruene, Texas" in Tyler, ed., *New Handbook of Texas*, vol. 3, p. 357.

86. Virginia Erickson and Sue Brandt McBee, *Austin: The Past Still Present* (Austin: Austin Heritage Society, 1975), p. 24. Sharon Greenhill, *Historic Austin: A Collection of Walking/Driving Tours* (Austin: Austin Heritage Society, 1981), p. 17.

87. Richard I. Dodge, *Our Wild Indians: Thirty-three Years' Personal Experience Among the Red Men of the Great West* (reprint from 1872, New York: Archer House, 1960), pp. 341–342.

88. John M. Findlay, *People of Chance: Gambling in American Society from Jamestown to Las Vegas* (New York: Oxford University Press, 1986), pp. 4–6, 50–51.

89. Lubbock, *Six Decades*, pp. 55–56. Also cited in David G. McComb, *Houston: a History* (Austin: University of Texas Press, 1981), p. 46.

90. Samuel Chamberlain, *My Confession: Recollections of a Rogue*, ed. William H. Goetzmann (Austin: Texas State Historical Association, 1996), p. 61.

91. Selcer et al., *Legendary Watering Holes*, p. 25.

92. Ty Cashion, "(Gun) Smoke Gets in Your Eyes: A Revisionist Look at 'Violent' Fort Griffin," *Southwestern Historical Quarterly*, vol. 99 (July 1995), p. 87.

93. Elton Cude, *The Free and Wild Dukedom of Bexar* (San Antonio: no pub., 1978), p. 95.

94. Cude, *Dukedom of Bexar*, p. 95.

95. The best accounts of the Thompson-Harris episode are: David Bowser, "Jack Harris's Vaudeville and San Antonio's 'Fatal Corner,'" in Selcer et al., *Legendary Watering Holes*, pp. 91–104; and Paul Adams, "The Unsolved Murder of Ben Thompson: Pistoleer Extraordinary," *Southwestern Historical Quarterly*, vol. 48 (January 1945), pp. 321–328.

96. Richard Selcer, "The White Elephant: Fort Worth's Saloon *par Excellence*," in Selcer et al., *Legendary Watering Holes*, pp. 253–254. William R. Cox, *Luke Short and His Era* (Garden City, New York: Doubleday, 1961), pp. 159–174.

97. Richard F. Selcer, *Hell's Half Acre: The Life and Legend of a Red-Light District* (Fort Worth: Texas Christian University Press, 1991), pp. 196, 201.

98. Selcer et al., *Legendary Water Holes*, pp. 274–275.

99. John S. Spratt Sr., *Thurber, Texas: The Life and Death of a Company Coal Town*, ed. Harwood P. Hinton (Austin: University of Texas Press, 1986), p. 15.

100. W. H. Timmons, *El Paso: A Borderlands History* (El Paso: Texas Western Press, 1990), pp. 225–226.

101. Frank H. Bushick, *Glamorous Days* (San Antonio: Naylor, 1934), p. 57.

102. Told in Carson, *Social History of Bourbon*, p. 1.

103. Thad Sitton, *The Texas Sheriff: Lord of the County Line* (Norman: University of Oklahoma Press, 2000), pp. 29–32, p. 29 (quote).

104. Spratt, *Thurber, Texas*, p. 16.

105. *Corpus Christi Caller-Times*, "Centennial Journey," January 23, 1983.

106. Sister Mary Keaveney, "The Depression Era in Fort Worth, Texas 1929–1934," MA thesis (Austin: University of Texas, 1974), p. 24.

107. *San Antonio Light*, September 16–23, 1929.

108. Denise M. Ford, "Deep Ellum," MA thesis (Dallas: Southern Methodist University, 1985), pp. 1–2, 7–12, p. 2 (quote). Also see Lisa C. Maxwell, "Deep Ellum" in Tyler, ed., *New Handbook of Texas*, vol. 2, p. 560.

109. *Austin American-Statesman*, March 9, 1990.

110. McComb, *Galveston*, pp. 161–166, 176–177, p. 177 (quote).

111. McComb, *Galveston*, pp. 185–187. Scott Arnold purchased the Balinese pier, still standing, in 2001 and reopened it with small shops and a sports bar.

112. *Fort Worth Press*, June 25, 1993. Quoted in Ann Arnold, *Gamblers & Gangsters: Fort Worth's Jacksboro Highway in the 1940s & 1950s* (Austin: Eakin Press, 1998), p. 9.

113. Arnold, *Gamblers & Gangsters*, pp. 59–67, 80–82.

114. Arnold, *Gamblers & Gangsters*, pp. 40–47.

115. *Austin American-Statesman*, January 18, 2001.

116. *Austin American-Statesman*, September 1, 1994.

117. *Austin American-Statesman*, January 18, 2001.

118. *Austin American-Statesman*, June 27, 1987.

119. Craig Hattersley, "Wither the Armadillo? And Where From?" *Texas Observer*, December 26, 1980.

120. *Austin American-Statesman*, September 1, 1994.

121. Frieda Werlin papers, "Gay Bars in Texas—Notes," Box AR 81–113, Center for American History, University of Texas at Austin.

122. *Dallas Times-Herald*, April 23, 1988.

123. *Austin American-Statesman*, June 25, 1995.

124. *Austin American-Statesman*, May 17, 1998.

125. *Washington Post*, January 4, 2006.

126. *Dallas Morning News*, January 30, 2000. See also Daniel G. Habib, "Online and Obsessed," *Sports Illustrated*, May 30, 2005, pp. 66–78.

127. *Dallas Times-Herald*, November 5, 1987. *Dallas Morning News*, January 30, 1995.

128. *Houston Chronicle Magazine*, September 14, 1986, p. 6.

CHAPTER TWO

1. John Van Der Kiste, *King George II and Queen Caroline* (Gloucestershire, UK: Sutton, 1997), p. 48. Roger Fulford, "Victorian and Edwardian London," in Arnold Toynbee, ed., *Cities of Destiny* (New York: Weathervane Books, 1967), p. 288.

2. David R. Goldfield and Blaine A. Brownell, *Urban America, a History* (Boston: Houghton Mifflin, 1990), pp. 26, 29, 30, 33–34.

3. John W. Reps, *The Forgotten Frontier: Urban Planning in the American West Before 1890* (Columbia: University of Missouri Press, 1981), pp. 11, 12, 13, 24–29.

4. David La Vere, *The Texas Indians* (College Station: Texas A&M University Press, 2004), pp. 188–189. T. R. Fehrenbach, *Lone Star: A History of Texas and the Texans* (New York: Macmillan, 1968), pp. 458–459. Mary A. Maverick, *Memoirs of Mary A. Maverick*, ed. Rena Maverick Green (Lincoln: University of Nebraska Press, 1989), pp. 25–31.

5. San Antonio American Institute of Architects, *A Guide to San Antonio Architecture* (San Antonio: San Antonio AIA, 1986), pp. 28, 29, 31. Charles Ramsdell, *San Antonio: A Historical and Pictorial Guide* (Austin: University of Texas Press, 1985), p. 115.

6. Martha Anne Turner, *Clara Driscoll: An American Tradition* (Austin: Madrona Press, nd), p. 17.

7. Writers' Program of the Work Projects Administration, *San Antonio: A History and Guide* (San Antonio: Clegg, 1941), p. 17.

8. Ramsdell, *San Antonio*, pp. 117–118.

9. Frederick Law Olmsted, *A Journey Through Texas* (Austin: University of Texas Press, 1978), p. 156. Scientist Ferdinand Von Roemer provides a brief description of Main Plaza in 1846. Ferdinand Von Roemer, *Texas*, trans. Oswald Mueller (San Antonio: Standard Printing, 1935), pp. 119–120. Roemer was also enamored with the sight of naked Mexican girls bathing in the crystal clear San Antonio River, pp. 124–125.

10. Sidney Lanier, *San Antonio de Bexar* (San Antonio: Mary Ann Guerra reprint, 1980), np.

11. Cornelia E. Crook, *San Pedro Springs Park, Texas' Oldest Recreation Area* (San Antonio: private printing, 1967), pp. 2–3, 5, 27, 41, 47–53, 55, 59, 69, 74, 80–81, 95.

12. Quoted in David C. Humphrey, *Austin, a History of the Capital City* (Austin: Texas State Historical Association, 1997), p. 52.

13. *Austin American-Statesman*, September 30, 2000.

14. *Austin American-Statesman*, April 29, 1983. *Daily Texan*, February 21, 1980.

15. *Austin American-Statesman*, May 3, 1992.

16. Paul Burka, "The Battle for Barton Springs," *Texas Monthly*, vol. 18 (August 1990), pp. 140–141. *Austin American-Statesman*, May 3, 1992.

17. *Austin American-Statesman*, June 7, 1991.

18. *Austin American-Statesman*, May 3, 1992. Burka, "The Battle for Barton Springs," p. 142 (quote).

19. *Austin American-Statesman*, November 19, 1994.

20. *Austin American-Statesman*, November 19, 1994; September 24, 1995; August 1, 1996; October 2, 1998; April 26, 1998.

21. *Austin American-Statesman*, March 2, 3, 2006.

22. Roemer, *Texas*, p. 42. See also Francis C. Sheridan, *Galveston Island; or, a Few Months Off the Coast of Texas: The Journal of Francis C. Sheridan, 1839–1840*, ed. Willis W. Pratt (Austin: University of Texas Press, 1954), p. 53; and M. C. Houstoun, *Texas and the Gulf of Mexico; or, Yachting in the New World* (London: John Murray, 1844), p. 275.

23. See David G. McComb, "Galveston as a Tourist City," *Southwestern Historical Quarterly*, vol. 100 (January 1997), pp. 330–360.

24. *Galveston Daily News*, May 24, 1959 (quote). McComb, "Galveston," pp. 353–354.

25. McComb, "Galveston," p. 354, p. 355 (quote).

26. Alexander Garvin, *Parks, Recreation, and Open Space: A Twenty-First Century Agenda* (Chicago: American Planning Association, 2000), p. 10. Charles Edward Doell and Gerald B. Fitzgerald, *A Brief History of Parks and Recreation in the United States* (Chicago: Athletic Institute, 1954), p. 27.

27. Vernon N. Kisling Jr., *Zoo and Aquarium History: Ancient Animal Collections to Zoological Gardens* (Boca Raton: CRC Press, 2001), pp. 8–28.

28. R. J. Hoage, Ann Roskell, and Jane Mansour, "Menageries and Zoos to 1900," in R. J. Hoage and William A. Deiss, eds., *New Worlds, New Animals: From Menagerie to Zoological Park in the Nineteenth Century* (Baltimore: Johns Hopkins University Press, 1996), p. 9.

29. Michael H. Robinson, "Foreword," in Hoage and Deiss, *New Worlds*, p. x. Harriet Ritvo, "The Order of Nature," in Hoage and Deiss, *New Worlds*, p. 50. I wish to thank T. Lindsay Baker for his suggestions about the importance of natural history museums in zoo history.

30. David Ehrlinger, "The Hagenbeck Legacy," in *International Zoo Yearbook, 1989*, vol. 29 (London: Zoological Society of London, 1989), pp. 6–9. Carl Hagenbeck, *Beasts and Men*, trans. Hugh S. R. Elliot and A. G. Thacker (New York: Longmans, Green, 1909), pp. 40–42, 234–236. Lorenz Hagenbeck, *Animals Are My Life*, trans. Alec Brown (London: Bodley Head, 1956), pp. 98–100. The idea of moats came from the use of a "sunken fence" or ditch to keep livestock away from eighteenth-century English country estates. The *Tierpark* was largely destroyed during World War II.

31. Paul Pearce, "The Fort Worth Zoological Park: A Sixty-Year History, 1909–1969," MA thesis (Fort Worth: Texas Christian University, 1969), pp. 17, 32–43, 49–54.

32. Pearce, "Fort Worth Zoological Park," pp. 63–66. *Dallas Morning News*, March 15, 1956.

33. Pearce, "Fort Worth Zoological Park," pp. 131–138. *Fort Worth Star-Telegram*, February 24, 1958.

34. *Fort Worth Star-Telegram*, April 4, 1992.

35. *Fort Worth Star-Telegram*, March 30, 1992; October 19, 1995; December 30, 1996; August 15, 1997 (quote). *Dallas Morning News*, December 25, 1997.

36. *Dallas Morning News*, December 25, 1997.

37. Elizabeth Hanson, *Animal Attractions: Nature on Display in American Zoos* (Princeton, NJ: Princeton University Press, 2002), p. 74.

38. Harry Jebsen Jr., Robert M. Newton, and Patricia R. Hogan, *Centennial History of the Dallas, Texas Park System, 1876–1976* (Lubbock: Department of History, Texas Tech University, 1976), p. 376. Maxine Holmes and Gerald D. Saxon, eds., *The WPA Dallas Guide and History* (Denton: University of North Texas Press, 1992), pp. 396–398. *Dallas Morning News*, May 19, 1957; April 4, 1966.

39. *Dallas Morning News*, December 26, 1982; July 10, 1985.

40. *Dallas Morning News*, March 1, 1983; June 17, 1983; November 5, 1984; July 28, 1986.

41. *Dallas Morning News*, October 24, 1994. Ann Zimmerman, "Survival of the Fittest," *Dallas Observer*, June 17–23, 1993.

42. *Los Angeles Times*, March 20, 2004. *New York Times*, June 20, 2004.

43. Hagenbeck, *Beasts and Men*, p. 235.

44. *Houston Post*, May 13, 14, 1988.

45. *Houston Chronicle*, May 31, 1988.

46. *USA Today*, June 3, 2005.

47. Hanson, *Animal Attractions*, p. 45, notes the comment of William M. Mann, director of the National Zoo in Washington, D.C., about its founding: that they marched two elephants from the circus, chained them to a tree, and "the zoo was a fact."

48. *Houston Press*, April 4, 1941.

49. *El Paso Times*, September 26, 1997. *El Paso Herald Post*, March 12, 1997. There is recent concern about the amount of space needed for elephants. See *USA Today*, November 1, 2006, and *New York Times*, November 5, 2006.

50. Fred A. Sullivan, ed., *Official Guide Book: San Antonio Zoological Park* (San Antonio: San Antonio Zoological Society, 1934), pp. vi–vii. Ron Tyler, ed., *The New Handbook of Texas*, vol. 5 (Austin: Texas State Historical Association, 1996), p. 816. Ramsdell, *San Antonio*, p. 184. *San Antonio Express-News*, August 26, 1988; September 19, 1993.

51. *Dallas Morning News*, January 13, 1974. *Zoo News* (Brownsville), vol. 21, no. 4 (1991), np; vol. 25, no. 4 (1995), np; vol. 26, no. 1 (1996), np.

52. *Zoo News* (Brownsville), vol. 22, no. 3 (1992), p. 5. The Houston Zoo has won the Bean Award four times, Brownsville twice, Dallas twice, and Fort Worth once.

53. *Zoo News* (Brownsville), vol. 24, no. 4 (1994), np.

54. *Austin American-Statesman*, June 21, 1992.

55. *San Antonio Express-News*, August 5, 1989. New York City established the first children's zoo in 1941. Houston opened its children's zoo in 1967.

56. See Peter Singer, *Animal Liberation: A New Ethics for Our Treatment of Animals* (New York: Avon Books, 1977). During the World War II bombing of the Hamburg Zoo, many of the enclosures ruptured and the animals were free to escape. Most of them remained near their quarters. See Hagenbeck, *Animals Are My Life*, p. 219.

57. Edward C. Schmitt, "Effects of Conservation Legislation on the Professional Development of Zoos," *International Zoo Yearbook*, vol. 27 (1987), pp. 3–4. At his wife's insistence, Charles Goodnight (1836–1929) became the first Texas preservationist by protecting a small herd of buffalo at his Palo Duro ranch.

58. *Dallas Times-Herald*, September 17, 1982.

59. *Dallas Morning News*, November 5, 1984.

60. *Dallas Morning News*, September 29, 2000.

61. *Houston Chronicle*, April 7, 1992. *San Antonio Express-News*, April 7, 1992.

62. Michael Satchell, "Cruel and Usual," *U.S. News and World Report* (August 5, 2002), pp. 28–33.

63. Peter Batten, *Living Trophies* (New York: Thomas Y. Crowell, 1976), pp. viii–ix, 1–2, 184–185. See also, Marvin L. Jones, "Mortality of Wild-Caught Animals After Arrival in the Zoo," *International Zoo Yearbook*, vol. 14 (1974), pp. 37–38.

64. *San Antonio Express-News*, August 18, 1985 (quote). *San Antonio Current*, August 8–21, 1991. Hermann Dembeck, *Animals and Men*, trans. Richard and Charles Winston (Garden City, New York: Natural History Press, 1965), pp. 283–287. For a sample of the ongoing argument, see *Dallas Morning News*, March 5, 2006.

65. Freeman Tilden, *The State Parks: Their Meaning in American Life* (New York: Knopf, 1962), p. 27 (quote). Ney C. Landrum, *The State Park Movement in America: A Critical Review* (Columbus: University of Missouri Press, 2004), pp. 1–2, 30, 39, 48–73, 81–94.

66. Dan K. Utley and James W. Steely, *Guided with a Steady Hand: the Cultural Landscape of a Rural Texas Park* (Waco: Baylor University Press, 1998), p. 6.

67. Utley and Steely, *Guided with a Steady Hand*, p. 23.

68. James W. Steely, *Parks for Texas: Enduring Landscapes of the New Deal* (Austin: University of Texas Press, 1999), pp. 6, 11, 29–36. James W. Steely, *The Civilian Conservation Corps in Texas State Parks* (Austin: Texas Parks and Wildlife, 1986), np. Sharon M. Toney, "The Texas State Parks System: An Administrative History, 1923–1984," PhD thesis (Lubbock: Texas Tech University, 1995), pp. 11–12, 22–24, 25, 28–30, 42–45. The number of parks is based upon a count in the *2004 Texas State Travel Guide* (Austin: Texas Department of Transportation, 2004?), pp. 251–252. Toney cites a number of 136.

69. Randolph B. Marcy, *Adventure on Red River*, ed. Grant Foreman (Norman: University of Oklahoma Press, 1937), pp. 90–91. Cited also by William C. Griggs, "Man and the Palo Duro Canyon: From Coronado to Goodnight," in Duane F. Guy, ed., *The Story of Palo Duro Canyon* (Lubbock: Texas Tech University Press, 2001), p. 122.

70. Marcy, *Adventure on Red River*, p. 91.

71. J. Evetts Haley, *Charles Goodnight: Cowman & Plainsman* (Norman: University of Oklahoma Press, 1936), pp. 262–263.

72. Haley, *Goodnight*, p. 296.

73. Ann Fears Crawford and Crystal Sasse Ragsdale, *Women in Texas: Their Lives, Their Experiences, Their Accomplishments* (Austin: Eakin Press, 1982), p. 115.

74. Crawford and Ragsdale, *Women in Texas*, p. 117 (first quote), p. 116 (second quote).

75. Peter L. Petersen, "A Park for the Panhandle: the Acquisition and Development of Palo Duro State Park," in Guy, ed., *The Story of Palo Duro Canyon*, pp. 145–146.

76. Petersen, "A Park for the Panhandle," pp. 153–156, 169–170, 172–173, 174–177.

77. Petersen, "A Park for the Panhandle," p. 177. Duane F. Guy, "An Amphitheater for the Panhandle," in Guy, ed., *The Story of Palo Duro Canyon*, pp. 185–192.

78. Letter from D. E. Colp to R. E. Townsend, January 11, 1930, MS/Int file Palo Duro Park, Panhandle-Plains Museum Archives.

79. John Jameson, *The Story of Big Bend National Park* (Austin: University of Texas Press, 1996), pp. 9–10, 15.

80. Ronnie C. Tyler, "The Little Punitive Expedition in the Big Bend," *Southwestern Historical Quarterly*, vol. 78 (January 1975), p. 284.

81. Roland H. Wauer and Carl M. Fleming, *Naturalist's Big Bend: An Introduction to the Trees and Shrubs, Wildflowers, Cacti, Mammals, Birds, Reptiles and Amphibians, Fish, and Insects* (College Station: Texas A&M University Press, 2002), pp. 13–14.

82. Elton Miles, *Tales of the Big Bend* (College Station: Texas A&M University Press, 1976), pp. 37–48, 90–98.

83. Miles, *Tales of the Big Bend*, pp. 114–132. Richard I. Dodge, *Our Wild Indians: Thirty-three Years' Personal Experience Among the Red Men of the Great West* (reprint from 1882, New York: Archer House, 1959), p. 245.

84. Odie B. Faulk, *The U.S. Camel Corps: An Army Experiment* (New York: Oxford University Press, 1976), p. 150.

85. Kenneth B. Ragsdale, *Big Bend Country: Land of the Unexpected* (College Station: Texas A&M University Press, 1998), p. 49. H. Joaquin Jackson and David Marion Wilkinson report a chilling random shooting of three American tourists rafting on the river in 1988 by Mexican teenagers in *One Ranger: A Memoir* (Austin: University of Texas Press, 2005), pp. 109–146.

86. Robert T. Hill, "Running the Cañons of the Rio Grande," *The Century Magazine*, vol. 61 (January 1901), pp. 371–372.

87. Walter Prescott Webb, "The Big Bend of Texas," *The Panhandle-Plains Historical Review*, vol. 10 (1937), p. 7.

88. *Dallas Morning News*, May 15, 1958; December 9, 1962 (quote).

89. Virginia Madison, *The Big Bend Country of Texas* (Albuquerque: University of New Mexico Press, 1955), pp. 229–230.

90. Robert M. Wagstaff, "Beginnings of the Big Bend Park," *The West Texas Historical Association Year Book*, vol. 44 (October 1968), pp. 3–14.

91. Madison, *The Big Bend Country of Texas*, p. 232.

92. Ron C. Tyler, *The Big Bend: A History of the Last Texas Frontier* (College Station: Texas A&M University Press, 2003), pp. 199–205, 207–210. Wauer and Fleming, *Naturalist's Big Bend*, pp. 4, 18–19.

93. Jameson, *The Story of Big Bend National Park*, pp. 88–93, 96–99.

94. *Austin American-Statesman*, October 7, 1999.

95. Tyler, *The Big Bend*, p. 206.

96. Barto Arnold III and Robert Weddle, *The Nautical Archeology of Padre Island: The Spanish Shipwrecks of 1554* (New York: Academic Press, 1978), pp. 22, 27, 28, 38–48. Much of this history of Padre Island can be found in David G. McComb, *The Historic Seacoast of Texas* (Austin: University of Texas Press, 1999), pp. 70–76.

97. Padre Island Boosters' Club press release, 1959, Padre Island vertical file, Center for American History, University of Texas at Austin.

98. *Padre Island National Park.* Hearings before the Senate Subcommittee on Public Lands, Committee on Interior and Insular Affairs, 86th Cong., 1st sess., Corpus Christi, Texas, December 14, 1959 (Washington: Government Printing Office, 1960), p. 9.

99. *Padre Island National Park.* Hearings, December 14, 1959, p. 80.

100. *Padre Island National Park.* Hearings, December 14, 1959, p. 82.

101. *Corpus Christi Caller*, April 9, 1968.

CHAPTER THREE

1. Quoted in David G. McComb, *Sports in World History* (London: Routledge, 2004), p. 24–25. See this book also for the influence of the Greeks and others, pp. 9–33.

2. Peter Quennell, *The Colosseum* (New York: Newsweek, 1971), pp. 16–31, 35–36.

3. Quennell, *The Colosseum*, pp. 36–41. Rosella Rea, "The Architecture and Function of the Colosseum," in Ada Gabucci, ed., *The Colosseum* (Los Angeles: J. Paul Getty Museum, 2000), p. 105. See also Gabucci, pp. 166–167, for an artist's rendition of the stadium.

4. Quoted in David G. McComb, *Sports: An Illustrated History* (New York: Oxford University Press, 1998), p. 38.

5. Quennell, *The Colosseum*, p. 97.

6. Quennell, *The Colosseum*, pp. 126–127, 142–151.

7. Dene Hofheinz Mann, *You Be the Judge* (Houston: Premier Printing, 1965), p. 79. Edgar W. Ray, *The Grand Huckster: Houston's Judge Roy Hofheinz, Genius of the Astrodome* (Memphis: Memphis State University Press, 1980), pp. 230–231.

8. McComb, *Sports: An Illustrated History*, pp. 101–102.

9. David G. McComb, *Houston, a History* (Austin: University of Texas Press, 1981), p. 104.

10. David G. McComb, *Galveston, a History* (Austin: University of Texas Press, 1986), p. 116.

11. Michael V. Hazel, ed. "Timeline," *Legacies*, vol. 17 (Spring 2005), pp. 6–7.

12. Jon Holmes, *Texas Sport* (Austin: Texas Monthly Press, 1984), p. 30.

13. Harry Jebsen Jr. "The Public Acceptance of Sports in Dallas, 1880–1930," *Journal of Sport History*, vol. 6 (Winter 1979), p. 11.

14. McComb, *Houston*, p. 102.

15. Nancy Wiley, *The Great State Fair of Texas* (Dallas: Taylor Publishing Company, 1985), pp. 49, 52, 70, 71, 86, 103.

16. Wiley, *State Fair*, pp. 105–106. *Dallas Morning News*, January 16, 1966; July 3, 2005.

17. *Dallas Morning News*, January 2, 1947; December 31, 1985; August 6, 1994 (quote).

18. *Dallas Morning News*, August 6, 1994.

19. *Dallas Morning News*, December 22, 1985.

20. *Dallas Morning News*, January 1, 1995. Carlton Stowers, *The Cotton Bowl Classic, The First Fifty Years* (Dallas: Host Communications, 1986), p. 35 (quote).

21. *Dallas Morning News*, December 31, 1989. SMU athletic Web site, "Walker Receives Heisman." The statistics vary slightly and the *ESPN Sports Almanac, 2003* indicates a tie game in the 1949 Cotton Bowl Classic.

22. *Dallas Morning News*, February 21, 1954; December 16, 1966; December 31, 1989 (quote); November 12, 1999. Stowers, *The Cotton Bowl Classic,* pp. 19, 150.

23. *Dallas Morning News*, November 12, 1999. All quotes from the article "Moving Memories" by Jodie Valade.

24. John Eisenberg, *Cotton Bowl Days: Growing Up with Dallas and the Cowboys in the 1960s* (New York: Simon & Schuster, 1997), pp. 15 (first quote), 72 (second quote).

25. *Austin American-Statesman*, December 19, 1993.

26. *Austin American-Statesman*, December 19, 1993 (first and second quotes); *Dallas Morning News*, January 1, 2004 (third quote).

27. *Austin American-Statesman*, December 19, 1993 (first and third quotes); *Dallas Morning News*, January 1, 2004 (second quote).

28. *Dallas Morning News*, January 2, 1970.

29. *Austin American-Statesman*, January 1, 1991.

30. *Dallas Morning News*, January 2, 1970.

31. Joe Montana with Dick Schaap, *Montana* (Atlanta: Turner Publishing, 1995), pp. 40, 43.

32. Stowers, *Cotton Bowl Classic*, p. 121.

33. Montana, *Montana*, p. 43.

34. Jodella K. Dyreson, "The Racial Dynamics of the Forgotten Texas Centennial Olympics." Paper delivered at the Texas State Historical Association annual meeting, San Antonio, March 10, 2007.

35. Charles H. Martin, "Integrating New Year's Day: The Racial Politics of College Bowl Games in the American South," *Journal of Sport History*, vol. 24 (Fall 1997), pp. 362–364, p. 363 (quote).

36. Martin, "Integrating New Year's Day," p. 365.

37. Alexander Wolff, "Ground Breakers," *Sports Illustrated*, vol. 103 (November 7, 2005), p. 62.

38. Wolff, "Ground Breakers," pp. 62, 64. Richard Pennington, *Breaking the Ice: The Racial Integration of Southwest Conference Football* (Jefferson, N.C.: McFarland, 1987), p. 109. For integration elsewhere in Texas see Ronald E. Marcello, "The Integration of Intercollegiate Athletics in Texas: North Texas State College as a Test Case, 1956," *Journal of Sport History*, vol. 14 (Winter 1987), pp. 286–316.

39. National Football Foundation, December 9, 2003. The quote came from the *Des Moines Register.*

40. Charles K. Ross, *Outside the Lines: African Americans and the Integration of the National Football League* (New York: New York University Press, 1999), pp. 128–130, 146.

41. Jane Wolfe, *The Murchisons: The Rise and Fall of a Texas Dynasty* (New York: St. Martin's Press, 1989), pp. 298–299.

42. Donald Chipman, Randolph Campbell, and Robert Calvert, *The Dallas Cowboys and the NFL* (Norman: University of Oklahoma Press, 1970), p. 145.

43. Quoted in Jon Morgan, *Glory for Sale* (Baltimore: Bancroft Press, 1997), p. 315. See also Costas Spirou and Larry Bennett, *It's Hardly Sportin': Stadiums, Neighborhoods, and the New Chicago* (DeKalb: Northern Illinois University Press, 2003), pp. 9–58.

44. Robert C. Trumpbour, "The New Cathedrals: The Sports Stadium and Mass Media's Role in Facilitating New Construction," thesis (State College: Penn State University, 2001), p. 1. Dean V. Baim, *The Sports Stadium as a Municipal Investment* (Westport, Conn.: Greenwood Press, 1994), p. 218. Roger G. Noll and Andrew Zimbalist, "Sports, Jobs, and Taxes: The Real Connection," in Roger G. Noll and Andrew Zimbalist, eds. *Sports, Jobs, and Taxes: The Economic Impact of Sports Teams and Stadiums* (Washington, D.C.: Brookings Institution Press, 1997), pp. 495–498.

45. See: Nelson W. Wolff, *Mayor: An Inside View of San Antonio Politics, 1981–1995* (San Antonio: Express-News, 1997). Francisca A. Gonzalez, "The San Antonio Multipurpose Domed Stadium: An Evaluation of its Economic Feasibility," MA thesis (San Antonio: Trinity University, 1989). *San Antonio Express-News*, June 18, 1987; August 6, 30, 1987; July 23, 1996; March 29, 1998. *San Antonio Light*, November 29, 1988.

46. Chipman, Campbell, and Calvert, *Dallas Cowboys*, p. 103.

47. Eisenberg, *Cotton Bowl Days*, pp. 173, 177.

48. Eisenberg, *Cotton Bowl Days*, pp. 14, 73, pp. 162–163 (quote).

49. *Dallas Times Herald*, November 26, 1967; December 28, 1967; January 3, 1968. *Dallas Morning News*, May 6, 1968.

50. *Dallas Morning News*, April 21, 1966.

51. *Dallas Morning News*, April 13, 1970.

52. Wolfe, *Murchisons*, pp. 300–303, p. 300 (quote).

53. Wolfe, *Murchisons*, pp. 305–307, p. 307 (quote).

54. Wolfe, *Murchisons*, p. 307. Because of financial difficulties, Murchison sold the Cowboys and the lease on Texas Stadium in 1983. His health broke and he declared bankruptcy in 1985. He died two years later.

55. Eisenberg, *Cotton Bowl Days*, pp. 92, 264 (third quote), 265 (first quote), 266 (second quote).

56. *Dallas Morning News*, November 12, 1999.

57. *Dallas Morning News*, June 29, 1994; March 29, 1995; January 2, 1996 (quote). *Austin American-Statesman*, August 5, 1994.

58. *Dallas Morning News*, May 31, 1953; October 12, 1989; July 3, 2005; August 17, 2005.

59. *Dallas Morning News*, February 28, 2007.

60. Geoffrey C. Ward and Ken Burns, *Baseball: An Illustrated History* (New York: Knopf, 1994), p. 13. Ward and Burns place Putnam in Texas, but he is clearly in Louisiana. See George H. Putnam, *Memories of My Youth, 1844–1865* (New York: G. P. Putnam's Sons, 1914).

61. McComb, *Galveston*, p. 115. McComb, *Houston*, p. 43. Bill O'Neal, *The Texas League, 1888–1987: A Century of Baseball* (Austin: Eakin Press, 1887), pp. 3–4, 60.

62. O'Neal, *Texas League*, pp. 16, 179. McComb, *Galveston*, p. 148.

63. O'Neal, *Texas League*, pp. 260–263.

64. *The Sporting News*, January 15, 1958.

65. Jason Bruce Chrystal, "The Taj Mahal of Sport: The Creation of the Houston Astrodome, 1957–1967." PhD thesis (Ames: Iowa State University, 2004), p. 19.

66. Chrystal, "Taj Mahal," pp. 26–29, 36, 44, 50, 68, 74–75, 79.

67. Ray, *Grand Huckster*, p. 263.

68. Ray, *Grand Huckster*, pp. 260–262, p. 260 (quote).

69. *USA Today*, September 21, 2005. R. Q. Praeger and John W. Waterburg, "Convertibility," *The American City*, vol. 81 (August 1966), p. 101. Robert J. Minchew to Edwin M. Long, April 29, 1964, in Minchew Papers, 92–274/1, Center for American History, University of Texas at Austin.

70. Frank X. Tolbert, "The Incredible Houston Dome," *Look*, vol. 29 (April 20, 1965), p. 98.

71. Chrystal, "Taj Mahal," pp. 133–139, 148–149.

72. Chrystal, "Taj Mahal," p. 236.

73. Ray, *Grand Huckster*, p. 308.

74. McComb, *Houston*, p. 188 (including quote).

75. Deposition of Alan C. Farnsworth, November 1973, and deposition of Robert Minchew, March 1974, in Minchew Papers, 94–274/13, Center for American History, University of Texas at Austin.

76. Ray, *Grand Huckster*, p. 334 (quote). John R. McDermott, "What a Wonder! What a Blunder!" *Life*, vol. 58 (April 23, 1965), p. 78. See also McComb, *Houston*, pp. 188–189.

77. Dan J. Forrestal, *Faith, Hope, and $5,000: The Story of Monsanto* (New York: Simon & Schuster, 1977), pp. 207–209. Ray, *Grand Huckster*, pp. 307, 344–345.

78. Larry McMurtry, "Love, Death, & the Astrodome," in *In a Narrow Grave: Essays on Texas* (Albuquerque: University of New Mexico Press, 1968), pp. 110 (first quote), 111 (third quote), 117 (second quote).

79. Roger Angell, "The Cool Bubble," *New Yorker*, vol. 42 (May 14, 1966), pp. 130, 131, 135, 141 (quote).

80. Quoted in Ray, *Grand Huckster*, p. 337.

81. "Daymares in the Dome," *Time*, vol. 85 (April 16, 1965), p. 98.

82. Ray, *Grand Huckster*, p. 437.

83. Ray, *Grand Huckster*, pp. 456, 460, 509, 515–519, 527–538.

84. *Dallas Morning News*, July 10, 2000. *Houston Chronicle*, October 22, 1995; September 15, 1996; October 22, 2005.

85. *Houston Chronicle*, October 1, 1995.

86. *Houston Chronicle*, March 3, 2000.

87. *Dallas Morning News*, September 15, 2000; October 27, 2000.

88. *Houston Chronicle*, October 3, 1999.

89. *Houston Chronicle*, August 4, 7, 2003; June 23, 2006. See also for Katrina refuge, John Spong, "Dome Away From Home," *Texas Monthly*, vol. 33 (November 2005), pp. 154–158, 261–268. If asked, I would suggest a mammoth sports museum that would include artifacts from baseball, football, and other sports.

90. *Houston Chronicle*, June 29, 1997.

91. *Houston Chronicle*, March 26, 2000. See Mickey Herskowitz column "Enron Field."

CHAPTER FOUR

1. R. E. Wycherley, *How the Greeks Built Cities*, 2nd ed. (Garden City, N.Y.: Doubleday & Company, 1969), pp. 39–220.

2. *USA Today*, December 27, 2004.

3. Harry Reasoner's quote is from *Before the Colors Fade* (New York: Knopf, 1981), p. 116. Moby is quoted in *Austin American-Statesman*, October 13, 2002. *Miami Herald*, October 13, 2002. Smith is quoted in Rhoda Thomas Tripp, comp., *The International Thesaurus of Quotations* (New York:

Thomas Y. Crowell, 1970), p. 92. Stevenson is quoted in Suzy Platt, ed., *Respectfully Quoted: A Dictionary of Quotations* (New York: Dorset Press, 1992), p. 29.

4. It was not a complete triumph and these statistics taken from U.S. census data may be questioned. Tests of World War I soldiers and sailors found literacy at 75 percent. The National Institute of Literacy reported in 1998 that 20 to 23 percent of adult Americans read at such a low level that they could not fill out a Social Security application or find their location on a map. See National Institute of Literacy, *The State of Literacy in America* (Washington, D.C.: U.S. Government Printing Office, 1998).

5. John Salmon Ford, *Rip Ford's Texas*, ed. Stephen B. Oates (Austin: University of Texas Press, 1963), p. 442.

6. Douglas C. McMurtrie, "Pioneer Printing in Texas," *Southwestern Historical Quarterly*, vol. 35 (January 1932), pp. 175–176. Lota M. Spell, "Samuel Bangs: The First Printer in Texas," *Southwestern Historical Quarterly*, vol. 35 (April 1932), pp. 268–273. Joseph Milton Nance, "Samuel Bangs," in Ron Tyler, ed., *The New Handbook of Texas*, vol. 1 (Austin: Texas State Historical Association, 1996), p. 367.

7. David G. McComb, *Galveston, a History* (Austin: University of Texas Press, 1986), p. 73.

8. James McEnteer, *Fighting Words: Independent Journalists in Texas* (Austin: University of Texas Press, 1992), p. 32. Charles Carver, *Brann and the Iconoclast* (Austin: University of Texas Press, 1957), pp. 4, 171.

9. Louise C. Allen, Ernest A. Sharpe, and John R. Whitaker, "Newspapers," in Tyler, ed. *The New Handbook of Texas*, vol. 4, pp. 1,000–1,002.

10. National Endowment for the Arts, *Reading at Risk: A Survey of Literary Reading in America*, Research Division Report #47 (Washington, D.C.: National Endowment for the Arts, 2004), p. 17.

11. Frederick Law Olmsted, *A Journey Through Texas* (Austin: University of Texas Press, 1978), pp. 117–118.

12. Kenneth W. Wheeler, *To Wear a City's Crown: The Beginnings of Urban Growth in Texas, 1836–1865* (Cambridge: Harvard University Press, 1968), p. 58.

13. Wheeler, *To Wear a City's Crown*, pp. 57, 58. Elizabeth Silverthorne, *Ashbel Smith of Texas: Pioneer, Patriot, Statesman 1805–1886* (College Station: Texas A&M University Press, 1982), p. 5. Ferdinand Roemer, *Texas* (San Antonio: Standard Printing, 1935, 1983), pp. 59–60.

14. Carl C. Wright, "Reading Interests in Texas from the 1830's to the Civil War," *Southwestern Historical Quarterly*, vol. 54 (January 1951), pp. 312–314.

15. Prescott C. Mabon, *Mission Communications: The Story of Bell Laboratories* (Murray Hill, N.J.: Bell Laboratories, 1975), pp. 7, 160, 169. It is curious that the role of libraries and education is often ignored in the process of invention. See for example, Harold Evans, *They Made America* (New York: Little, Brown, 2004).

16. Fred Lerner, *The Story of Libraries: From the Invention of Writing to the Computer Age* (New York: Continuum, 1998), p. 112.

17. Harry H. Ransom, *The Other Texas Frontier* (Austin: Texas, 1984), pp. 59–68, p. 68 (quote).

18. Walter Muir Whitehall, *Boston Public Library: A Centennial History* (Cambridge: Harvard University Press, 1956), pp. 29–33. Michael H. Harris, *History of Libraries in the Western World*, 4th ed. (Lanham, Md.: Scarecrow Press, 1995), pp. 241, 243–244.

19. Quoted in Whitehall, *Boston Public Library*, p. 193.

20. Quoted in Susan Allen Toth and John Coughlan, eds., *Reading Rooms* (New York: Doubleday, 1991), pp. 421, 422.

21. Christine A. Jenkins, "Children's Services, Public," in Wayne A. Wiegand and Donald G. Davis Jr., eds., *Encyclopedia of Library History* (New York: Garland, 1994), p. 128 (first quote), p. 129 (second quote).

22. Quoted in Toth and Coughlan, eds., *Reading Rooms*, pp. 423–424.

23. Quoted in Toth and Coughlan, eds., *Reading Rooms*, pp. 212–215.

24. Dan Rather with Peter Wyden, *I Remember: Growing Up in Texas* (Boston: Little, Brown, 1991), p. 193 (first and second quotes), p. 194 (third and fourth quotes).

25. Kenneth B. Ragsdale, *Big Bend Country: Land of the Unexpected* (College Station: Texas A&M University Press, 1998), pp. 56–69, p. 66 (first quote), p. 69 (second quote). Jefferson Morgenthaler, *The River Has Never Divided Us* (Austin: Texas, 2004), pp. 3–4, 240.

26. Quoted in Abigail A. Van Slyck, *Free to All: Carnegie Libraries & American Culture, 1890–1920* (Chicago: University of Chicago Press, 1995), p. 208.

27. Quoted in Toth and Coughlan, eds., *Reading Rooms*, pp. 65–66.

28. Slyck, *Free to All*, pp. 125–128.

29. Slyck, *Free to All*, p. 163.

30. Mary Miles Maack, "Gender Issues in Librarianship," in *Encyclopedia of Library History*, p. 229.

31. Paul S. Boyer, *Purity in Print: Book Censorship in America from the Gilded Age to the Computer Age* (Madison: University of Wisconsin Press, 2002), pp. 324–327, 329.

32. Jean Preer, "Censorship," in *Encyclopedia of Library History*, p. 121.

33. *Galveston Daily News*, January 29, 1871.

34. "Fiction Song," *Library Journal*, vol. 15 (November 1890), p. 325. Also quoted in Rosemary R. Du Mont, *Reform and Reaction: The Big City Public Library in American Life* (Westport, Conn.: Greenwood Press, 1977), pp. 116–117.

35. Du Mont, *Reform and Reaction*, p. 41.

36. William S. Gray and Ruth Monroe, *The Reading Interests and Habits of Adults: A Preliminary Report* (New York: Macmillan, 1929), pp. 15, 19, 49–50.

37. National Endowment for the Arts, *Reading at Risk*, pp. 3–4.

38. Whitehall, *Boston Public Library*, 74.

39. Quoted in Slyck, *Free to All*, pp. 196–197. The Lillian Gunter diary is in the Texas State Archives.

40. Slyck, *Free to All*, pp. 22, 25, 64–66, 76. Robert Sidney Martin, ed., *Carnegie Denied: Communities Rejecting Carnegie Library Construction Grants, 1898–1925* (Westport, Conn.: Greenwood Press, 1993), pp. viii–ix.

41. Donald G. Davis Jr. and Ronald C. Stone Jr., "Poverty of Mind and Lack of Municipal Spirit: Rejection of Carnegie Public Library Grants by Seven Southern Communities," in Martin, *Carnegie Denied*, pp. 138–140, 145–149. Robert Edward Lee, "Texas Library Development: Its Relation to the Carnegie Movement, 1898–1915," MA thesis (Austin: University of Texas, 1959), pp. 6, 67, 71. Cities fulfilling their obligations in 1916 were Abilene, Cleburne, Corsicana, Dallas, El Paso, Fort Worth, Houston, San Antonio, and Waco. See also Paul M. Culp Jr., "Carnegie Libraries of Texas: The Past Still Present," *Texas Libraries*, vol. 43 (Summer 1981), pp. 81–96.

42. Darwin Payne, *Dallas: An Illustrated History* (Woodland Hills, Calif.: Windson Publications, 1982), p. 174.

43. Michael V. Hazel, *The Dallas Public Library: Celebrating a Century of Service, 1901–2001* (Denton: University of North Texas Press, 2001), pp. 2–9, p. 6 (first quote), p. 9 (second quote).

44. Hazel, *Dallas Public Library*, pp. 12–13.

45. Hazel, *Dallas Public Library*, pp. 13–15, p. 15 (quote).

46. Tommie Dora Barker, *Libraries of the South: A Report on Developments, 1930–1935* (Chicago: American Library Association, 1936), p. 201, pp. 101–102 (quote).

47. Hazel, *Dallas Public Library*, pp. 59–66.

48. E. J. Jose, "Race Issues in Library History," in Wiegand and Davis, *Encyclopedia*, p. 535.

49. Hazel, *Dallas Public Library*, pp. 87–92.

50. Hazel, *Dallas Public Library*, pp. 108–111.

51. Ronald L. Davis, *John Rosenfield's Dallas: How the Southwest's Leading Critic Shaped a City's Culture, 1925–1966* (Dallas: Three Forks Press, 2002), pp. 252–253, pp. 302–303 (quote).

52. Hazel, *Dallas Public Library*, pp. 169, 204.

53. Doug Tomlinson and David Dillon, *Dallas Architecture, 1936–1986* (Austin: Texas Monthly Press, 1985), p. 100.

54. Tomlinson and Dillon, *Dallas Architecture*, p. 103.

55. Slyck, *Free to All*, p. 5 (first quote), p. 37 (second quote).

56. In the 1990s, at my home campus at Colorado State University, the president authorized a monumental addition to the library designed by Boston architects. The huge three-story concave entry façade, designed to represent the open pages of a book, funneled the cold winter northwest winds through the front door so effectively that the people working at the circulation desk had to wear their parkas. Curved walls along one side indicated that the designers forgot that books are rectangular in shape. The architects, moreover, designed a moat to allow light into the basement floor on a campus known to flood. In 1997 floodwaters filled the moat, broke into the basement, and destroyed about one-fourth to one-third of the collection.

57. William Albert Trembley, "Henry Rosenberg, a Texas Builder," MA thesis (Houston: University of Houston, 1953), pp. 1, 3, 9, 65, 77, 78. Quote is from the cornerstone of the Rosenberg Library.

58. *Galveston Daily News*, January 26, 1858; December 9, 1870; January 20, 1871; January 29, 1871; February 5, 1871; December 14, 1873; September 15, 1878; June 2, 1880; October 2, 1885; March 8, 1888. Melbourne Jordan, "Frank Chauncy Patten: the Galveston Years," MLS report, University of Texas, 1966, pp. 25–27.

59. Glynell S. Barnes, "A History of Public Library Services to Negroes in Galveston, Texas, 1904–1955," thesis (Atlanta, GA: Atlanta University, 1957), pp. 2, 20–22, 34.

60. Jordan, "Patten," pp. 32, 73–75, pp. 54–55 (quote).

61. Jane Kenamore, "Texas History at Rosenberg Has History of Its Own," *Texas Libraries*, vol. 41 (Spring 1979), pp. 28–30. Casey Edward Greene, "Foresight Built the Rosenberg Library's Archives," *Houston Review*, vol. 19 (1997), pp. 65–66.

62. *Galveston Daily News*, March 5, 1967.

63. Kenamore, "Texas History at Rosenberg," p. 31. Greene, "Foresight," p. 67. *Galveston News*, March 5, 1967 (first quote). Bob Dalehite quote with author, 1966.

64. Tyler, ed., *The New Handbook of Texas*, vol. 6, p. 428.

65. Harriet Smither and Dorman H. Winfrey, "Texas State Archive," in Tyler, ed., *The New Handbook of Texas*, vol. 6, pp. 428–430.

66. Louis R. Wilson and Edward A. Wight, *County Library Service in the South: A Study of the Rosenwald County Library Demonstration* (Chicago: University of Chicago Press, 1935), p. 94. *Texas Almanac, 2002–2003* (Dallas: *Dallas Morning News*, 2001), pp. 498–507.

67. Lerner, *Story of Libraries*, pp. 120–121.

68. Quoted in Louis C. Moloney, "A History of the University Library at the University of Texas, 1883–1934," doctorate of library science thesis (New York: Columbia University, 1970), p. 273.

69. Carolyn Bucknall, "Texas. University of Texas Libraries," in Allen Kent, Harold Lancour, and Jay E. Daily, *Encyclopedia of Library and Information Science,* vol. 30 (New York: Dekker, 1980), pp. 359–360. Felex D. Almaraz Jr., *Knight Without Armor: Carlos Eduardo Castañeda, 1896–1958* (College Station: Texas A&M University Press, 1999), p. 160.

70. Bucknall, "Texas," p. 359. Don E. Carleton and Katherine J. Adams, "'A Work Peculiarly Our Own': Origins of the Barker Texas History Center, 1883–1950," *Southwestern Historical Quarterly,* vol. 86 (October 1982), pp. 209–210.

71. Jack Maguire, "Harry Ransom: the Liveliest Experimenter of Them All," *Alcalde,* vol. 69 (March 1961).

72. Ronnie Dugger, *Our Invaded Universities: Form, Reform and New Starts* (New York: W. W. Norton, 1974), p. 76.

73. UT News and Information Service release, May 31, 1962. Dugger, *Universities,* p. 77.

74. *Daily Texan,* May 1, 1987.

75. Carlton Lake, "Ed the Collector, Jake the Dentist and Beckett: A Tale That Ends in Texas," *New York Times Book Review,* September, 6, 1987, p. 2.

76. Bucknall, "Texas," p. 364. *Austin American-Statesman,* January 22, 1986. "The Great Paper Chase," *Time,* vol. 79 (April 6, 1962), p. 77.

77. Bucknall, "Texas," p. 358. Moloney, "A History of the University Library," pp. 181–190, 351–354.

78. Bucknall, "Texas," pp. 361, 363–364, p. 364 (quote).

79. David G. McComb, *Texas: A Modern History* (Austin: University of Texas Press, 1989), p. 173.

80. *Austin American-Statesman,* December 16, 1978. *Daily Texan,* June 5, 1978.

81. Bucknall, "Texas," pp. 367–368.

82. Gene Lyons, "The Last of the Big-Time Spenders," *Texas Monthly,* vol. 6 (January 1978), p. 145 (both quotes).

83. Norman D. Stevens, "Library Equipment," in Wiegand and Davis, *Encyclopedia,* p. 363.

84. Marylaine Block, "Keepers of the Flame," *American Libraries,* vol. 32 (June/July 2001), p. 65–66.

85. B. Varvek, "Wanted! Entertainment Director," *American Libraries,* vol. 32 (June/July 2001), pp. 69–71, p. 70 (quote).

86. Malcolm Jones, "Waiting for the Movie," *Newsweek,* vol. 164 (July 19, 2004), p. 58.

87. Frank Ahrens, "Hard News to Digest," *Washington Post National Weekly Edition,* February 28–March 6, 2005, p. 19. National Endowment for the Arts, *Reading at Risk,* p. ix. "The Decline of the American Newspaper," *The Week,* vol. 7 (January 19, 2007), p. 11. *Fort Collins Coloradoan,* October 31, 2006.

88. *USA Today,* August 10, 2004.

89. E. Rodger, G. D'Elia, and C. Jorgensen, "The Public Library and the Internet: Is Peaceful Coexistence Possible?" *American Libraries,* vol. 32 (May 2001), p. 58.

90. Patricia Cohen, "Spaces for Social Study," Education Life, *New York Times,* August 1, 2004, p. 19.

91. National Endowment for the Arts, *Reading at Risk,* p. vii.

92. *USA Today,* February 23, 2007.

93. *Washington Post,* January 21, 2007.

94. *USA Today,* August 3, 2004.

CHAPTER FIVE

1. Oscar G. Brockett and Franklin J. Hildy, *History of Theatre*, 9th ed. (Boston: Allyn and Bacon, 2003), pp. 1, 5, 13, 18, 95, 121, 163, 216, 218.

2. Brockett and Hildy, *History of Theatre*, p. 5.

3. Charles Hackett, "The Marquis of San Miguel de Aguayo and his Recovery of Texas from the French, 1719–1723," *Southwestern Historical Quarterly*, vol. 49 (October 1945), p. 209.

4. Stephen B. Oates, ed., *Rip Ford's Texas* (Austin: University of Texas Press, 1987), pp. 15–17, p. 17 (quote).

5. W. Eugene Hollon and Ruth Lapham Butler, eds. *William Bollaert's Texas* (Norman: University of Oklahoma Press, 1956), p. 86.

6. Darwin Payne, "Camp Life in the Army of Occupation: Corpus Christi, July 1845 to March 1846," *Southwestern Historical Quarterly*, vol. 73 (January 1970), p. 337.

7. Joseph Jefferson, *The Autobiography of Joseph Jefferson* (New York: Century Co., 1889), pp. 58–65.

8. Sue Dauphin, *Houston by Stages: A History of Theatre in Houston* (Burnet, Tex.: Eakin Press, 1981), pp. 5–9.

9. David Bowser, "Jack Harris's Vaudeville and San Antonio's 'Fatal Corner,'" in Richard Selcer, David Bowser, Nancy Hamilton, and Chuck Parsons, *Legendary Watering Holes: The Saloons that Made Texas Famous* (College Station: Texas A&M University Press, 2004), pp. 65–79.

10. Ronald L. Davis, "Sopranos and Six Guns: The Frontier Opera House as a Cultural Symbol," *American West*, vol. 7 (November 1970), p. 63.

11. Willard B. Robinson, *Gone from Texas: Our Lost Architectural Heritage* (College Station: Texas A&M University Press, 1981), p. 125. David G. McComb, *Galveston, a History* (Austin: University of Texas Press, 1986), pp. 107–108.

12. John S. Kendall, *The Golden Age of the New Orleans Theater* (Baton Rouge: Louisiana State University Press, 1952), pp. 584–593.

13. Frederick Warde, *Fifty Years of Make Believe* (Los Angeles: Times-Mirror Press, 1923), p. 193.

14. Warde, *Fifty Years*, pp. 195–196.

15. Elizabeth C. Ramírez, *Footlights Across the Border: A History of Spanish-Language Professional Theatre on the Texas Stage, 1875–1935* (New York: Peter Lang Publishing Group, 1990), pp. 11, 14, 29.

16. Edwina Booth Grossmann, *Edwin Booth: Recollections by His Daughter* (New York: Benjamin Blom, 1884, 1969), p. 271.

17. David Robinson, *From Peep Show to Palace: The Birth of American Film* (New York: Columbia University Press, 1996), pp. 7, 14, 34, 45–46, 63.

18. Robinson, *Peep Show to Palace*, pp. 89, 90. Richard Schroeder, *Lone Star Picture Shows* (College Station: Texas A&M University Press, 2001), p. 8.

19. Schroeder, *Lone Star Picture Shows*, pp. 4–5, 13–14, 28.

20. Robinson, *Peep Show to Palace*, pp. 146–147.

21. Schroeder, *Lone Star Picture Shows*, pp. 61–65.

22. Schroeder, *Lone Star Picture Shows*, pp. 59–72.

23. William H. Crain, "Karl St. John Hoblitzelle," in Ron Tyler, ed., *The New Handbook of Texas*, vol. 3 (Austin: Texas State Historical Association, 1996), p. 642.

24. Schroeder, *Lone Star Picture Shows*, pp. 82, 84.

25. Schroeder, *Lone Star Picture Shows*, pp. 93, 107–108, 129–132.

26. Schroeder, *Lone Star Picture Shows*, pp. xiii, 149–172.

27. Syd Field, *Going to the Movies* (New York: Dell, 2001), pp. xvi–xvii.

28. See the segment "Pictures" in Don Graham, *Giant Country: Essays on Texas* (Fort Worth: TCU Press, 1998) pp. 213–285.

29. Robinson, *Peep Show to Palace*, p. 109. Foster Rhea Dulles, *A History of Recreation: America Learns to Play*, 2nd ed. (New York: Appleton-Century-Crofts, 1965), pp. 290, 291.

30. *Houston Post-Dispatch*, April 12, 1929.

31. Ronald L. Davis, *John Rosenfield's Dallas: How the Southwest's Leading Critic Shaped a City's Culture, 1925–1966* (Dallas: Three Forks Press, 2002), p. 53.

32. Leonard J. Leff and Jerold L. Simmons, *The Dame in the Kimono; Hollywood, Censorship, and the Production Code* (Lexington: University of Kentucky Press, 2001), pp. 259–261, 274–275.

33. Lewis Coe, *Wireless Radio: A Brief History* (Jefferson, N.C.: McFarland, 1996), pp. 7, 10, 11, 26, 28. Tom Lewis, *Empire of the Air: The Men Who Made Radio* (New York: Harper Collins, 1991), pp. 162–163.

34. Richard Schroeder, *Texas Signs On: The Early Days of Radio and Television* (College Station: Texas A&M University Press, 1998), pp. 9–11, pp. 32–34 (quotes).

35. Schroeder, *Texas Signs On*, pp. 14, 20. Tyler, "Radio," in *The New Handbook of Texas*, vol. 5, p. 405.

36. Schroeder, *Texas Signs On*, pp. 61, 63.

37. Gene Fowler and Bill Crawford, *Border Radio* (Austin: University of Texas Press, 2002), pp. 111–114, 168.

38. Betty Casey, *Dance Across Texas* (Austin: University of Texas Press, 1985), p. 43.

39. Schroeder, *Texas Signs On*, p. 25.

40. George Ansbro, *I Have a Lady in the Balcony: Memoirs of a Broadcaster in Radio and Television* (Jefferson, N.C.: McFarland, 2000), pp. 186–187. Gerald Nachman, *Raised on Radio* (New York: Pantheon Books, 1998), p. 325.

41. Ronald Garay, *Gordon McLendon: The Maverick of Radio* (New York: Greenwood Press, 1992), p. 95.

42. Lewis, *Empire of the Air*, p. 1.

43. Garay, *Gordon McLendon*, pp. 1–18, p. 19 (quote).

44. Willie Morris, *North Toward Home* (Jackson: University Press of Mississippi, 1999), p. 109.

45. Morris, *North Toward Home*, p. 119.

46. Garay, *Gordon McLendon*, pp. 20–21, 25–30, 54–63, 67–72, 90–94, 131, 136, 147–149, p. 150 (quote). Gene Fowler and Bill Crawford provide in *Border Radio* a history of the super stations along the Mexican border that includes the unregulated advertising of goat glands for fertility.

47. Garay, *Gordon McLendon*, p. 189.

48. Schroeder, *Texas Signs On*, pp. 134–150, p. 138 (quote).

49. Tyler, "Television," in *The New Handbook of Texas*, vol. 6, p. 246.

50. *New York Post*, September 22, 1963 (quote). Also see Gary Cross, *A Social History of Leisure Since 1600* (State College, Pa.: Venture Publishing, 1990), p. 180, and Robert D. Putnam, *Bowling Alone* (New York: Simon and Schuster, 2000), pp. 216–246.

51. Dauphin, *Houston by Stages*, p. 155.

52. Davis, *Rosenfield's Dallas*, p. 71.

53. Nicolas Kanellos, *Mexican American Theatre: Legacy and Reality* (Pittsburgh: Latin American Literary Review Press, 1987), pp. 22, 23, 36, 50, 51, 59.

54. Dauphin, *Houston by Stages*, p. 32.

55. Dauphin, *Houston by Stages*, p. 32.

56. Brockett and Hildy, *History of the Theatre*, pp. 405, 457.

57. Hallie Flanagan, *Arena: The History of the Federal Theatre* (New York: Arno Press, 1980), p. 93 (both quotes).

58. Jan Jones, *Billy Rose Presents . . . Casa Manana* (Fort Worth: Texas Christian University Press, 1999), pp. xii (second quote), 36, 37, 64 (first quote), 115, 154.

59. Helen Sheehy, *Margo: The Life and Theatre of Margo Jones* (Dallas: Southern Methodist University Press, 1989), pp. 4, 12, 17, 34, 19, 28, 37, 38, 87.

60. Sheehy, *Margo*, pp. 21, 32, 35, 36.

61. Margo Jones, *Theatre-in-the-Round* (New York: McGraw-Hill Book Company, 1965), pp. 92–93.

62. Jones, *Theatre-in-the-Round*, p. 49.

63. Sheehy, *Margo*, p. 41.

64. Sheehy, *Margo*, p. 49.

65. Jones, *Theatre-in-the-Round*, p. 52.

66. Sheehy, *Margo*, pp. 67, 68, 76, 89, 132–133.

67. Sheehy, *Margo*, pp. 252–255. Kay Cattarulla, "I'm Doing It, Darling!" *Legacies*, vol. 16 (Fall 2004), p. 46 (quote).

68. This information and the quotes are taken from the *Dallas Theater Center Brochure* (1959?). There are no page numbers, no date, and no place of publication.

69. David Dillion and Doug Tomlinson, *Dallas Architecture, 1936–1986* (Austin: Texas Monthly Press, 1985), p. 35.

70. Ronald L. Davis, *La Scala West: The Dallas Opera Under Kelly and Rescigno* (Dallas: Southern Methodist University Press, 2000), pp. 2 (quote), 7, 9.

71. Joan Sutherland, *A Prima Donna's Progress* (Washington, D.C.: Regnery Publishing, 1997), p. 94.

72. Davis, *La Scala West*, pp. 17, 95 (quote).

73. Davis, *La Scala West*, pp. 14 (first quote), 2 (second quote).

74. *Dallas Morning News*, June 19, 1994. Chester Rosson, "Sound Investments," *Texas Monthly*, vol. 17 (November 1989), pp. 140, 142.

75. A. C. Greene, *Dallas USA* (Austin: Texas Monthly Press, 1984), pp. 239 (first quote), 240 (second quote).

76. Sheehy, *Margo*, p. 36.

77. Dauphin, *Houston by Stages*, pp. 84–89.

78. *Houston Post*, January 26, 1949.

79. Dauphin, *Houston by Stages*, p. 94.

A Bibliographic Note

The sources for recreational history in the United States are meager, but there are a few places to start. The venerable Foster Rhea Dulles, *A History of Recreation: America Learns to Play*, 2nd. ed. (New York: Appleton-Century-Crofts, 1965); the more recent Gary Cross, *A Social History of Leisure Since 1600* (State College, Pa.: Venture Publishing, 1990); Witold Rybczynski, *Waiting for the Weekend* (New York: Penguin, 1991); and David Nasaw, *Going Out: The Rise and Fall of Public Amusements* (New York: Basic Books, 1993) are fundamental. The standard encyclopedias or enumerations of great books offer almost nothing about recreation. Gary Cross, however, has edited a special two-volume *Encyclopedia of Recreation and Leisure in America* (New York: Charles Scribner's Sons, 2004). Of particular value is the article by John L. Hemingway, "Theory of Leisure" (vol. 1, pp. 517–525) that summarizes the various concepts about spare time. The theories tend to place emphasis upon social, philosophical, and psychological aspects. Martin Scarrott, ed. in *Sport, Leisure, and Tourism Information Sources* (Oxford: Butterworth Heinemann, 1999) provides basic data about English language journals (pp. 90–117) that touch upon recreation, but it is clear that sociologists, the travel industry, and parks administrators, not historians, dominate the content. There is no specific journal of recreational history.

Recreation, however, is closely related to the narrower subjects of sports history and physical education, and there is a vast discourse for those topics. Ready access to the literature can be found in the three volumes of the *Encyclopedia of World Sport* (Santa Barbara, Calif.: ABC-CLIO, 1996), edited by David Levinson and Karen Christensen; the *Journal of Sport History* (1973–); the *International Journal of the History of Sport* (1983–); and some of the standard texts, such as Benjamin G. Rader, *American Sports,* 3rd ed. (Englewood Cliffs, N.J.: Prentice Hall, 1996); and Allen Guttmann, *Sports: the First Five Millennia* (Amherst: University of Massachusetts Press, 2004). These books can lead the reader to further bibliographic sources.

Also akin to recreation is the trickle of tourism studies that started with Earl Pomeroy, *In Search of the Golden West: The Tourist in Western America* (New York: Knopf, 1957) and continued with Warren J. Belasco, *Americans on the Road: From Autocamp to Motel, 1910–1945 (Cambridge: MIT Press, 1979);* John A Jakle, *The Tourist: Travel in Twentieth-Century America* (Lincoln: University of Nebraska Press, 1985); Hal K. Rothman, *Devil's Bargains: Tourism in the Twentieth-Century American West* (Lawrence: University Press of Kansas, 1998); and Cindy S. Aron, *Working at Play: A History of Vacations in the United States* (New York: Oxford University Press, 1999). There are increasing numbers of books about specific tourist destinations, such as John Kasson, *Amusing the Millions: Coney Island at the Turn of the Century* (New York: Hill & Wang, 1978); Eugene P. Moehring, *Resort City in the Sun Belt: Las Vegas, 1930–1970* (Reno: University of Nevada Press, 1989); Jon Sterngass,

First Resorts: Pursuing Pleasure at Saratoga Springs, Newport and Coney Island (Baltimore: Johns Hopkins Press, 2001); Thomas A. Chambers, *Drinking the Waters: Creating an American Leisure Class at Nineteenth-Century Mineral Springs* (Washington, D.C.: Smithsonian Institution Press, 2002) that compares Virginia and New York; and Gary S. Cross and John K. Walton, *The Playful Crowd: Pleasure Places in the Twentieth Century* (New York: Columbia University Press, 2005) that is mainly about Coney Island and Blackpool, England.

Explorations of health spas in Texas include Gene Fowler, *Crazy Water: the Story of Mineral Wells and Other Texas Health Resorts* (Fort Worth: Texas Christian University Press, 1991), and Janet M. Valenza, *Taking the Waters in Texas: Springs, Spas, and Fountains of Youth* (Austin: University of Texas Press, 2000). A few scholars have touched upon tourism such as David G. McComb, who wrote "Galveston as a Tourist City," *Southwestern Historical Quarterly*, vol. 100 (January 1997), pp. 330–360; Char Miller, who examined the Alamo City in "Tourist Trap: Visitors and the Modern San Antonio Economy" in Hal K. Rothman, ed., *The Culture of Tourism, the Tourism of Culture: Selling the Past to the Present in the American Southwest* (Albuquerque: University of New Mexico Press, 2003) pp. 206–228; and Thomas S. Bremer, who probed the interrelationship of tourism and religion in San Antonio in *Blessed with Tourists: The Borderlands of Religion and Tourism in San Antonio* (Chapel Hill: University of North Carolina Press, 2004).

Such studies of tourism and recreation in Texas, however, are limited and random; there is no thoroughgoing coverage even in the textbooks. Nonetheless, slivers and scraps can be sifted from various biographies, newspapers, theses, articles, and special topic histories. For licit and illicit matters, several sources are especially helpful: Granville Price, "A Sociological Study of a Segregated District," MA thesis (Austin: University of Texas, 1930); David C. Humphrey, "Prostitution in Texas: From the 1830's to the 1960's," *East Texas Historical Journal*, vol. 33 (1995), pp. 27–33; and Richard Selcer, David Bowser, Nancy Hamilton, and Chuck Parsons, *Legendary Watering Holes: The Saloons That Made Texas Famous* (College Station: Texas A&M University Press, 2004).

In regard to Texas parks, James W. Steely's *Parks for Texas: Enduring Landscapes of the New Deal* (Austin: University of Texas Press, 1999) is quite helpful. It provides comprehensive information about the establishment of the state parks system. Duane F. Guy, ed., *The Story of Palo Duro Canyon* (Lubbock: Texas Tech University Press, 2001); Kenneth B. Ragsdale, *Big Bend Country: Land of the Unexpected* (College Station: Texas A&M University Press, 1998); Ron C. Tyler, *The Big Bend: A History of the Last Texas Frontier* (College Station: Texas A&M University Press, 2003); and David G. McComb's discussion about Padre Island in *The Historic Seacoast of Texas* (Austin: University of Texas Press, 1999), pp. 70–80, help to fill in the gaps about park history. An outstanding book about the development of Fair Park in Dallas is Kenneth B. Ragsdale's *The Year America Discovered Texas: Centennial '36* (College Station: Texas A&M University Press, 1987).

Sports historians have not been particularly interested in the construction and significance of stadiums, but information about the Astrodome can be found in Edgar W. Ray, *The Grand Huckster: Houston's Judge Roy Hofheinz, Genius of the Astrodome* (Memphis: Memphis State University Press, 1980), and Jason Bruce Chrystal, "The Taj Mahal of Sport: The Creation of the Houston Astrodome, 1957–1967," PhD thesis (Ames: Iowa State University, 2004). Nancy Wiley, *The Great State Fair of Texas* (Dallas: Taylor Publishing Company, 1985), and Jane Wolfe, *The Murchisons: The Rise and Fall of a Texas Dynasty* (New York: St. Martin's Press, 1989) provide some information about the Cotton Bowl.

There is no general history of libraries in Texas, but beneficial for parts of the story are the following: Robert Edward Lee, "Texas Library Development: Its Relation to the Carnegie Movement, 1898–1915," MA thesis (Austin: University of Texas, 1959); Michael V. Hazel, *The Dallas Public Library: Celebrating a Century of Service, 1901–2001* (Denton: University of North Texas Press, 2001); William

Albert Trembley, "Henry Rosenberg, a Texas Builder," MA thesis (Houston: University of Houston, 1953); Casey Edward Greene, "Foresight Built the Rosenberg Library's Archives," *Houston Review*, vol. 19 (1997) pp. 65–75; and Don E. Carleton and Katherine J. Adams, "'A Work Peculiarly Our Own': Origins of the Barker Texas History Center, 1883–1950," *Southwestern Historical Quarterly*, vol. 86 (October 1982), pp. 197–230.

There is no comprehensive history of theater in Texas, but the following books help to fill in blank spots: Elizabeth C. Ramírez, *Footlights Across the Border: A History of Spanish-Language Professional Theatre on the Texas Stage, 1875–1935* (New York: Peter Lang Publishing Group, 1990); Sue Dauphin, *Houston by Stages: A History of Theatre in Houston* (Burnet, Tex.: Eakin Press, 1981), which includes amateur theater efforts in the Bayou City; Jan Jones, *Billy Rose Presents . . . Casa Manana* (Fort Worth: Texas Christian University Press, 1999), which covers the Fort Worth extravaganza during the Texas Centennial; Ronald L. Davis, *La Scala West: The Dallas Opera Under Kelly and Rescigno* (Dallas: Southern Methodist University Press, 2000); and Helen Sheehy, *Margo: The Life and Theatre of Margo Jones* (Dallas: Southern Methodist University Press, 1989). Fortunately, Richard Schroeder, who once taught communications, has provided two books that cover much about radio, television, and movies: *Lone Star Picture Shows* (College Station: Texas A&M University Press, 2001) and *Texas Signs On: The Early Days of Radio and Television* (College Station: Texas A&M University Press, 1998). The data in these books can be enriched with information from Gene Fowler and Bill Crawford, *Border Radio* (Austin: University of Texas Press, 2002), and Ronald Garay, *Gordon McLendon: the Maverick of Radio* (New York: Greenwood Press, 1992).

There is no general history of recreation for Texas, only these bits and pieces. For students and scholars, therefore, there is much original work that can be done to create this new mosaic of history. It is a wonderful opportunity.

Index

Underlined page numbers refer to photographs.

Image Credits

1a Institute of Texan Cultures at University of Texas at San Antonio.
1b Erwin E. Smith, Erwin E. Smith Collection, Library of Congress, on deposit at the Amon Carter Museum, Fort Worth, Texas.
1c Erwin E. Smith, Erwin E. Smith Collection, Library of Congress, on deposit at the Amon Carter Museum, Fort Worth, Texas.
2 Courtesy of Amarillo Public Library.
3 Photograph by author.
4 Western History Collections, University of Oklahoma Libraries.
5 San Antonio Public Library, Texana Collection.
6 Western History Collections, University of Oklahoma Libraries.
7 Western History Collections, University of Oklahoma Libraries.
8 Western History Collections, University of Oklahoma Libraries.
9 Institute of Texan Cultures at University of Texas at San Antonio.
10 San Antonio Public Library, Texana Collection.
11 Daughters of the Republic of Texas Library.
12 Photograph by author.
13 Photograph by author.
14 Institute of Texan Cultures at University of Texas at San Antonio.
15 From the Collection of the Texas/Dallas History and Archives Division, Dallas Public Library.
16 Photograph by author.
17 Photograph by author.
18 Photograph by author.
19 Photograph by author.
20 Photograph by author.
21 Austin History Center, Austin Public Library.
22 Photograph by author.
23 Photograph by author.
24 San Antonio Public Library, Texana Collection.
25 Western History Collections, University of Oklahoma Libraries.
26 Western History Collections, University of Oklahoma Libraries.
27 Institute of Texan Cultures at University of Texas at San Antonio.
28 Photograph by author.

29 Daughters of the Republic of Texas Library.
30 Photograph by author.
31 Photograph by author, permission by Old City Park, Dallas, Texas.
32 Photograph by author.
33 Austin History Center, Austin Public Library.
34 Austin History Center, Austin Public Library.
35 Photograph by author.
36 Daughters of the Republic of Texas Library.
37 Photograph by author.
38 Photograph by author.
39 Photograph by author.
40 Courtesy, *Fort Worth Star-Telegram* Collection, Special Collections, The University of Texas at Arlington, Arlington, Texas.
41 Courtesy, *Fort Worth Star-Telegram* Collection, Special Collections, The University of Texas at Arlington, Arlington, Texas.
42 Courtesy, *Fort Worth Star-Telegram* Collection, Special Collections, The University of Texas at Arlington, Arlington, Texas.
43 Photograph by author.
44 Photograph by author.
45 Courtesy of Amarillo Public Library.
46 Courtesy of Amarillo Public Library.
47 Photograph by author.
48 Courtesy of Amarillo Public Library.
49 Photograph by author.
50 Courtesy, *Fort Worth Star-Telegram* Collection, Special Collections, The University of Texas at Arlington, Arlington, Texas.
51 Courtesy, Photo Collection, LBJ Library & Museum.
52 Photograph by author.
53 Courtesy, Photo Collection, LBJ Library & Museum.
54 Courtesy, Photo Collection, LBJ Library & Museum.
55 Photograph by author.
56 Center for American History, University of Texas at Austin.
57 Austin History Center, Austin Public Library.
58 From the Collection of the Texas/Dallas History and Archives Division, Dallas Public Library.
59 From the Collection of the Texas/Dallas History and Archives Division, Dallas Public Library.
60 From the Collection of the Texas/Dallas History and Archives Division, Dallas Public Library.
61 From the Collection of the Texas/Dallas History and Archives Division, Dallas Public Library.
62 From the Collection of the Texas/Dallas History and Archives Division, Dallas Public Library.
63 Courtesy, *Fort Worth Star-Telegram* Collection, Special Collections, The University of Texas at Arlington, Arlington, Texas.
64 Photograph by author.

65 From the Collection of the Texas/Dallas History and Archives Division, Dallas Public Library.
66 Austin History Center, Austin Public Library.
67 Austin History Center, Austin Public Library.
68 Minchew Papers, Box 3V257, Center for American History, University of Texas at Austin.
69 Minchew Papers, Box 3V257, Center for American History, University of Texas at Austin.
70 Courtesy, Houston Metropolitan Research Center, Houston Public Library.
71a Minchew Papers, Box 3V257, Center for American History, University of Texas at Austin.
71b Minchew Papers, Box 3V257, Center for American History, University of Texas at Austin.
72 Photograph by author.
73 Photograph by author.
74 Photograph by author.
75 From the Collection of the Texas/Dallas History and Archives Division, Dallas Public Library.
76 Photograph by author.
77 Photograph by author.
78 Courtesy of Amarillo Public Library.
79 Photograph by author.
80 From the Collection of the Texas/Dallas History and Archives Division, Dallas Public Library.
81 Photograph by author.
82 Photograph by author.
83 Photograph by author.
84 Photograph by author.
85 Photograph by author.
86 From the Collection of the Texas/Dallas History and Archives Division, Dallas Public Library.
87 Photograph by author.
88 Photograph by author.
89 Photograph by author.
90 Photograph by author.
91 Photograph by author.
92 From the Collection of the Texas/Dallas History and Archives Division, Dallas Public Library.
93 Photograph by author.
94 Courtesy, Houston Metropolitan Research Center, Houston Public Library.
95 Photograph by author.
96 Courtesy, Houston Metropolitan Research Center, Houston Public Library.
97 Austin History Center, Austin Public Library.
98 Courtesy, Houston Metropolitan Research Center, Houston Public Library.
99 From the Collection of the Texas/Dallas History and Archives Division, Dallas Public Library.
100 From the Collection of the Texas/Dallas History and Archives Division, Dallas Public Library.
101 Photograph by author.
102 Photograph by author.
103 Austin History Center, Austin Public Library.

104 Austin History Center, Austin Public Library.

105 Austin History Center, Austin Public Library.

106 Institute of Texan Cultures, University of Texas at San Antonio. Courtesy of the Hearst Corporation.

107 From the Collection of the Texas/Dallas History and Archives Division, Dallas Public Library.

108 Courtesy, *Fort Worth Star-Telegram* Collection, Special Collections, The University of Texas at Arlington Library, Arlington, Texas.

109 From the Collection of the Texas/Dallas History and Archives Division, Dallas Public Library.

